IMAGES
of America

HOOPESTON

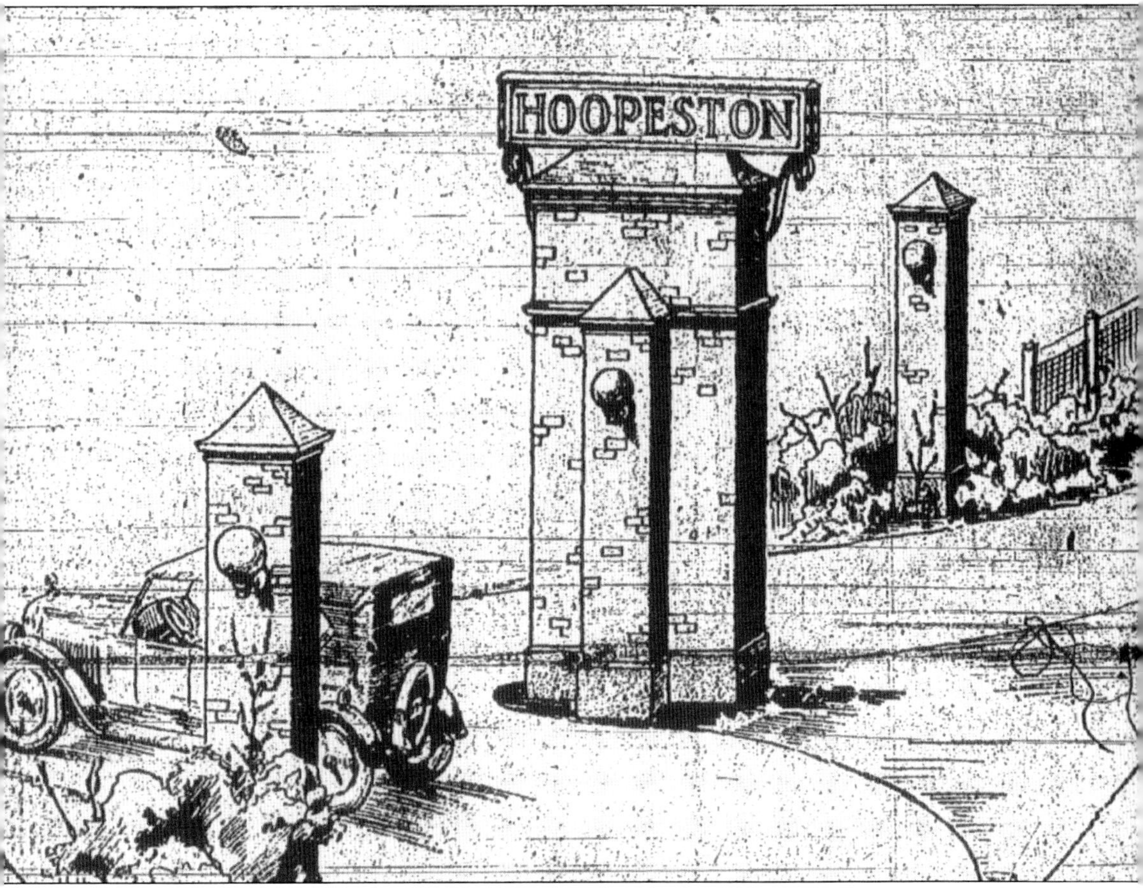

In 1923, the Hoopeston Chamber of Commerce decided to sponsor a gateway on West Main Street and the Dixie Highway to bring attention to the village of Hoopeston growing a couple miles down Main Street. The idea and a tentative rendering of the gateway were presented to the Hoopeston city council and approved. Construction started in 1923 and finished in May 1924. This rendering showed how the gateway would look. In 1925, the gateway was lighted to lead visitors to downtown Hoopeston. (Courtesy of the Hoopeston Public Library.)

On the Cover: Maple Grade School children gather on the steps of Maple School for a class photograph in 1951. These students graduated from Hoopeston High School in 1961 and are now in their early 70s. (Courtesy of John Musson.)

IMAGES
of America

HOOPESTON

Carol Hicks, Jean Minick, and Nora Gholson

ARCADIA
PUBLISHING

ISBN 978-1-4671-1424-0

Published by Arcadia Publishing
Charleston, South Carolina

Printed in the United States of America

Library of Congress Control Number: 2014959582

For all general information, please contact Arcadia Publishing:
Telephone 843-853-2070
Fax 843-853-0044
E-mail sales@arcadiapublishing.com
For customer service and orders:
Toll-Free 1-888-313-2665

Visit us on the Internet at www.arcadiapublishing.com

This book is dedicated to all the historians in Hoopeston who continue to research, copy, and write the history to keep it alive in the hearts and minds of the residents. May there always be a historian in Hoopeston.

Contents

Acknowledgments

The authors would like to thank the Hoopeston Public Library for allowing us to monopolize the microfilm machine, the Illinois room, and their time in our research. The authors also want to thank Alex Houmes for all his special work resizing the photographs used in this book, Susie Sheppard for answering the many questions posed to her on businesses start dates, and all the owners involved in sending fantastic photographs. All images in this book are from the authors' private collections, unless otherwise noted.

Introduction

Hoopeston had its early beginnings in 1871. It was laid out at the junction of two railroads, the Chicago, Danville & Vincennes Railroad and the Lafayette & Bloomington Railroad. Developers saw the advantages the railroads presented and began laying out sections of Hoopeston to build a village.

Three small villages were marked off by three different groups. The first, Hoopeston, was laid out by Thomas Hoopes and comprised 18 acres of land on the southeast corner of the railroad junction owned by two men named Davis and Satterthewait. The second village, North Hoopeston, was laid out by the Thompson brothers on the northeast section of the junction. And the last village was laid out on the southwest corner of the railroad junction and comprised 160 acres of land; it became known as Leeds and was owned by Snell, Taylor and Co., and a Mr. Mix.

Although 50 acres of the northwest corner were bought by two gentlemen by the name of Moore and Brown, and 10 acres by R. McCracken, those sections did not become a fourth village. Plans by the three men were to convert them into additions to the town.

Hoopeston was named after Thomas Hoopes, who donated the land on which the railroads were built. The moniker was supposedly chosen by the railroad men. Hoopeston was incorporated in 1874, and North Hoopeston and Leeds then became additions as part of the newly incorporated town.

Many photographs of the buildings and businesses have been lost to fires, deterioration, and removal. Those presented in this book show a way of life that revolved around downtown Hoopeston. Everything was located downtown, except a few gas stations, Baer's Motel, and the trailer parks.

Hoopeston was a wealthy town in its early history, and its name was bandied about in the New York newspapers on several occasions. Once in particular when the mayor of Hoopeston and its aldermen decided not to accept pay for serving the city. This was a great cause for amazement across the country in the early 1900s. Hoopeston, nicknamed the "Holy City" or "White City," supported more than 13 churches of all denominations. It also became famous as a dry town. No saloons were allowed in the city, and Hoopeston remained a dry community until the mid-1930s.

Since Hoopeston was located at the railroad junction, many who drove by on the Dixie Highway, also known as Route 1, did not realize a town existed a mile or so east of the roadway. Early newspapers tell that a gateway was proposed by the Hoopeston Chamber of Commerce and, once approved by the council, was erected at the corner of West Main Street and the Dixie Highway (or Route 1) in 1924. The specific purpose was to guide drivers to downtown Hoopeston. Later, the Hoopeston Chamber of Commerce decided to add some lighting to the gateway and along the roadway leading downtown as an additional incentive to bring people into their growing village. This would help travelers at night find a place to stop and rest. Hoopeston in 1925 had several hotels in the downtown area.

As all towns grow, they develop growing pains. Hoopeston's included fires and an insufficient water supply to put them out. Most early buildings were built of wood and heated with woodstoves. Woodstoves caused many fires during the early years of Hoopeston's growth spurt. As these disasters occurred, the town rebuilt using mortar and stone for safer buildings. Once electricity and gas arrived, woodstoves were eliminated, which lessened the risk. It did not totally eliminate fires, but it did cut down on the number in the downtown area.

The problem of water was eventually solved with the addition of a larger water tower to replace the first one located at the end of East Main and Fourth Streets, along with a water works department, sewer and water system, and water mains. The once-dirt streets were bricked over, sidewalks were added, a city hall was built on the corner of Davis (later renamed Seminary) and Market Streets in about 1897, and, eventually, telephone service was added. There were also several hotels, opera houses, nickelodeons, theaters, and more to maintain the good life for the Hoopeston residents.

The town was known to have an active Ku Klux Klan presence in the early 1920s. The Klan not only held parades in downtown Hoopeston but also held rallies at McFerren Park in 1925–1926, according to the local *Chronicle-Herald* newspaper.

Canning factories were the mainstay of the town. The Illinois Canning Company (later known as Joan of Arc) incorporated in 1877, and the Hoopeston Canning Company (which became Stokely Van Camp) was established in 1878. The Union Can Company was another early business. It remained Union Can Company until it was sold to the American Can Company. American Can was later sold to Silgan. Another factory, the Sprague-Sells Manufacturing Company, was formed and eventually became Food Machinery Corporation (FMC); it was closed several years ago.

All of these companies made Hoopeston a very self-sufficient little town, and all were located within a few blocks of the downtown area. Equipment used in the canning industry was made at FMC, cans and lids were made at American Can Company, and area farmers provided a lot of the product that was canned in the factories.

Fires were Hoopeston's worst enemies. Downtown Hoopeston burned twice, nearly wiping out the area; however, the business owners rebuilt sturdier structures. Stokely had at least two fires; the last one devastated the offices, boiler room, and part of one warehouse. They rebuilt. A year or two later, Chiquita Brand bought the business and closed it. Joan of Arc also announced its closing around that same time; however, employees bought the business, changed the name to Hoopeston Foods, and kept the doors open. A California-based business bought Hoopeston Foods, which is still in production today as Teasdale Foods.

Hoopeston is still a viable town. It keeps changing to find its specialty niche, adding unique stores and different types of businesses in the health field. It has become more of a retirement community, with the biggest employers being the Hoopeston Regional Health Center, Heritage Nursing Home, Hoopeston Area School District, Silgan Corporation, Teasdale Foods, IGA, and Schumacher's. Hoopeston also added a Danville Area Community College campus that offers transferable credit courses as well as trade courses for everyone interested in learning a trade or going on to a regular college. Hoopeston is evolving.

One

Hoopeston Businesses

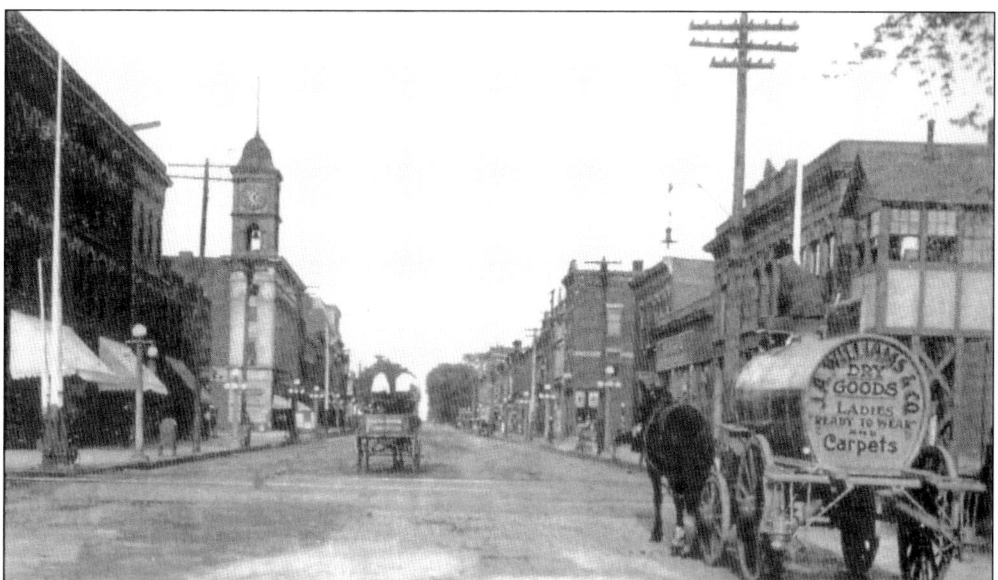

This photograph, taken around 1900, shows that horses were still used in transporting goods at the turn of the 20th century. J.A. Williams & Co. was an early seller of ladies' ready-to-wear items, dry goods, and carpeting, and Williams would travel door-to-door to homes in Hoopeston with his wares.

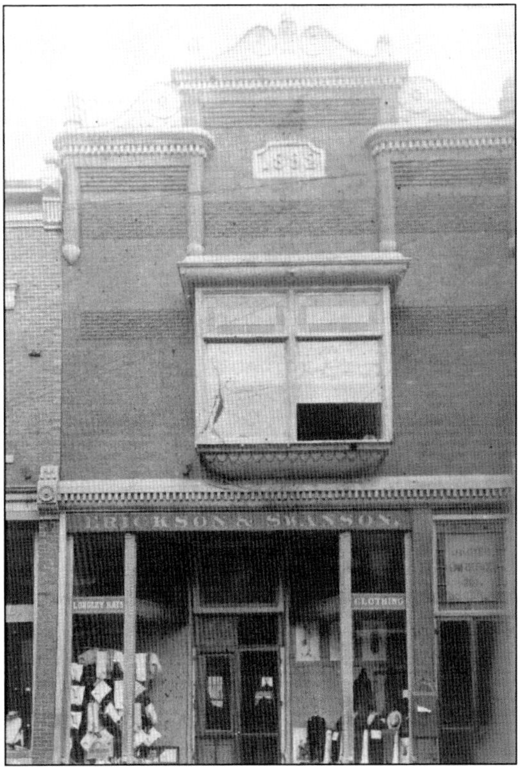

The Erickson & Swanson store was built in 1882. It not only sold clothing to the residents of Hoopeston, but also specialty hats. The building was located in the Dyer block on the 100 block of East Main Street. (Courtesy of the Hoopeston Public Library.)

This 1902 photograph of the First National Bank shows a better view of the early building on the southeast corner of Main and Market Streets. In 1902, the structure only had two stories; a third was added in 1903. (Courtesy of the Hoopeston Public Library.)

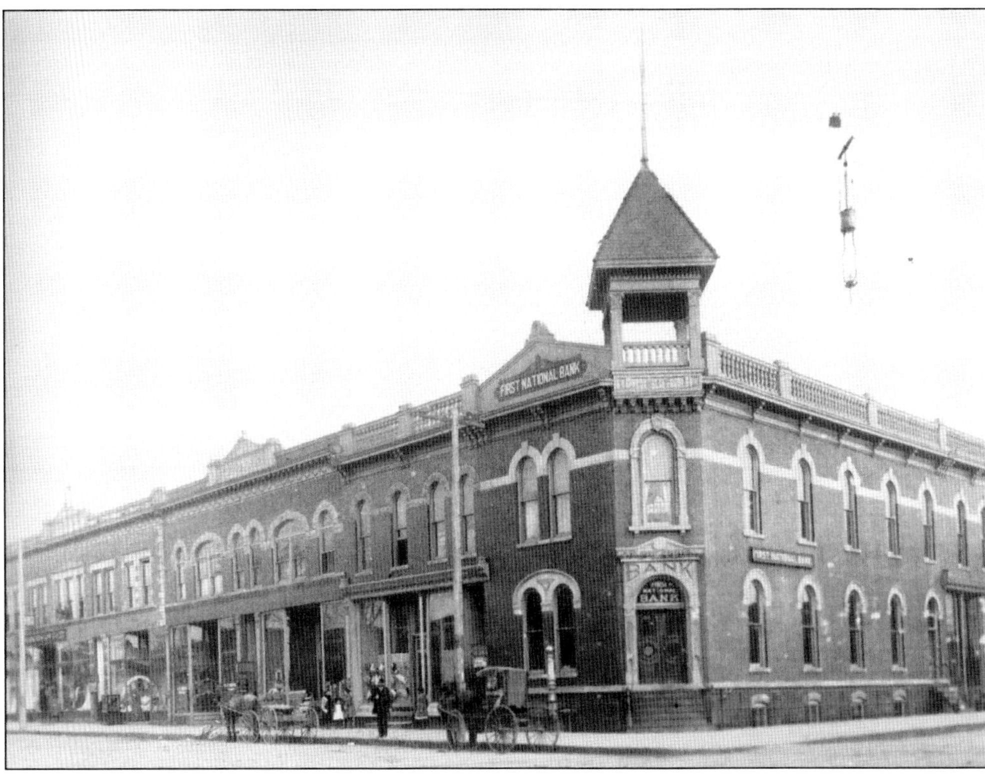

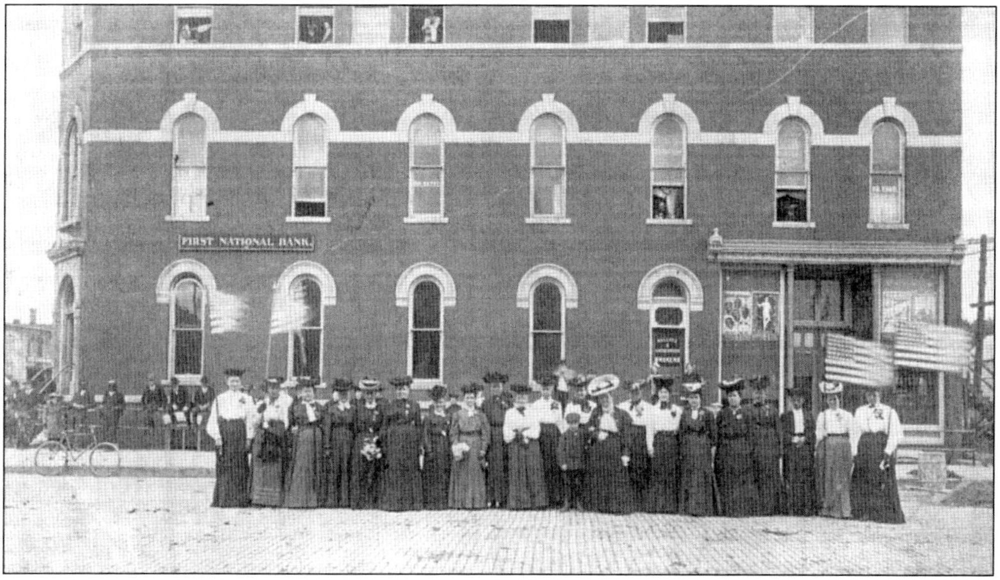

The First National Bank was established in 1872 by J.S. McFerren with a capitalization of $25,000. McFerren was the president until his death in 1921, when his son William McFerren became president. In this photograph, a ladies' organization poses on South Market Street in front of the bank. (Courtesy of the Hoopeston Public Library.)

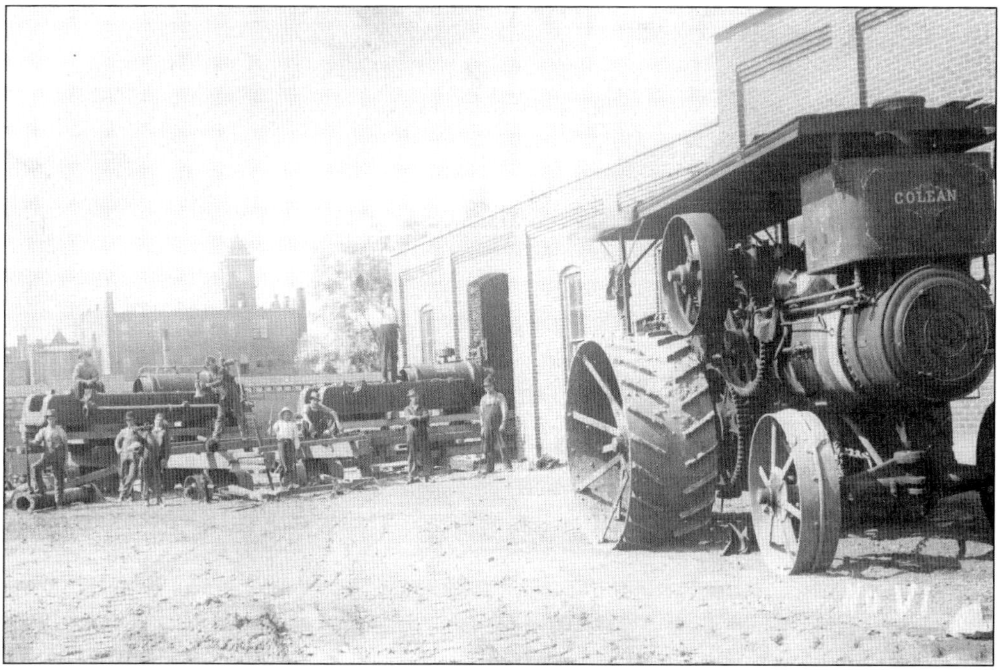

The Hoopeston Electric Plant, organized in 1891 by J.S. McFerren and A.H. Trego, is shown in this 1898 photograph. C. James Wakeman later received a 50-year franchise to supply residents' electricity and gas. Central Illinois Public Service Company acquired the plant in 1941, and it was later acquired by Ameren. A Colean steam engine stored at the plant is shown here. The offices on Bank and East Main Streets relocated to North Market Street, eventually closing except for the maintenance crew.

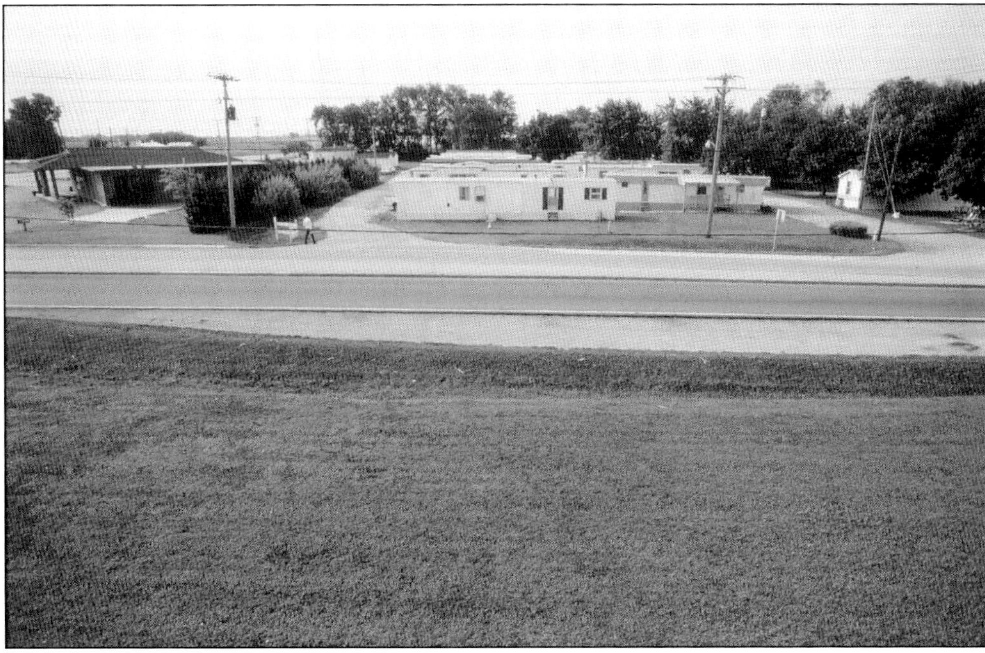

This 1989 photograph shows Baer's Trailer Park, which was south of Baer's Motel on Route 9 and west of Route 1. The trailer park was demolished in 2004 to make room for CVS. (Courtesy of Scott Baer.)

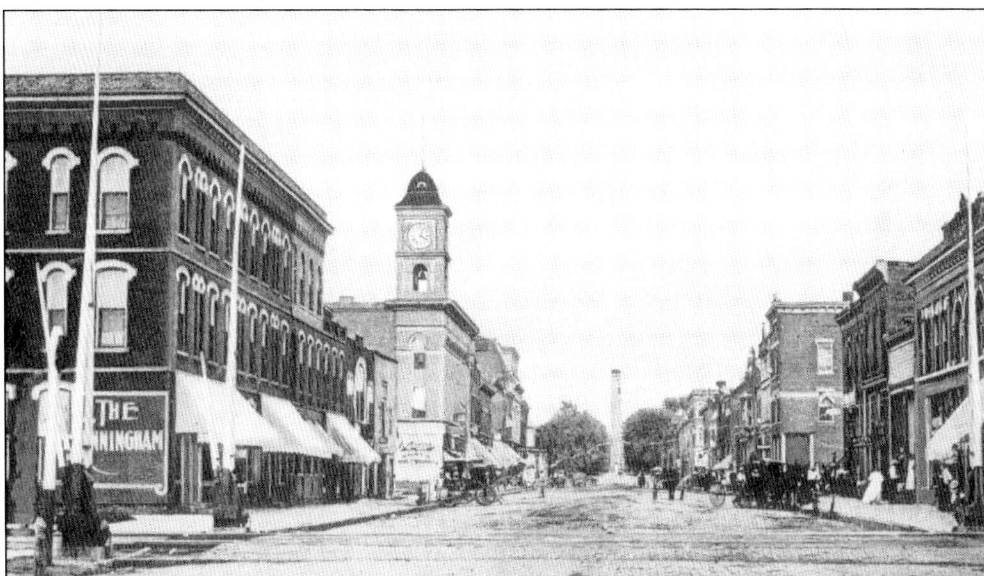

Pictured here at far left, the Arlington House—built by David Prutsman in about 1885, with Civil War veteran Capt. J.S. Agle as landlord—was a two-story building. Later, a third story was added. The name was changed to the Cunningham Hotel when it came into the possession of the Cunningham family. When R.L. Cragg took ownership, the hotel was briefly the Cragg-Cunningham Hotel. Much later, it was known only as the Cragg Hotel and housed a beauty shop and coffee shop. The Cragg Hotel burned down on March 17, 1965.

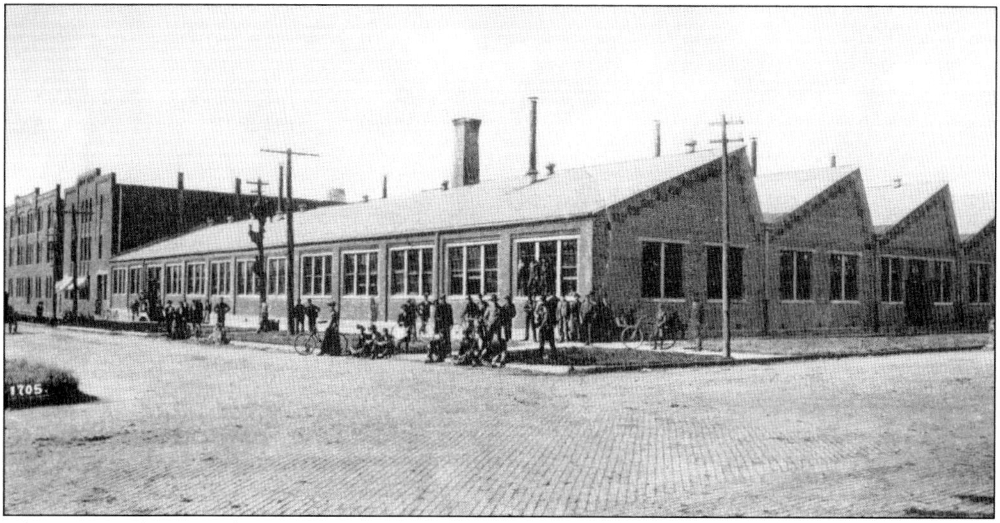

This 1900s photograph shows the American Can Company, which had its early beginnings as the Union Can Company. Two additions were built onto the plant in 1925—one on the west end, and the other on the east end—expanding it for the storage of tin cans. The American Can Company provided cans for both the Stokely and Illinois Canning Companies during canning seasons. Silgan Container Manufacturing Corporation bought the business, downsized, and continues to operate in Hoopeston.

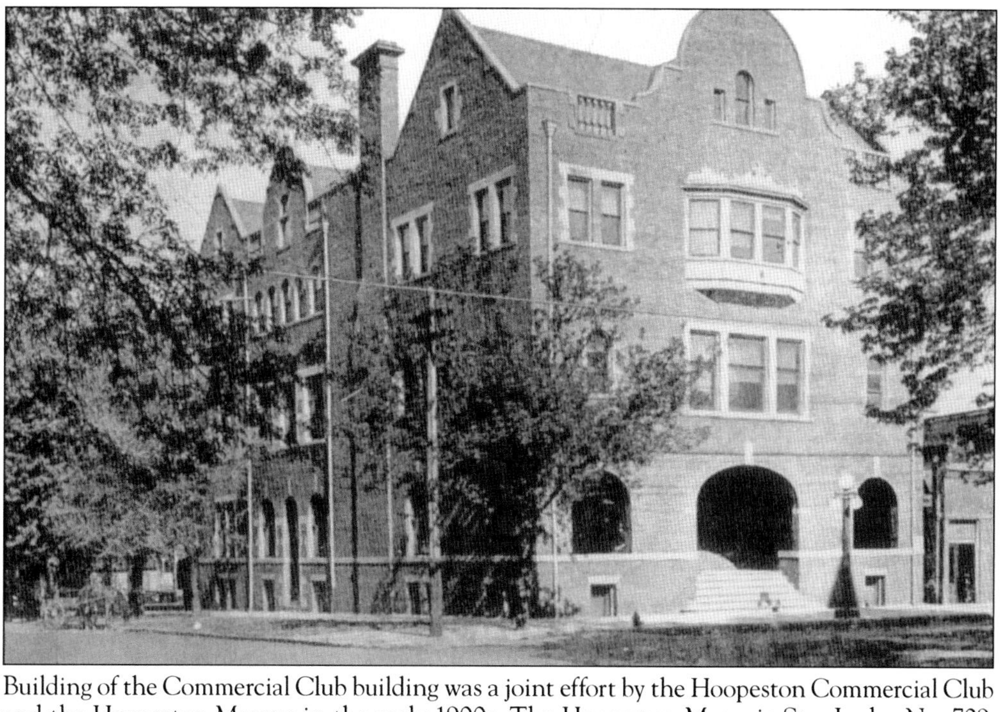

Building of the Commercial Club building was a joint effort by the Hoopeston Commercial Club and the Hoopeston Masons in the early 1900s. The Hoopeston Masonic Star Lodge No. 709, chartered in 1872, owned its own quarters in the Commercial Club building. (Courtesy of the Hoopeston Public Library.)

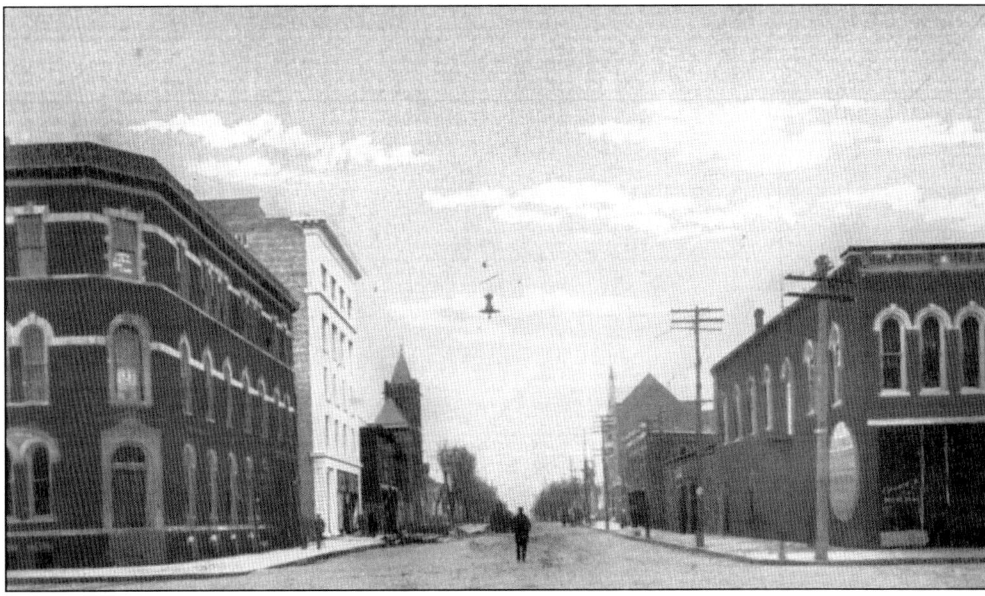

This postcard photograph looks south on South Market Street from Main Street in about 1910. The McFerren Building, Willdon Building, the telephone company, and the United Presbyterian Church are located on the left. The Clark Building is the first building on the right. In the background, the Commercial Club and Universalist church are seen. Two other unknown buildings are between the Clark Building and Commercial Club.

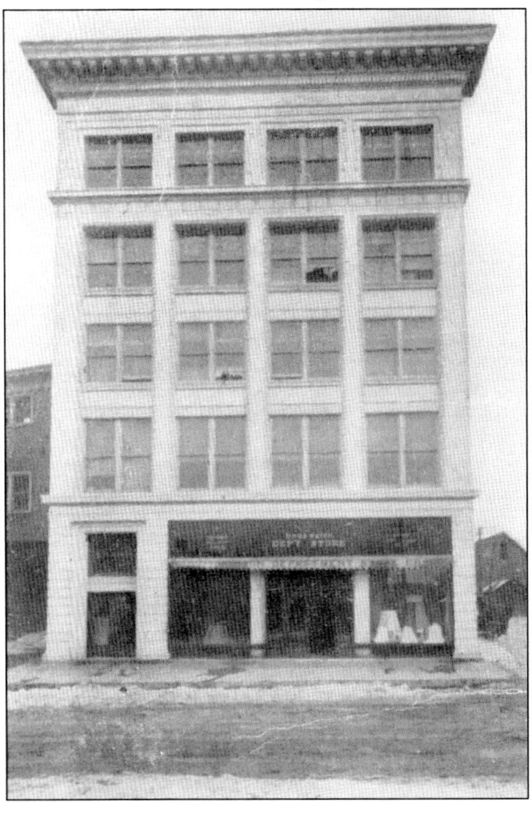

The Willdon Building was built in 1905 by J.S. McFerren. The building, named after his sons William and Donald McFerren, first opened with a department store on the bottom floor. Later, the first floor contained the Palmer Bank and City National Bank. The Hoopeston Chamber of Commerce, doctors' and lawyers' offices, and the offices of the Lorraine Theatre group were located in the top four floors. With five floors, it is Hoopeston's only "skyscraper."

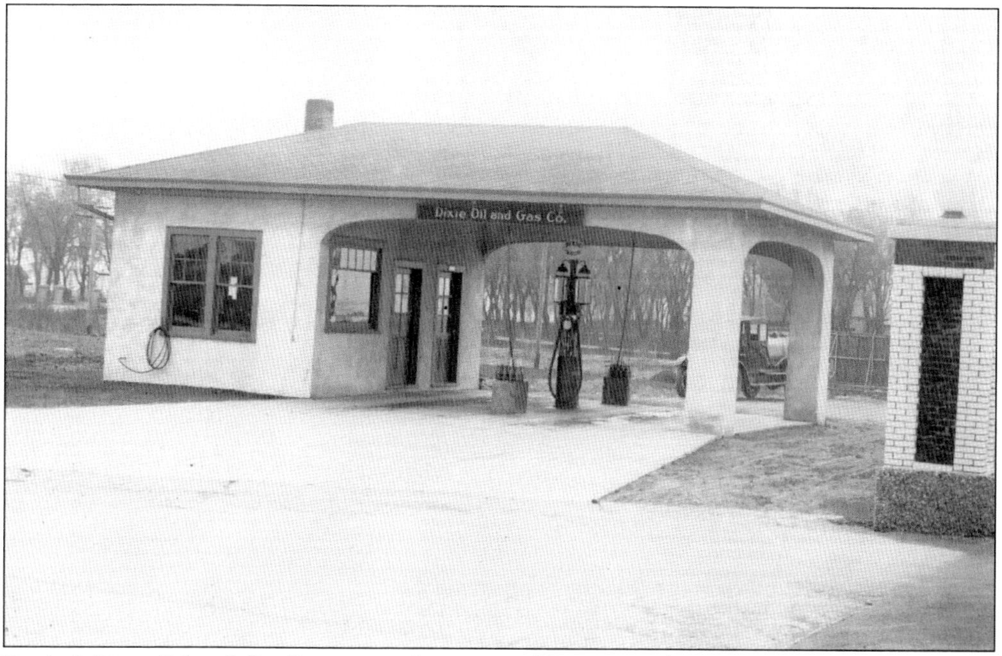

Powley's Dixie Oil and Gas Station on the corner of Route 1 and Main Street was located where BJ's Pump now stands. Floyd and Lon Powley purchased the property in the 1920s and built the gas station. McFerren Park can be seen in the background.

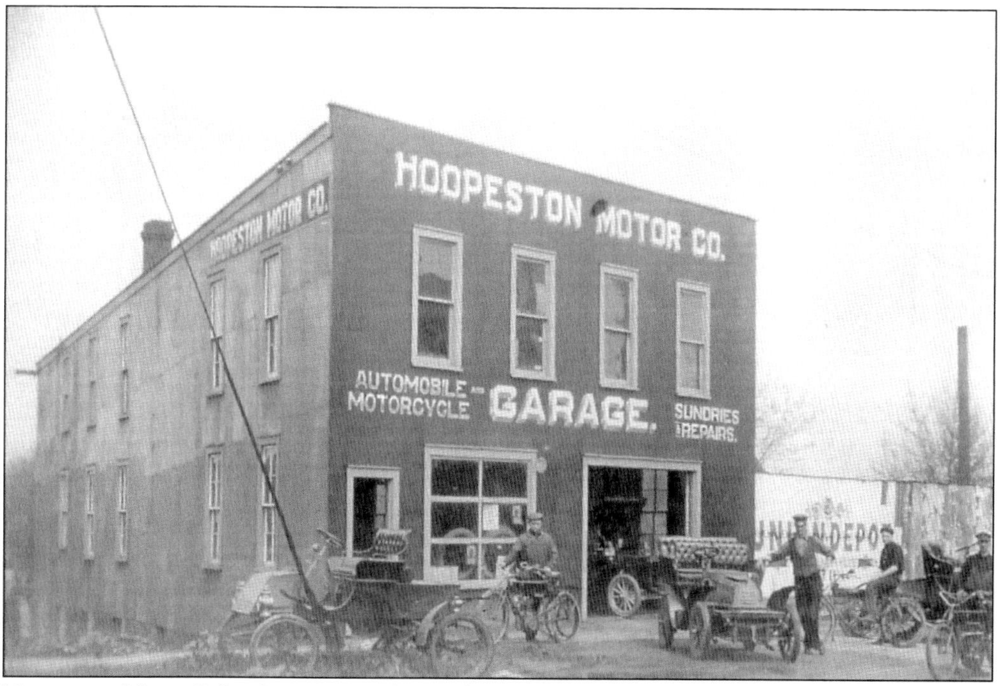

Hoopeston Motor Sales Company is shown during the early 1900s near the Union Train Depot. The company sold and repaired cars and early motorcycles. It later became the Ford garage and moved to 316 East Main Street. (Courtesy of the Hoopeston Public Library.)

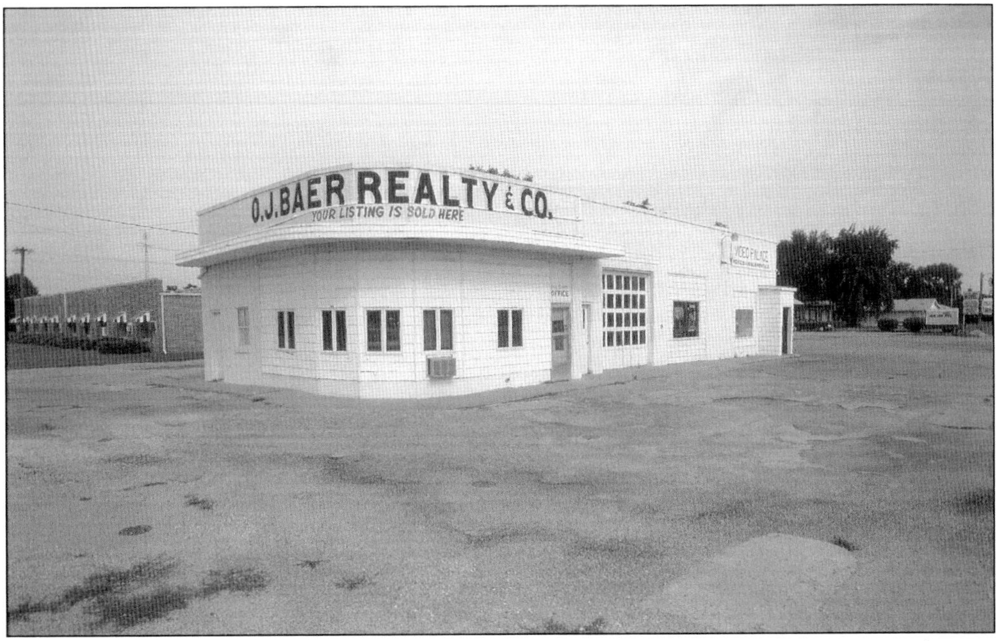

Ora J. Baer repurposed the old Texaco station on the northwest corner of Routes 1 and 9 as a realty office in 1989. It also housed the Video Palace business, which rented VCR tapes. (Courtesy of Scott Baer.)

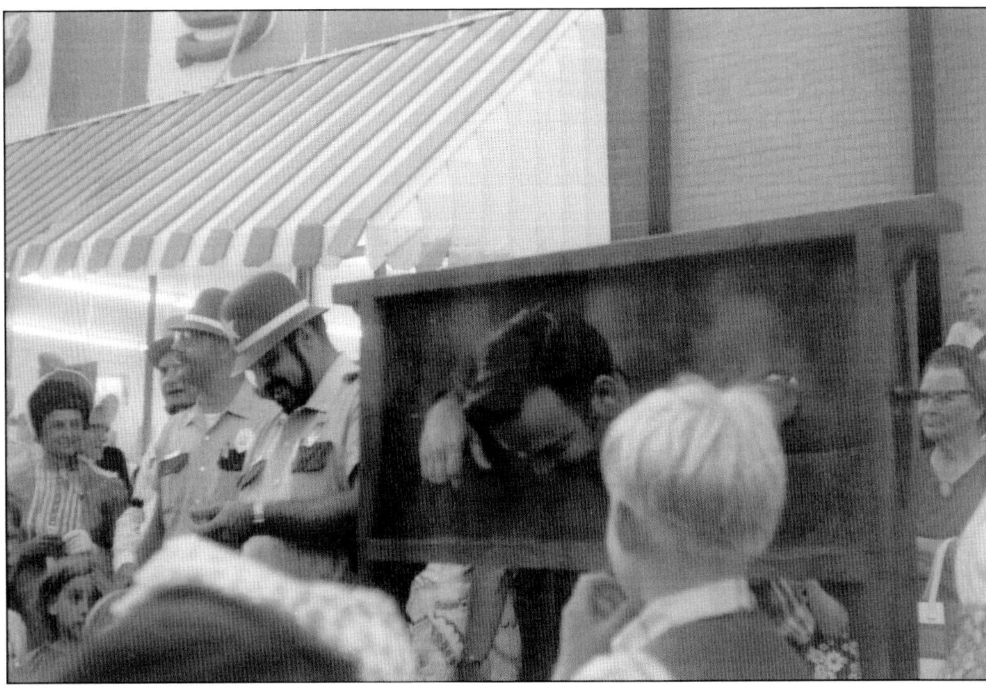

Downtown Hoopeston during the 1971 centennial was a busy thoroughfare for folks dressed in period clothing, as well as visitors checking out the scenes in front of the Carps store in the 200 block of East Main Street. The police department in this 1971 photograph has placed a man in stocks for an infraction. (Courtesy of Scott Baer.)

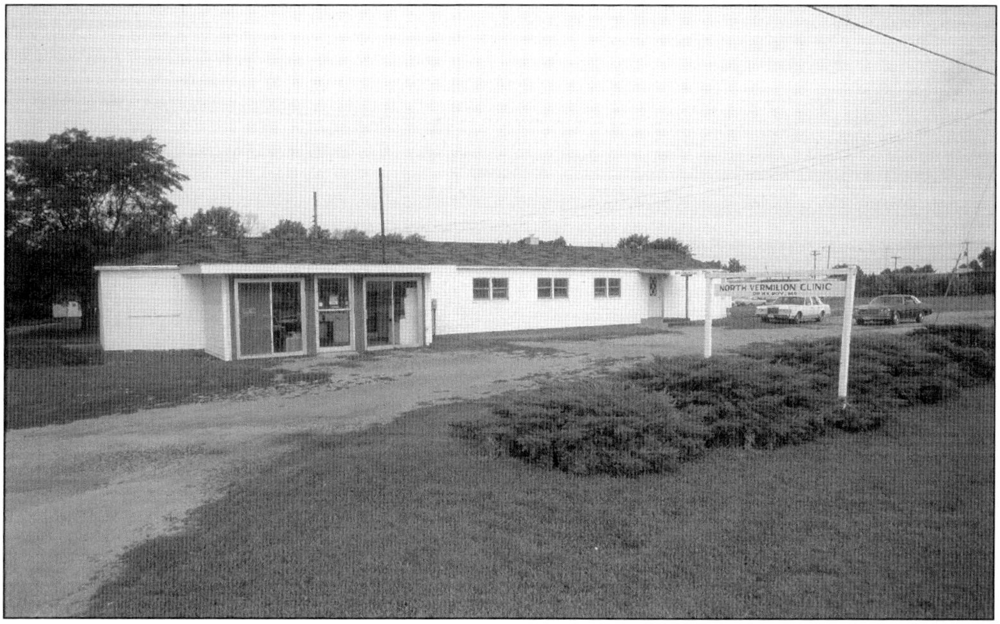

Ora J. Baer's former office on Route 1 became the North Vermilion Clinic in 1989. Dr. H.K. Roy was the physician who ran the office. (Courtesy of Scott Baer.)

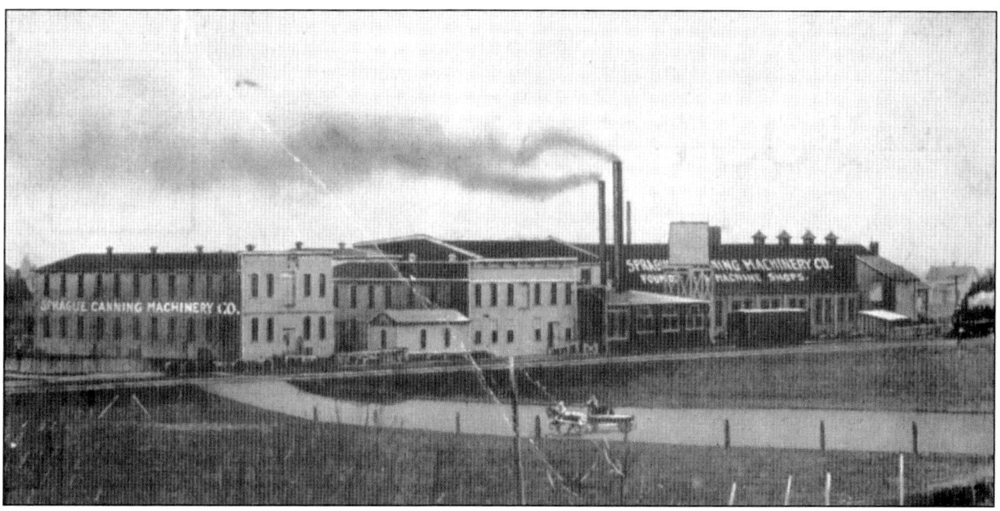

Built in 1897, the Sprague Manufacturing Company shown in this 1904 photograph later became Food Machinery Corporation, 103 East Maple Street. The plant was organized by Daniel G. Trench and B.P. Crane of New York in 1892. Ogden S. Sells bought it in 1923 and renamed it the Sprague-Sells Corporation, but in 1932, it became the Food Machinery Corporation. The company downsized and eventually closed on February 3, 2004. J&R Tire Recycling Service bought it. (Courtesy of the Hoopeston Public Library.)

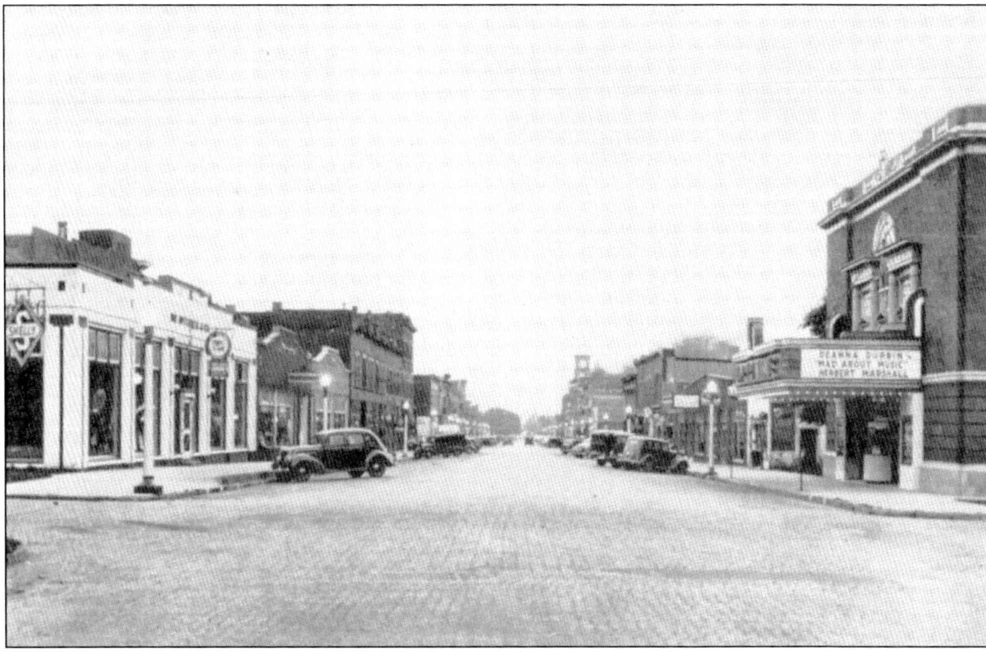

This photograph of East Main Street from Third Street shows the Lorraine Theatre in about 1938, the year after the theater was completely remodeled. Across the street is Sim's Garage, 317–323 East Main Street, and next door is Wood and Stocker's Furniture Store.

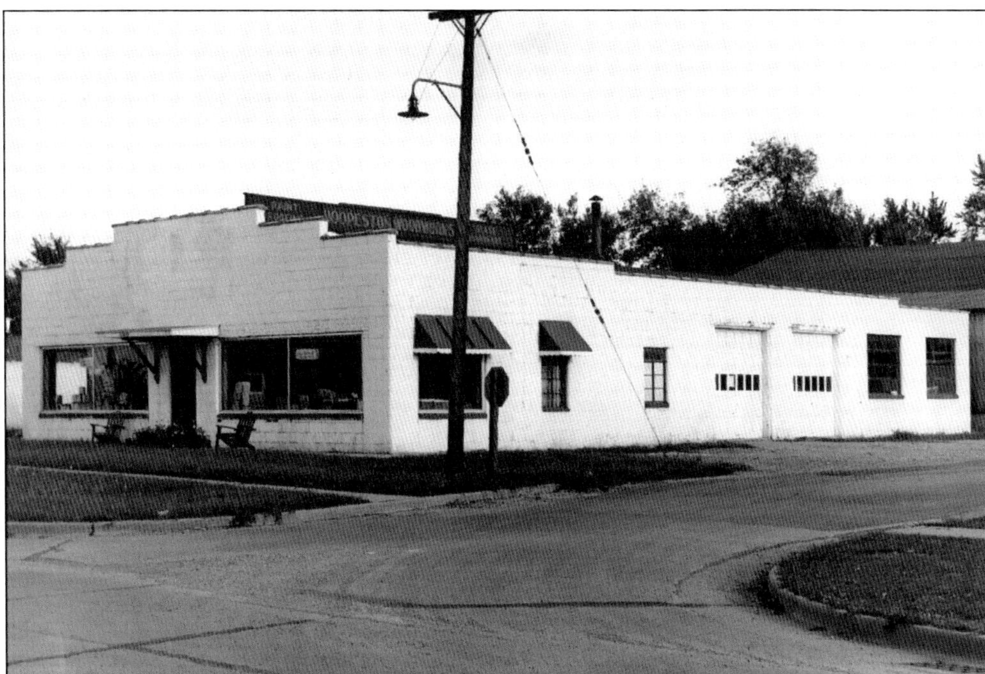

Brown's Cash and Carry, 815 East Thompson Avenue, was established as a partnership between Orville Brown and Robert Brown in 1946 as Hoopeston Woodworks. Robert's son Scott Brown and Scott's wife, Traci, took over the business once he retired. (Courtesy of Scott and Traci Brown.)

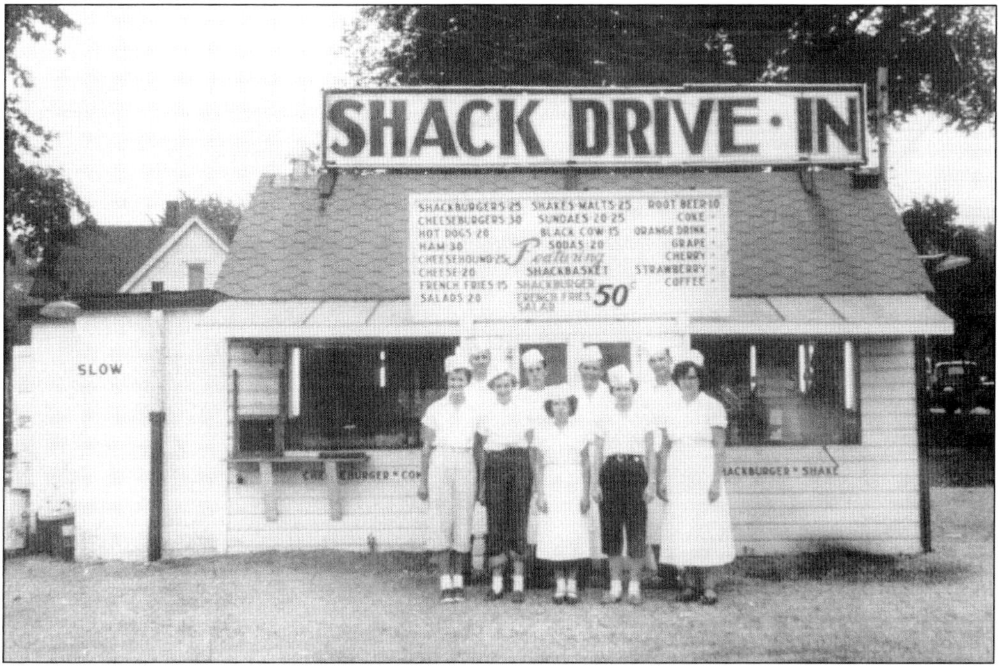

The Shack Drive-In on Seventh Avenue and Penn Street was originally a root beer stand run by Ralph Lloyd and Ron Ripley. When Ripley went into business for himself in Paxton, Earl Smock bought his share. However, after three years, Smock decided it was not the business for him. Since he and Lloyd also both owned the Darb pool hall, they split the two businesses. The Shack later expanded its menu to include steaks, seafood, chicken meals, and a full-service bar and lounge by 1969, and its name was changed to Mr. L's. When Lloyd retired in 1975, it was bought by Jesse Stark of Danville, Illinois. Pictured here are, from left to right, (first row) Barbara Garner Lewis, Joyce Curry, Joanne Glover, Mary Lou Taylor, and Phyllis Goyette; (second row) Ralph Lloyd, Danny Wood, John Veneble, and Earl Smock. (Courtesy of Margarite Lloyd.)

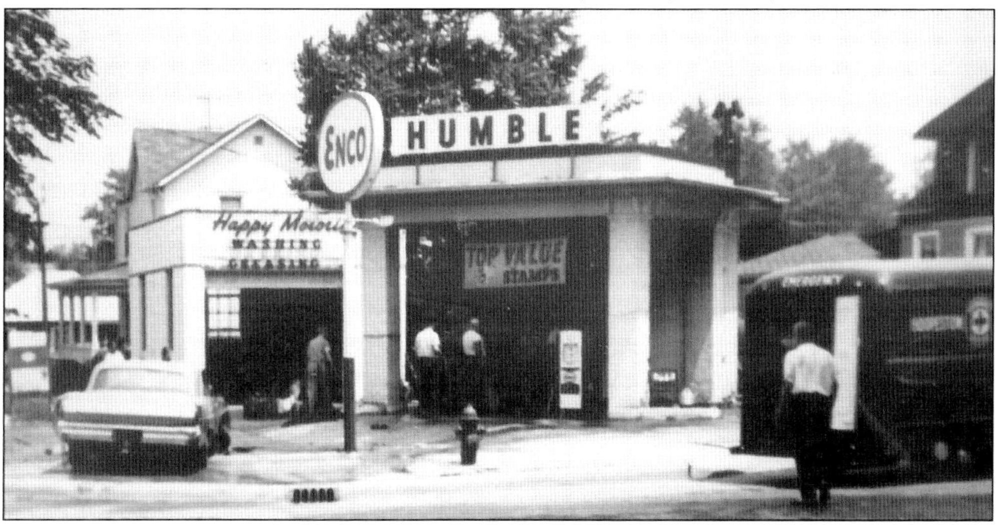

The Enco Humble gas station was located on the northeast corner of South Third and East Main Streets, across from the Lorraine Theatre. This photograph was taken following an accident that had occurred there. (Courtesy of John Musson.)

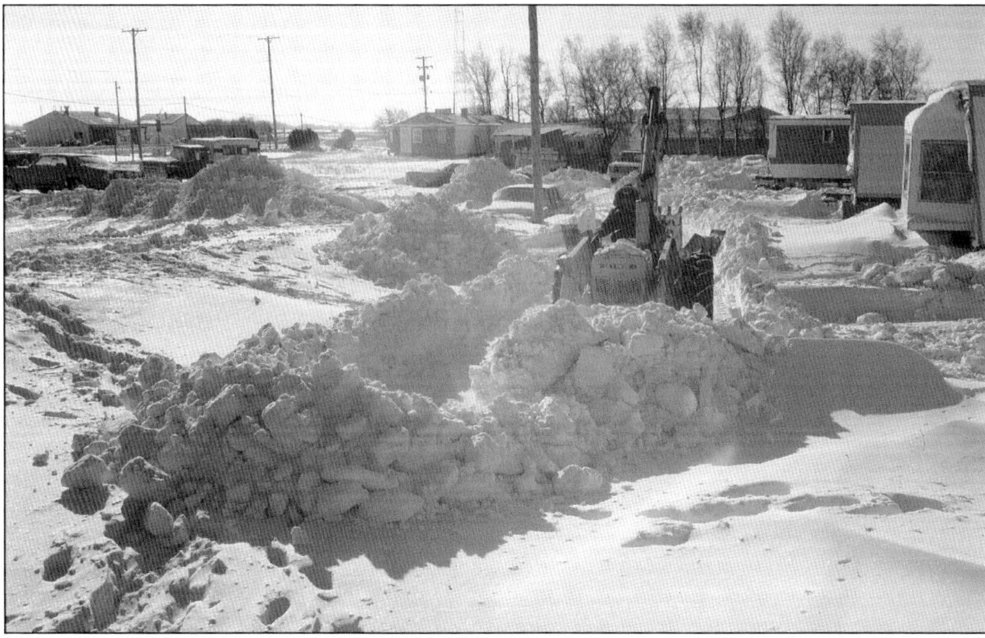

This photograph of Baer's Trailer Park shows a worker trying to clear more than a foot of snow after 1978's major snowstorm. The drifts caused by the wind were the major factor in this storm. (Courtesy of Scott Baer.)

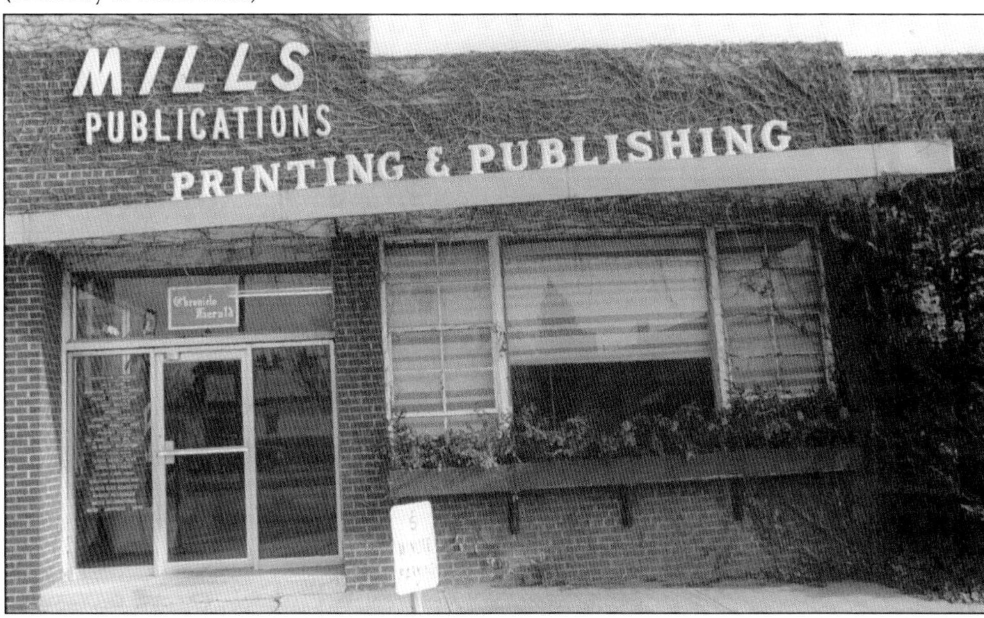

The *North Vermilion Chronicle*, launched by Gideon W. Seavey and Dale Wallace in January 1872, was located in the second story of Moore and Brillhart's hardware store on the northwest corner of Market Street and East Thompson Avenue. It later moved opposite the United Presbyterian Church and was later housed in a frame building that became Worthens, in the basement of the First National Bank, in a building on First Avenue (now the MultiAgency), then at 308 East Main Street. Other early newspapers were the *Hoopeston Herald*, *Hoopeston News*, *Evening Herald*, *Hoopeston Daily*, *Weekly Chronicle*, *Hoopeston Evening Times*, and the *Chronicle-Herald* (pictured here).

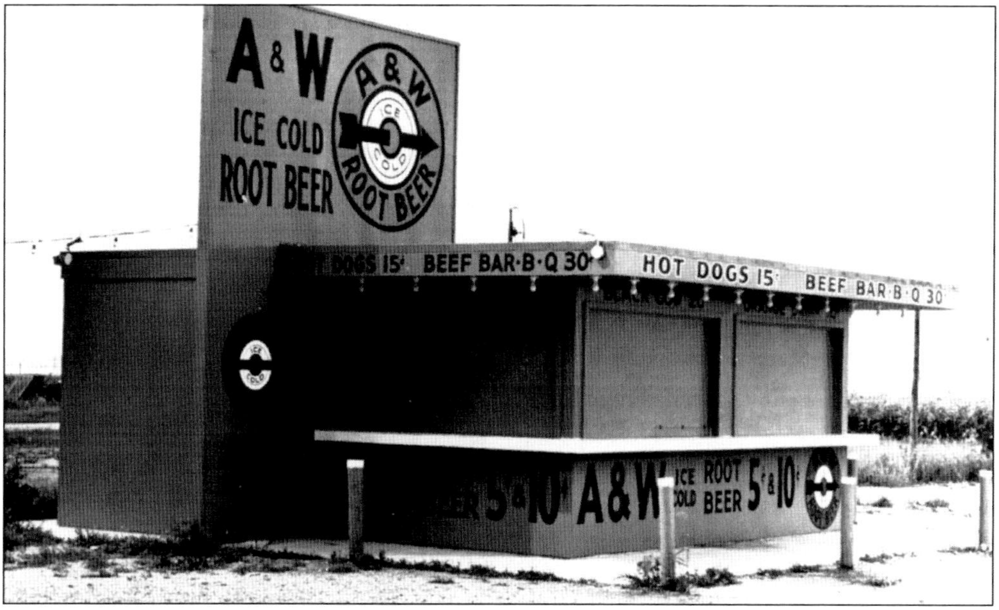

The A&W Root Beer stand was built by Brown's Woodwork in 1953. The Cartwright family owned the business and sold it to Don and Adalaide Henning in 1968. Henning owned it until 1984, when Dan Eckert bought the business. The Hennings bought it back in 1986. Following Don Henning's death, it was sold to Shirley Harper in 1990. (Courtesy of Scott and Traci Brown.)

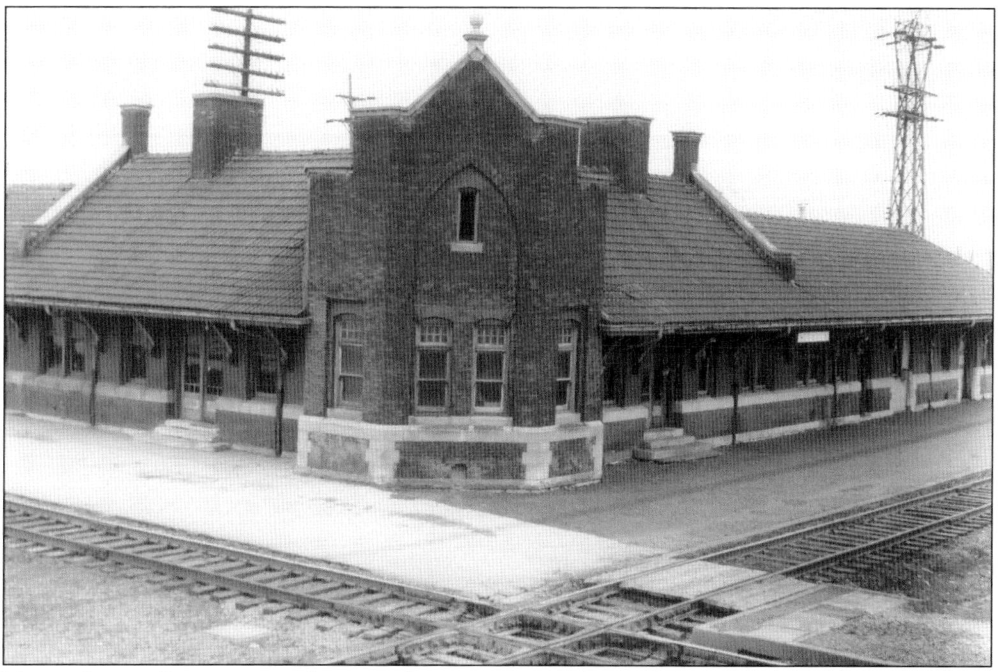

Union Station Depot was at first two depots. In 1876, the Nickel Plate depot was on the south side of the tracks, just east of Second Avenue. The Chicago, Danville & Vincennes Railroad station was located on the west side of the tracks, just north of Penn Street. Before 1880, both depots were moved to the west corner junction of the railroads. Later, the brick Union Station Depot was built. (Courtesy of Hoopeston Public Library.)

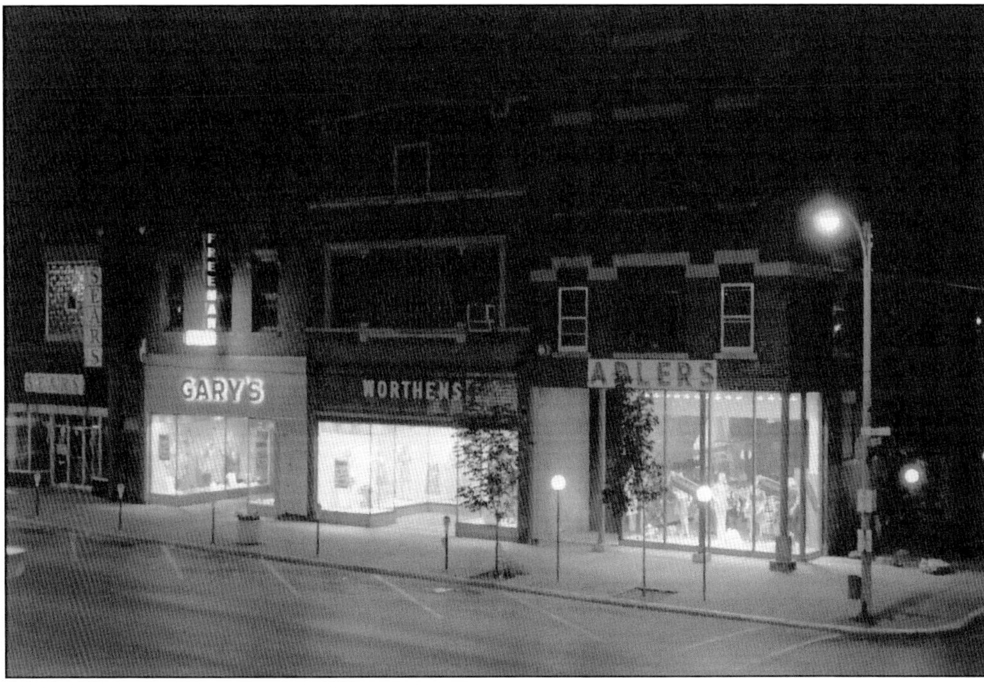

This nighttime photograph taken in 1972 shows the south side of the 200 block of East Main at Bank Street. The businesses of Sears, Gary's, Worthens, and Adlers are shown. (Courtesy of Scott Baer.)

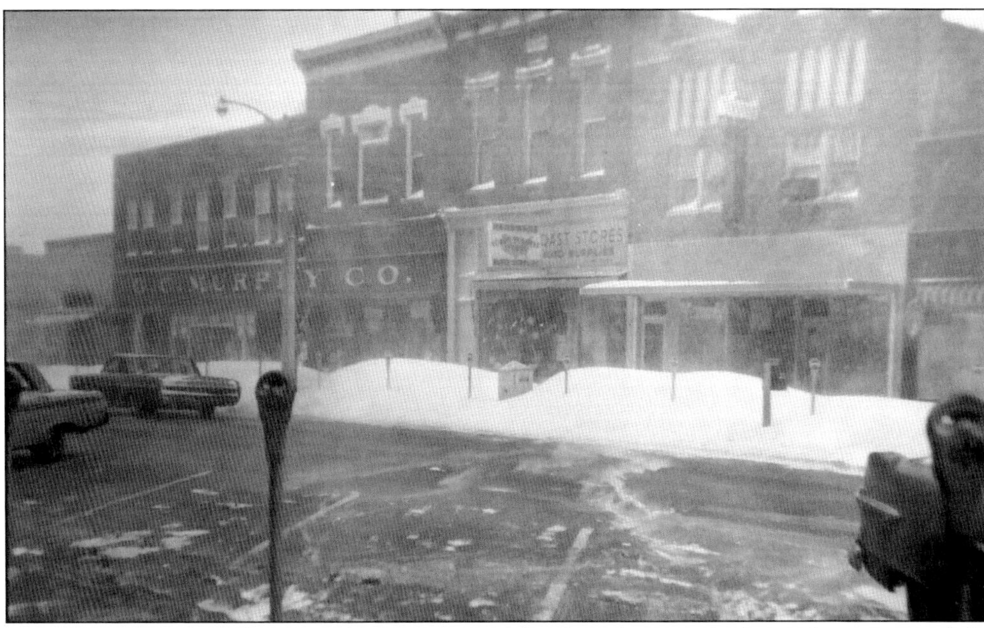

The winter of 1978 had a record-breaking snowfall. This photograph shows the remains of the snow along the 200 block of East Main Street in front of the G.C. Murphy Co., also known as the Little Dimestore, and the Coast to Coast hardware store. The parking meters were also part of Hoopeston's downtown during this time. They have since been removed. (Courtesy of Scott Baer.)

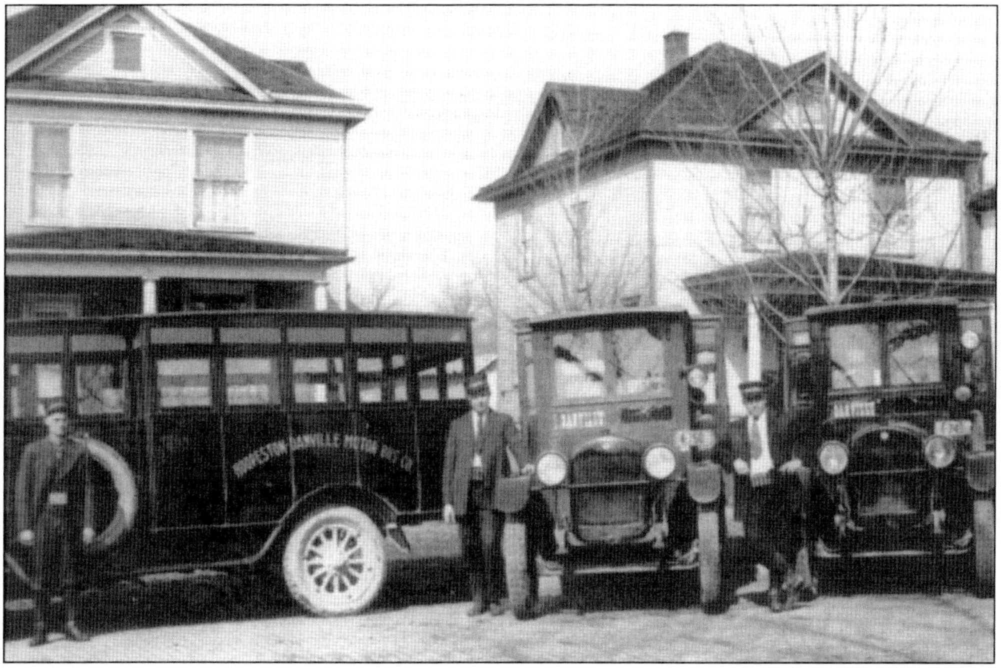

The Hoopeston-Danville Motor Bus Company is shown on Main Street in Hoopeston in 1922. The bus company ran on the Dixie Highway/Route 1 through Rossville to downtown Danville, providing workers, shoppers, and others a convenient way to go from city to city. (Courtesy of the Hoopeston Public Library.)

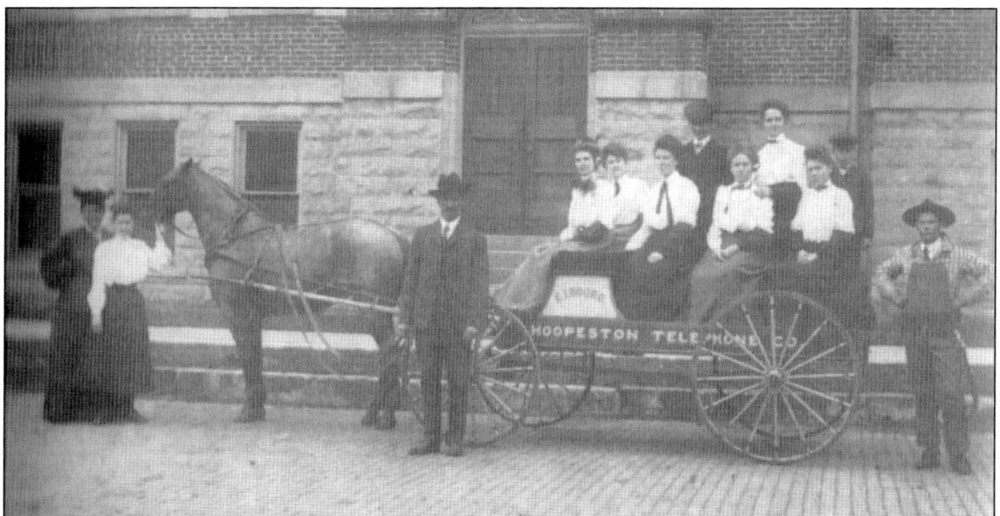

Chamberlin's Telephone Exchange was opened in 1895, on the second floor of the Montgomery Ward building. This photograph taken at the turn of the 20th century and shows the Boorde family, owners at that time. Standing from left to right are Anna Boorde, daughter Mabel Boorde Harris, Elijah J. Boorde, and lineman Albert Sims. In the wagon, from left to right, are Olive Newburn Boughton, Belle Hussey Boburn, Francis Bradley, John Rosslyn Boorde (the family's son), Alice Potter Scott, Lucy Potter Yates, Mary Fickle, and a boy cousin of John and Mable Boorde. (Courtesy of the Hoopeston Public Library.)

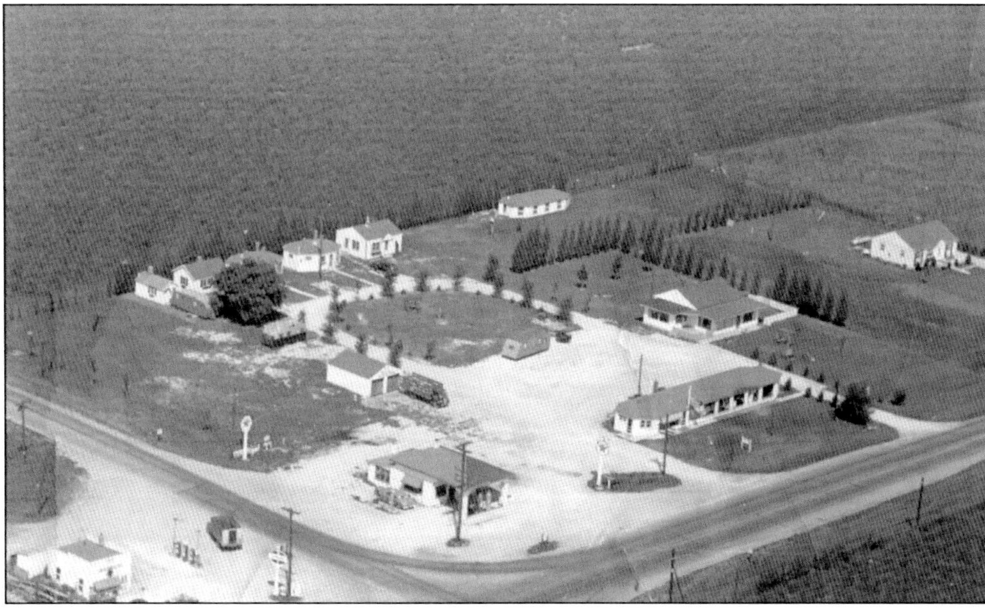

This aerial photograph shows the northwest corner of Routes 1 and 9 in September 1949. Most of the buildings toward the back are Economy tourist cabins, which were products of the Economy Portable Building Company of Chicago. The two homes to the right are Baer's National Home, which Ora J. Baer lived in, built in the autumn of 1945, and another rental home. The front two buildings are the original Texaco station and Baer Norse Appliance dealership. (Courtesy of Scott Baer.)

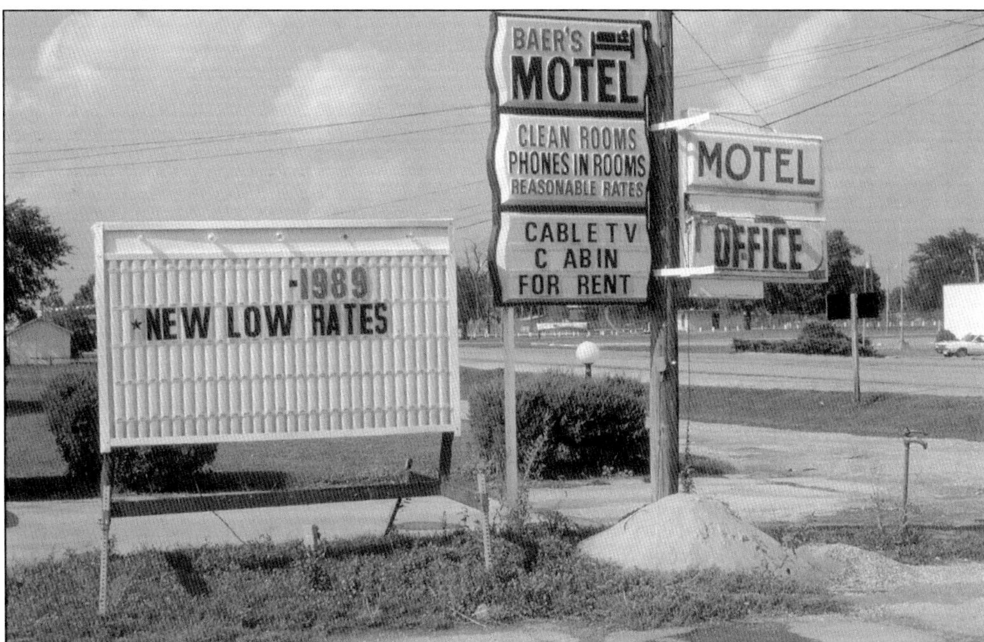

Baer's Motel was a staple in Hoopeston from 1945, when Ora J. Baer built a motel on the corner of Routes 1 and 9, until 2004. This sign advertises the amenities offered by Baer during his ownership of the motel. (Courtesy of Scott Baer.)

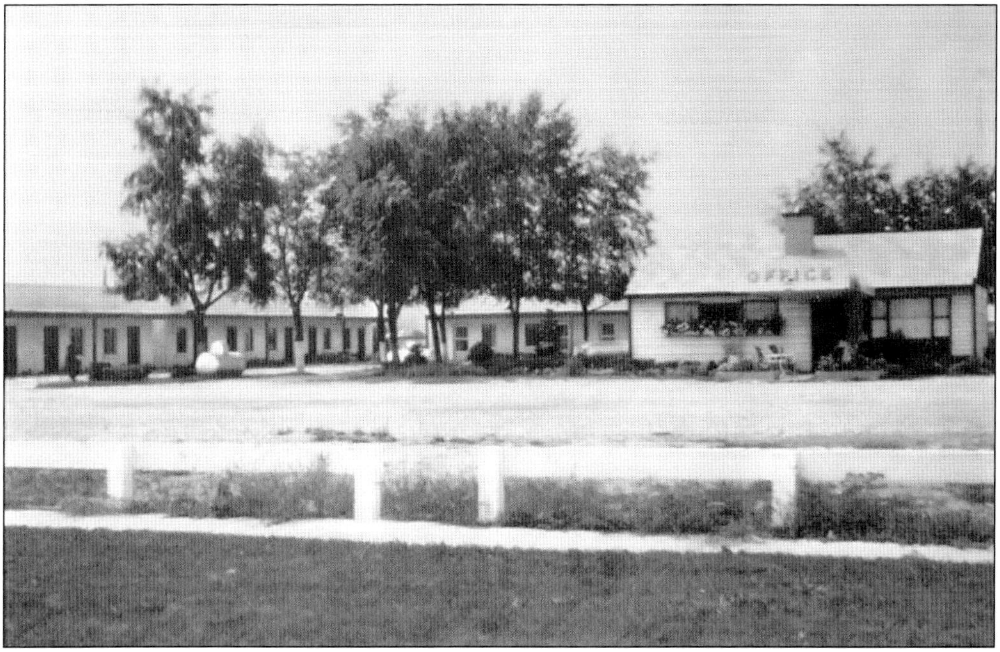

This photograph shows several units of Baer's Motel, which sat behind the home of Ora J. Baer. Baer not only owned the motel but also had a trailer park and a store selling kitchen appliances. Additionally, he built many of the homes around Hoopeston, including most of those on Scott Drive, named after his youngest son, Scott.

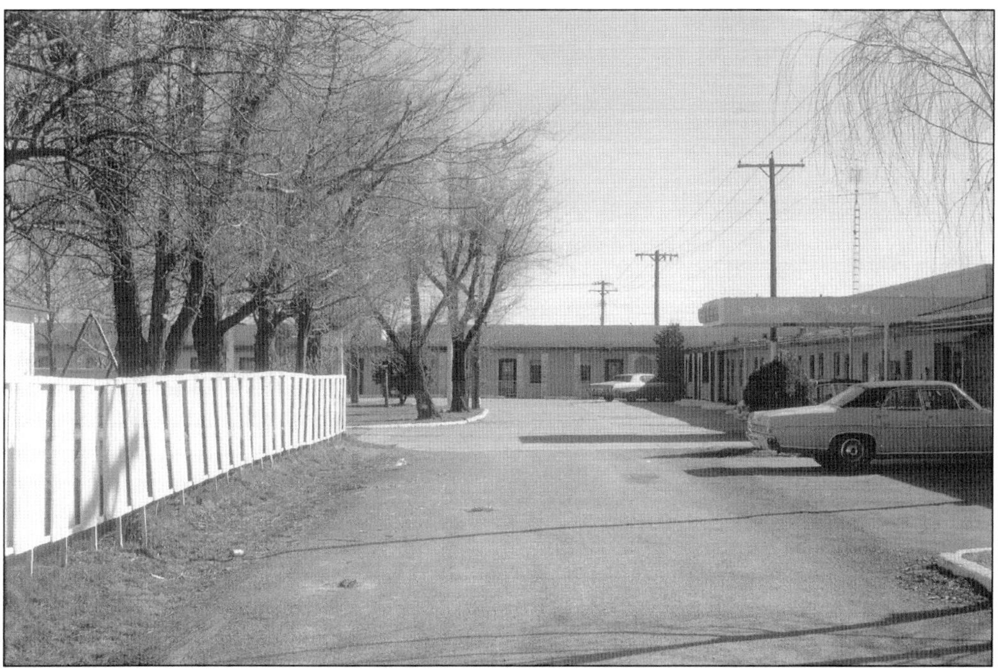

The office of Baer's Motel is shown in this photograph. Besides the motel section, Baer offered several little one- and two-bedroom cottages for families to rent. (Courtesy of Scott Baer.)

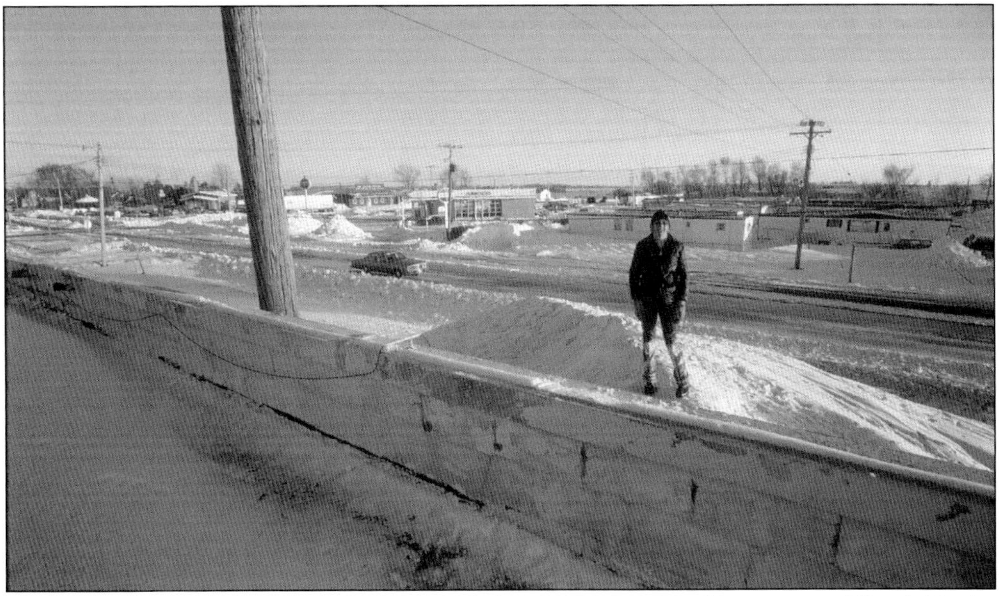

This photograph of the January 1978 blizzard shows the amount of snow around Baer's Trailer Park, the Amoco station, Dick Jones Auto Sales, and Cox Building Systems on the south corner of Routes 1 and 9. Scott Baer, son of Ora J. Baer, stands on a pile of snow south of the motel. (Courtesy of Scott Baer.)

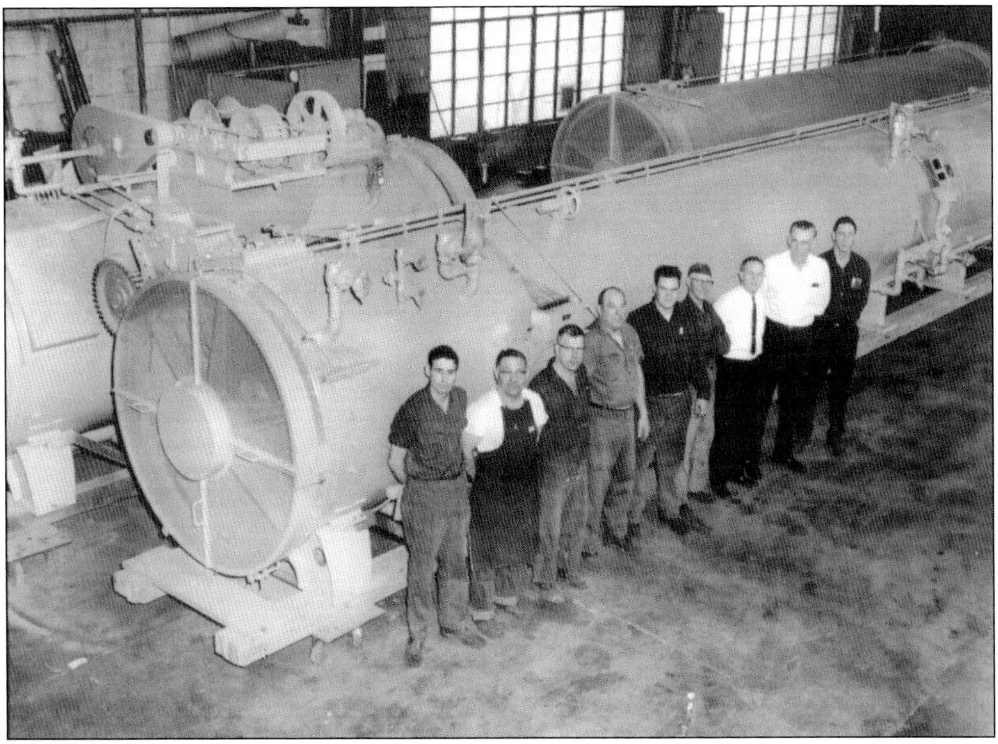

Food Machinery Corporation made many items used in the canning industry. This 1963 photograph shows the different cookers the company produced for local and worldwide canning industries. The plant closed in February 2004.

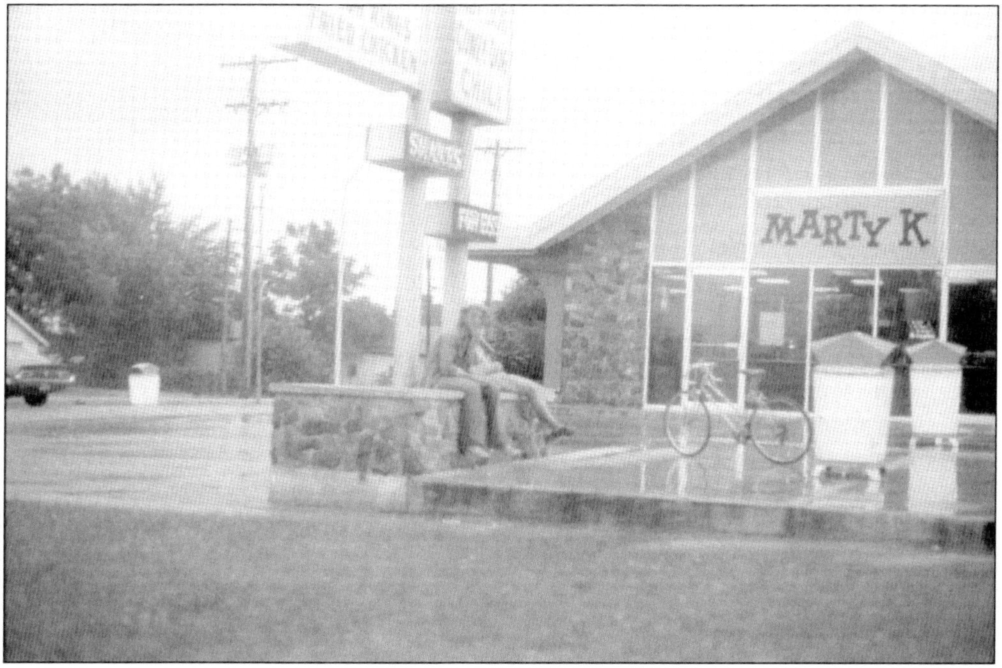

Marty K's, located on the northeast corner of Penn Street, later became known as the Around the Flame restaurant owned by Joseph Jusefi. It burned down in approximately 1976. (Courtesy of Scott Baer.)

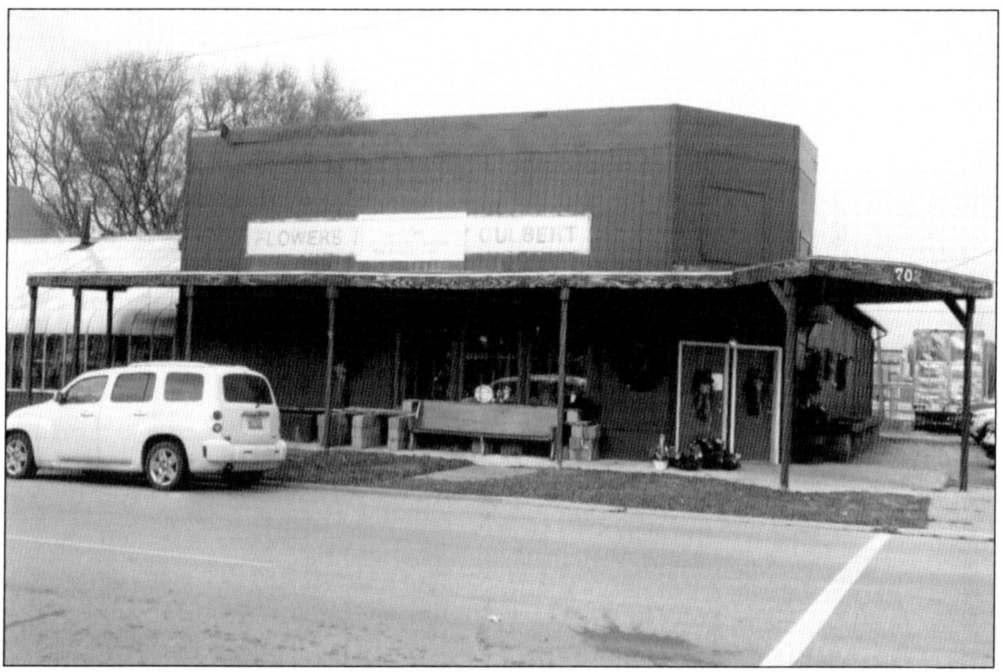

Molly Culbert's Flowers and Gifts by Molly was located at 702 West Main Street for 54 years, having moved to Hoopeston in 1962. The Culbert family was in business a total of 72 years, starting in Rossville in the 1890s. The business sold in December 2014 to Elaine and Brandon Tyler, who renamed it The Flower Shop.

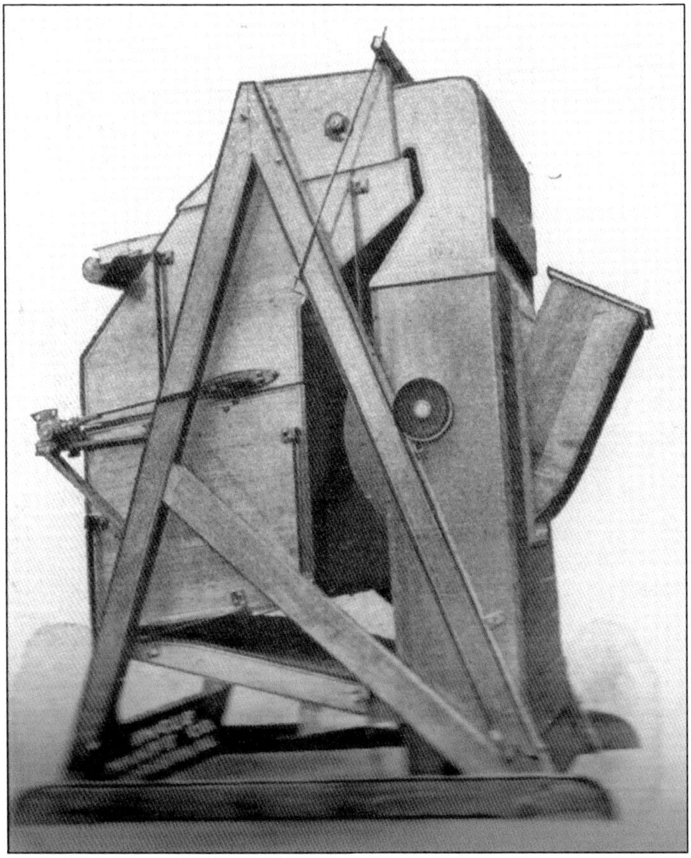

The Ingle Manufacturing Company was organized by Scott Ingle and E.C. Bird in 1899. This photograph shows the succotash mill; succotash was one of the products produced here.

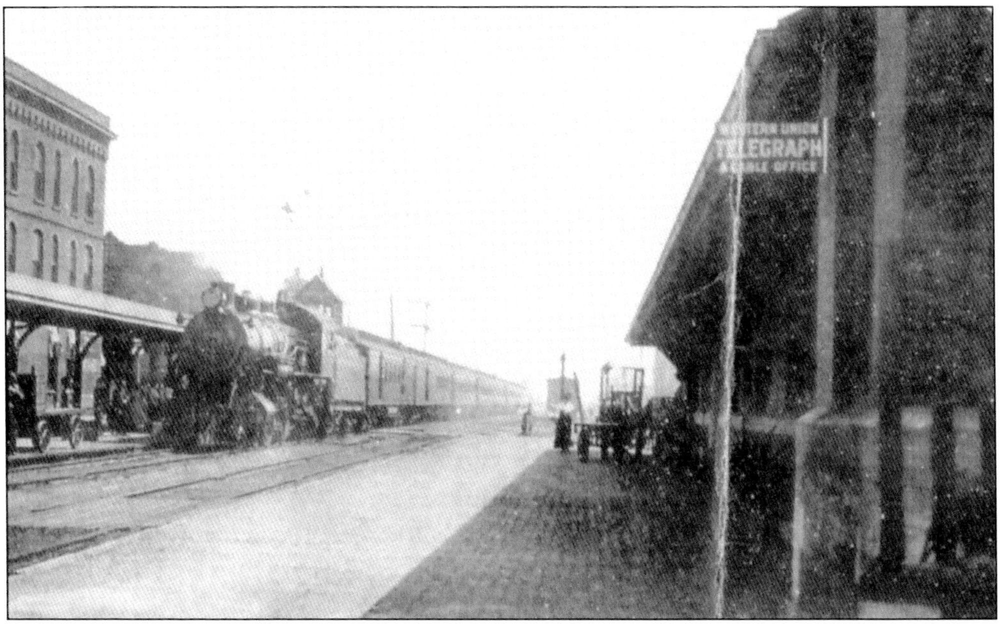

The Union Train Depot is shown in this early 1900s photograph, with people waiting to board the train. The Western Union Telegraph & Cable Office is also visible.

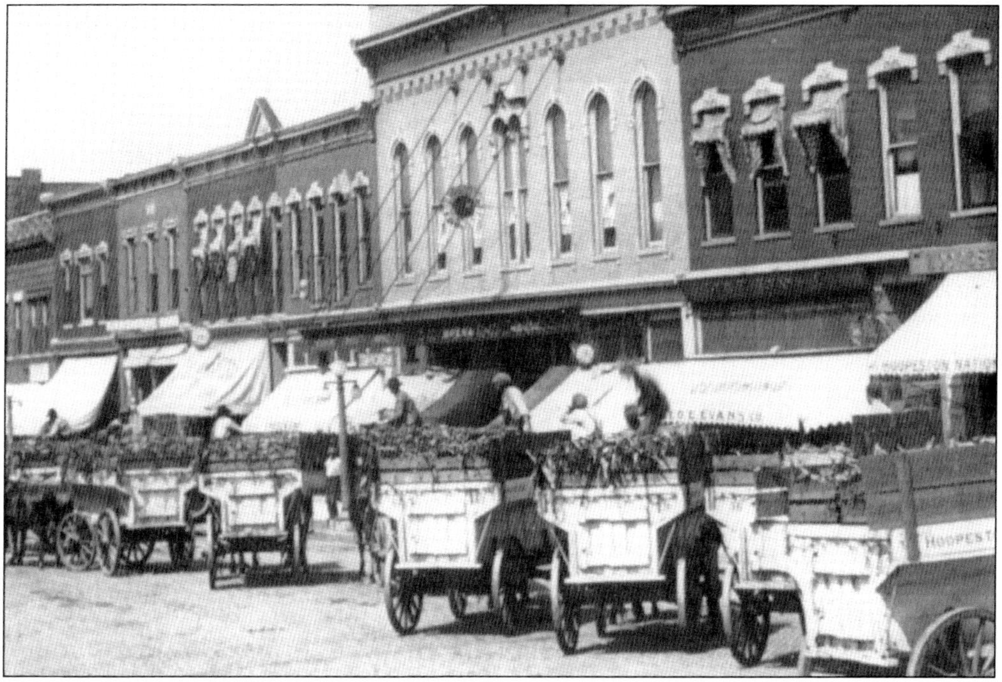

In the early years of the canning industry, mule-driven wagons on their way to deliver corn frequently lined Main Street. The Evans Clothing Store and opera house are shown in this early 1900s photograph.

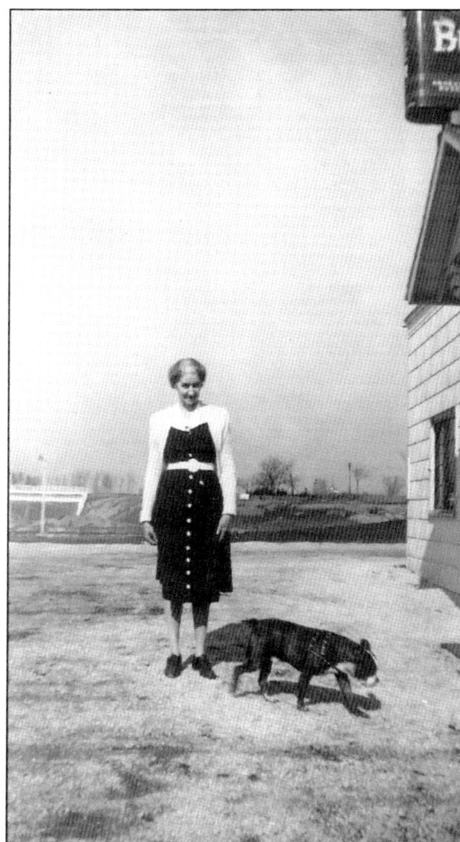

Lona Morgan Hayes stands with her dog in front of her 1940s business, the original tavern on Route 1. The tavern was known as Sweet's Tavern from 1941–1946 and became Vance Tavern in 1946. Today, it is BJ's Pump. In the background, the viaduct can be seen. (Courtesy of Scott Baer.)

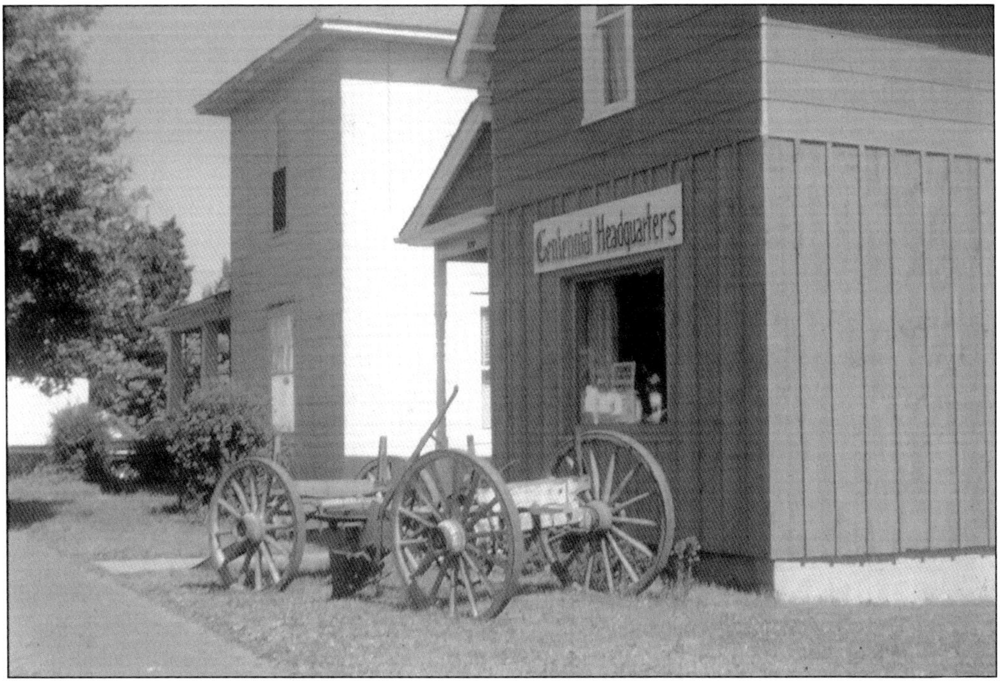

In 1971, the headquarters for Hoopeston's centennial was located at 219 West Main Street. (Courtesy of Scott Baer.)

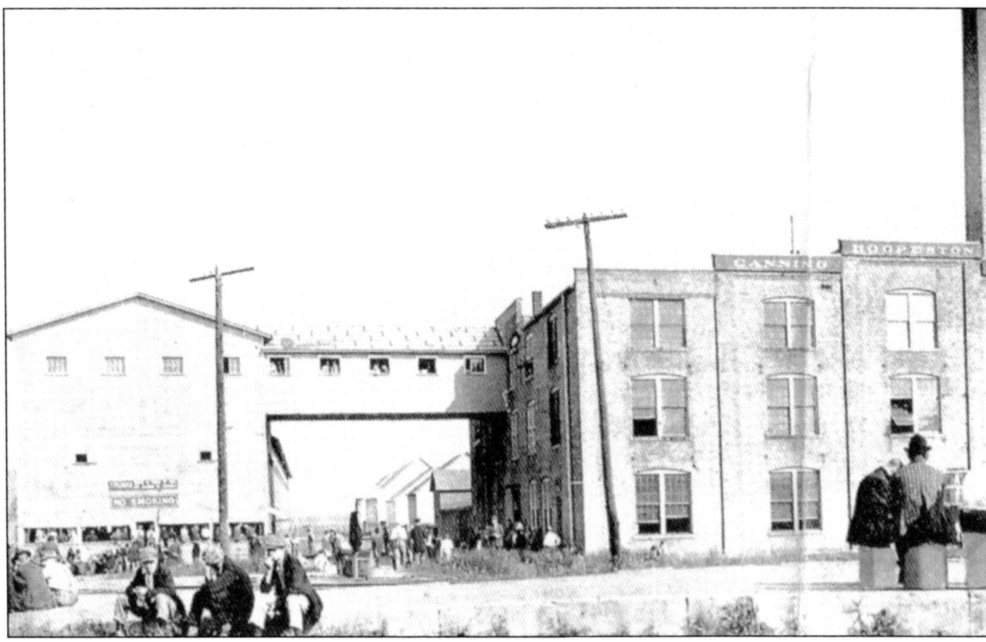

The Hoopeston Canning Company, founded in 1876 by J.S. McFerren, A.H. Trego, and A.T. Catherwood, did not incorporate until 1911. This 1913 photograph shows the workers on lunch break. In 1946, the Hoopeston Canning Company was sold to Stokely-Van Camp. In 1985, it was sold to Oconomowoc Canning Company, which changed the name to Stokely USA. Chiquita Brands International bought Stokely USA late in 1997 and closed the plant in 1998.

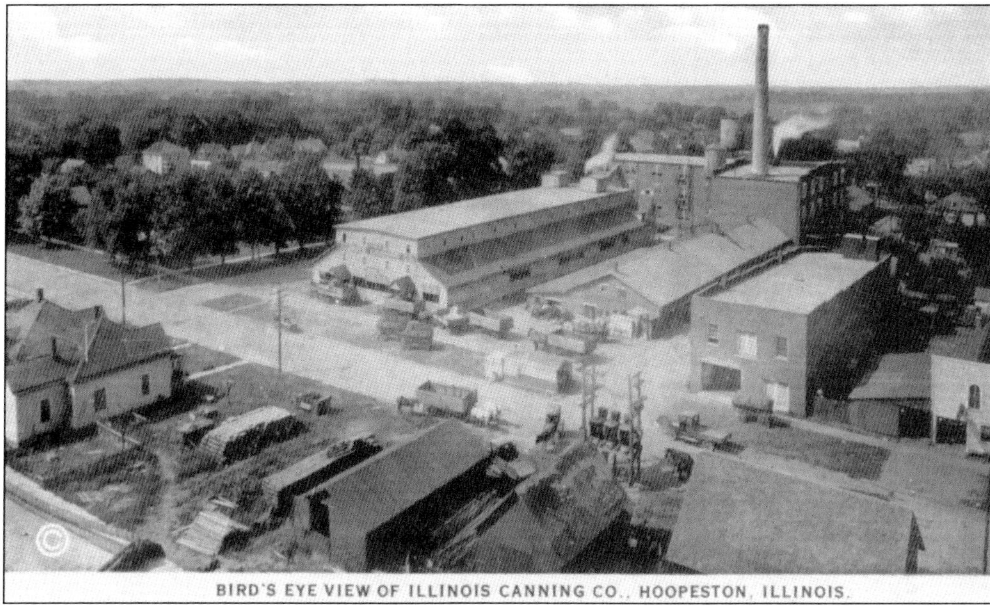

The Illinois Canning Company was the first business enterprise established in Hoopeston. S.S. McCall of New York established the company in 1875. It later was purchased by Joan of Arc, then by Pillsbury. When it was put up for sale in 1995, the employees bought the company and renamed it Hoopeston Foods. Teasdale Quality Foods of California acquired Hoopeston Foods in September 2012.

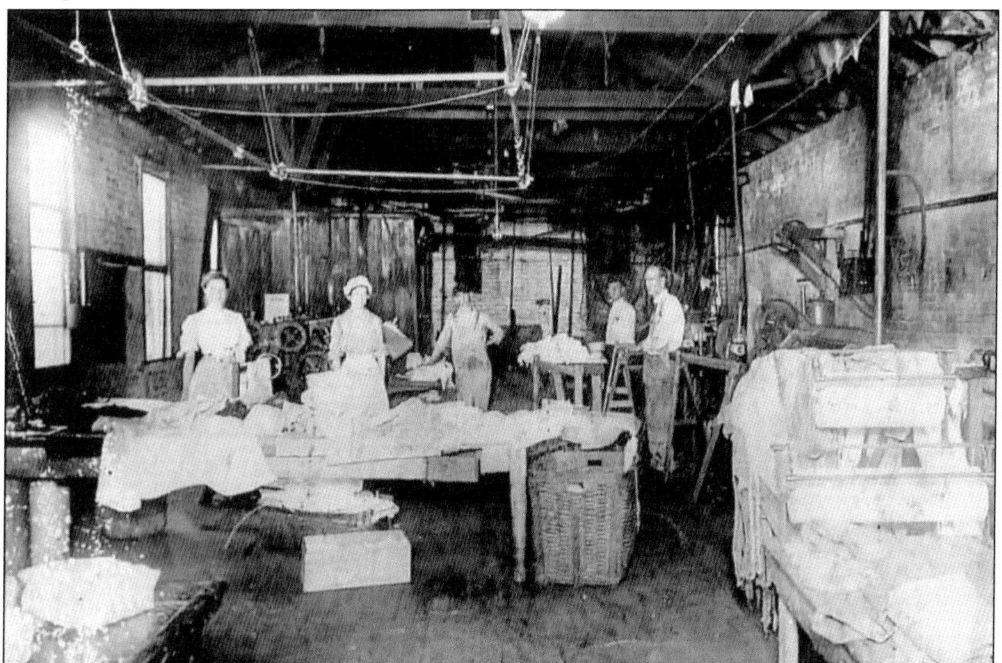

Parkway Laundry and Dry Cleaners, 201 North Market Street, served Hoopeston beginning in 1897. This early photograph shows the back room of the business and its employees working with the laundry. Fleta Park Evans was the owner in 1974.

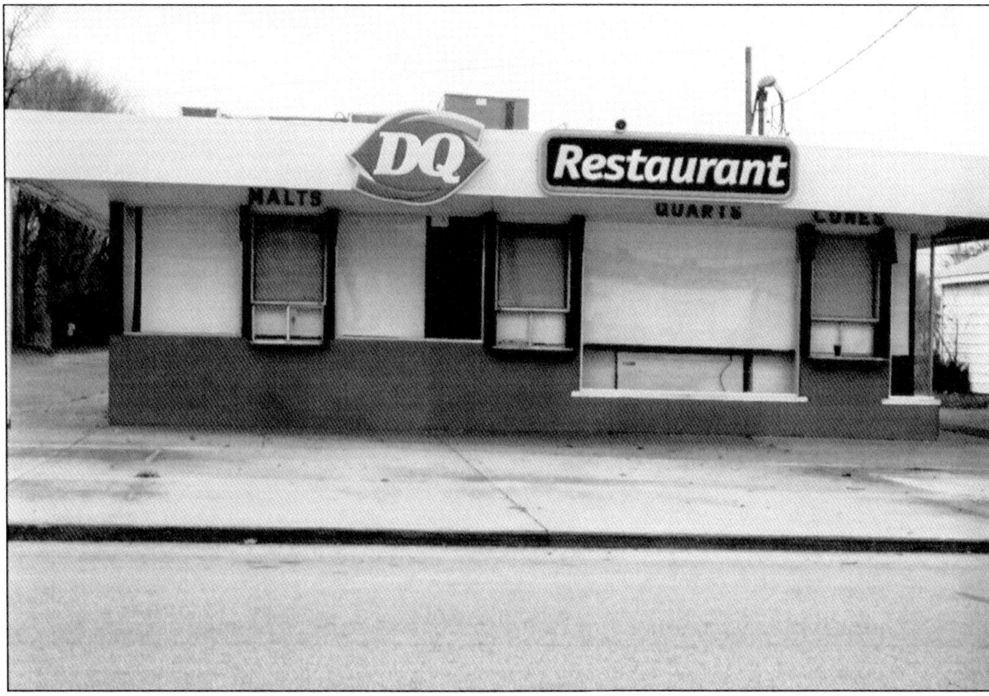

Simpson's Dairy Queen at 715 West Main Street was first built and opened in 1950 by Art and Eileen Murray. Arthur and Mary Simpson bought the business in 1958. Their son Harold and his wife, Cathy, bought the business in 1981. It continues as a family-owned business, open March to October each year.

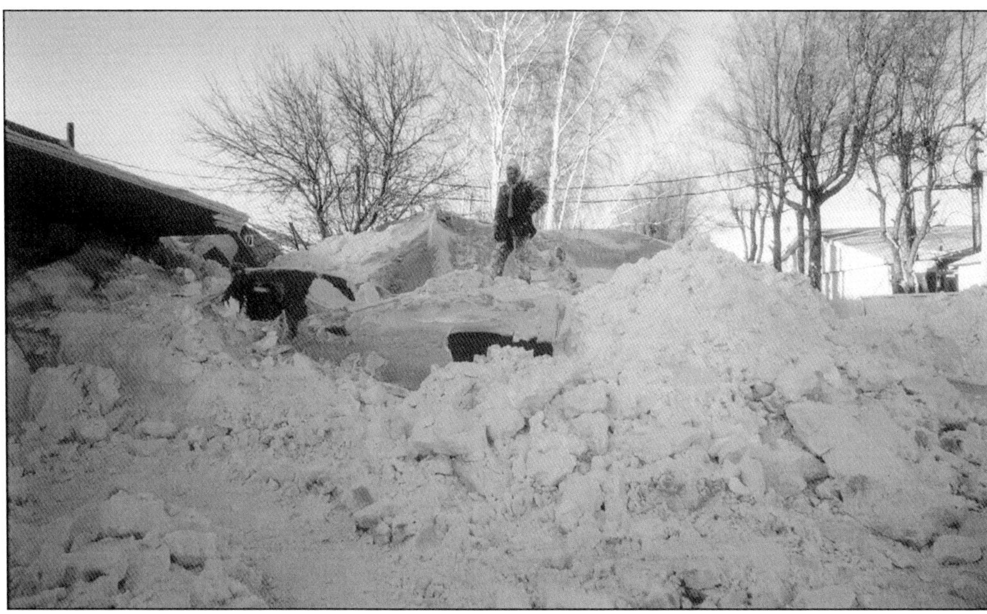

This 1978 photograph was taken at Baer's Motel. Snow-covered vehicles are visible under the drifts. Scott Baer stands on top of the pile of snow. (Courtesy of Scott Baer.)

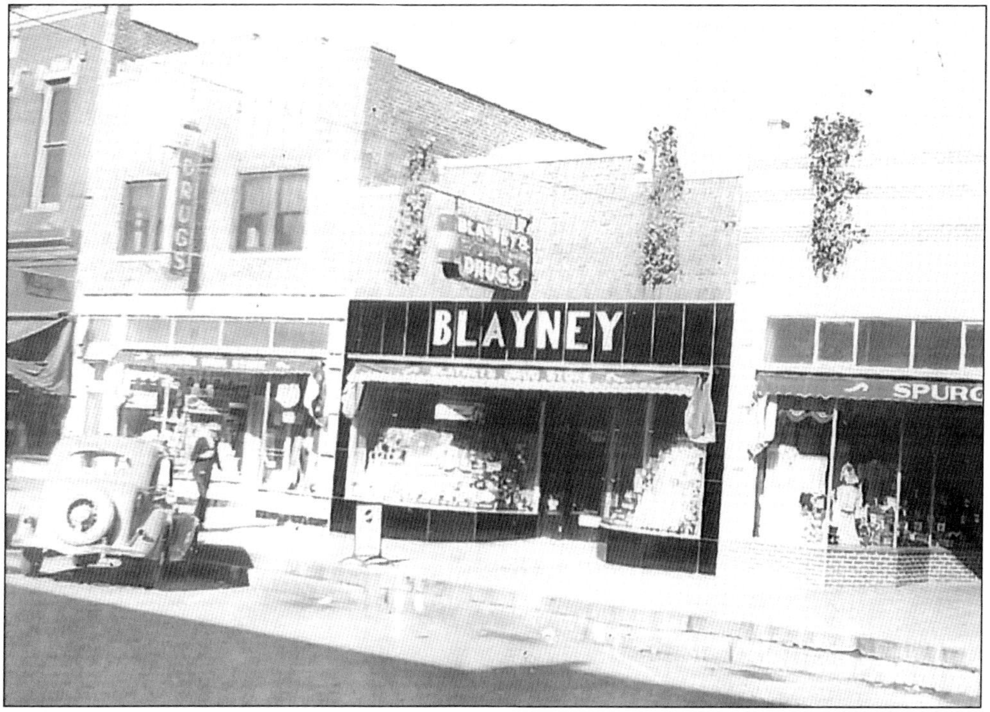

Pictured here are Blayney's drugstore, Lester's Drug Store, part of Spurgeons (to the right), and G.C. Murphy's (to the left) in the 200 block of East Main Street in 1940s.

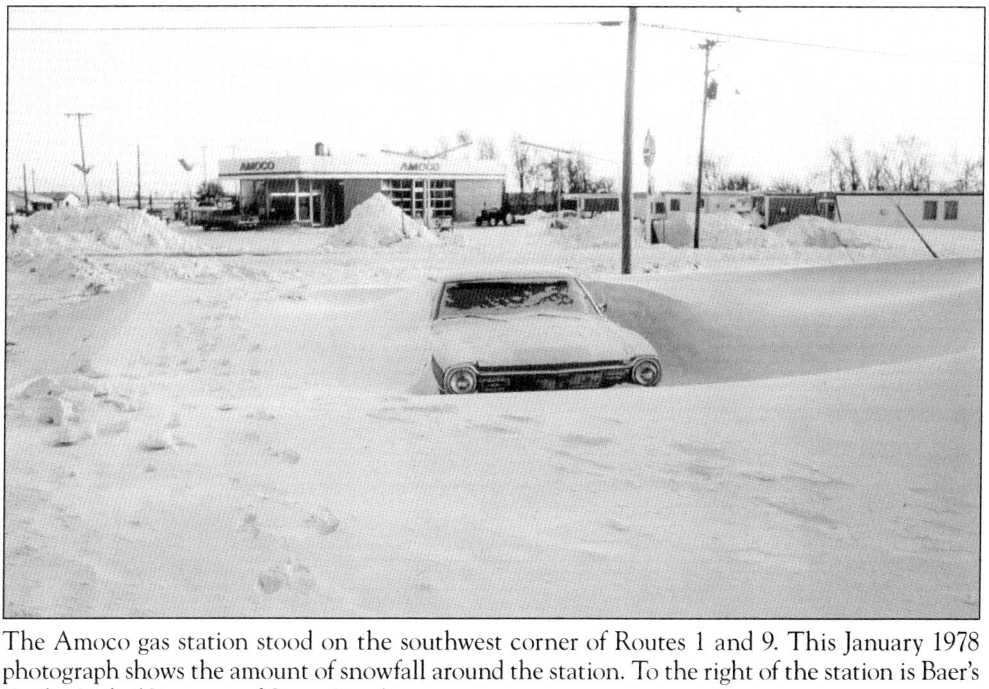

The Amoco gas station stood on the southwest corner of Routes 1 and 9. This January 1978 photograph shows the amount of snowfall around the station. To the right of the station is Baer's Trailer Park. (Courtesy of Scott Baer.)

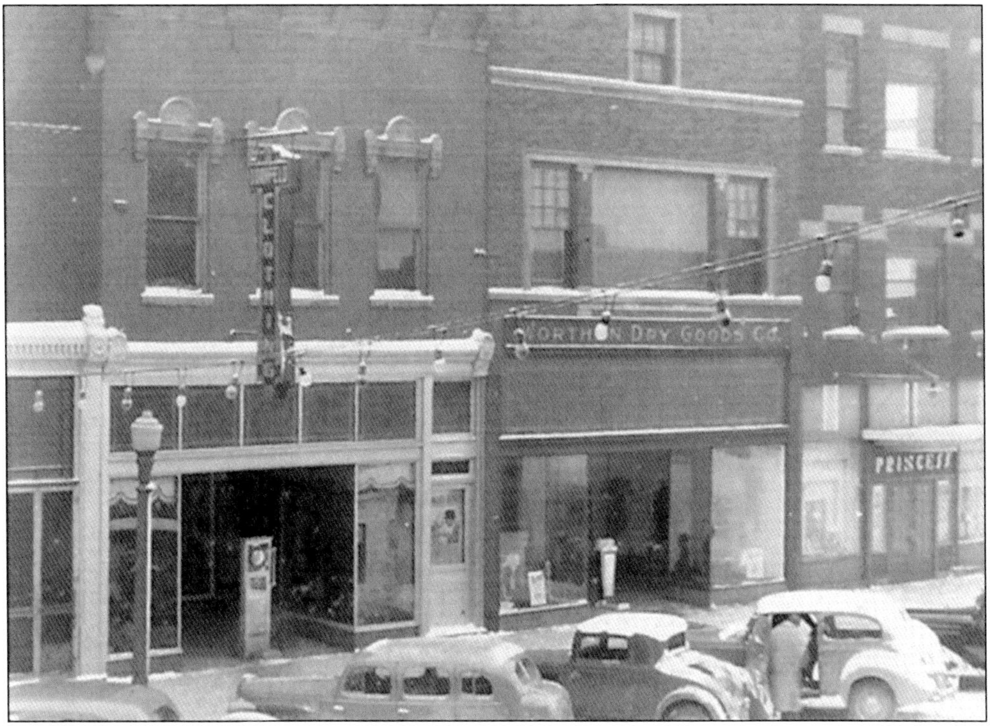

This 1940s photograph of the 200 block of downtown Hoopeston shows Dornfield Clothing, Worthen Day Goods Co., and the Princess Theatre. The Princess opened in 1935.

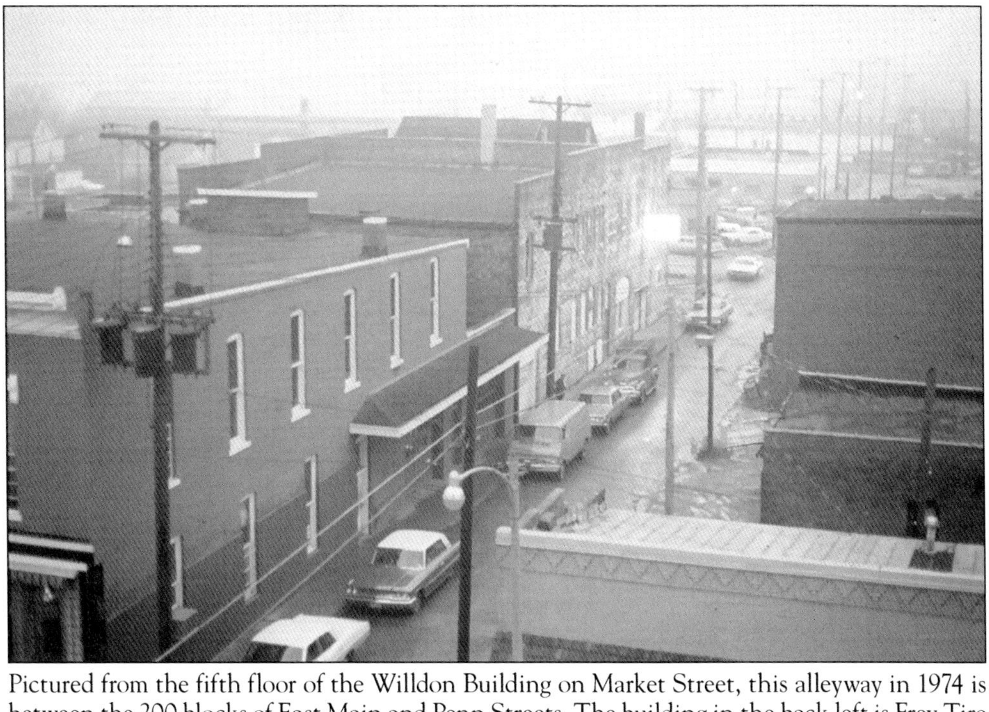

Pictured from the fifth floor of the Willdon Building on Market Street, this alleyway in 1974 is between the 200 blocks of East Main and Penn Streets. The building in the back left is Frey Tire Company. (Courtesy of Scott Baer.)

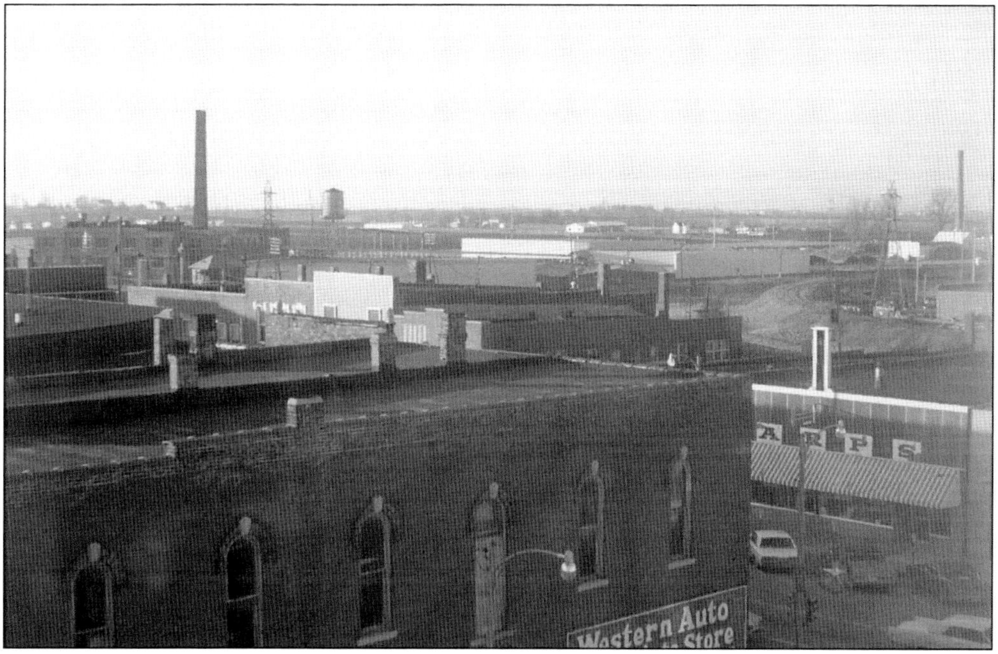

Carps and Western Auto can be recognized by their signage in this 1974 photograph taken from the fifth floor of the Willdon Building in the 200 block of East Main and Market Streets. Stokely's and its warehouses can be seen in the background. (Courtesy of Scott Baer.)

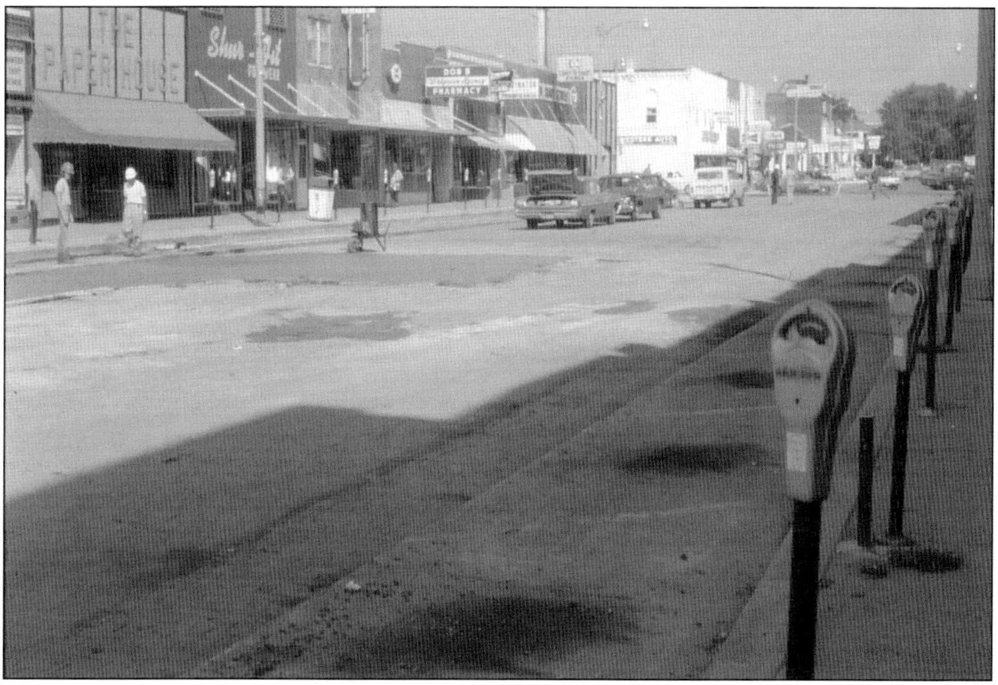

In 1974, the City of Hoopeston repaired the 200 block of East Main Street. Along the north side of the road are the Paper House (now the Little Lorraine Theatre), Shur-Fit, Lester's Drug Store, Don B's Pharmacy, Sheridan's, Coast to Coast, and Russell Leigh & Associate. Today, Western Auto is located on the northeast corner of Main and Market Streets. (Courtesy of Scott Baer.)

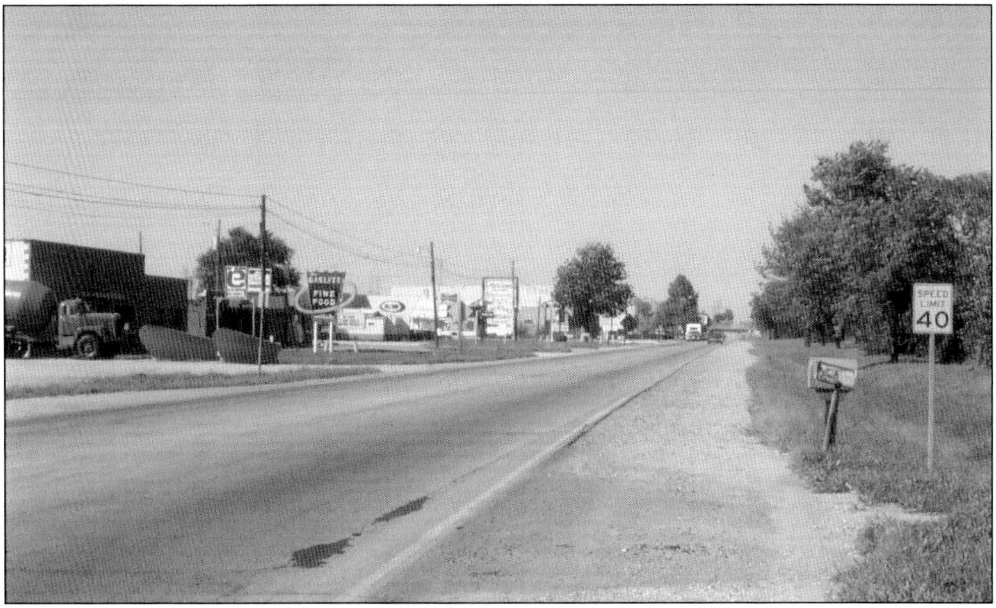

This photograph taken in 1974 of the west side of Route 1, north of the Route 9 intersection, shows the Ford dealership, the Gaslite Fine Food Restaurant, the A&W, Bob Smythe's gas station, and Essex Wire Corporation. (Courtesy of Scott Baer.)

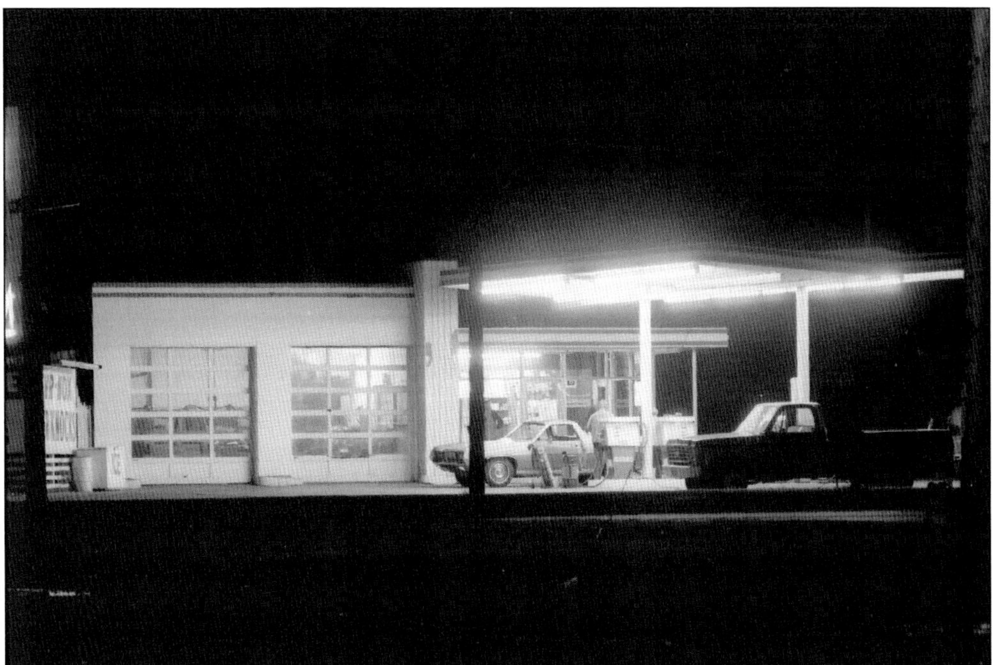

Sorenson's Freeway Gas Station was located at Routes 1 and 9 in 1975 on the same corner as Baer's Motel. At one time, there were gas stations on all four corners of Routes 1 and 9. Today, there are none in the area. (Courtesy of Scott Baer.)

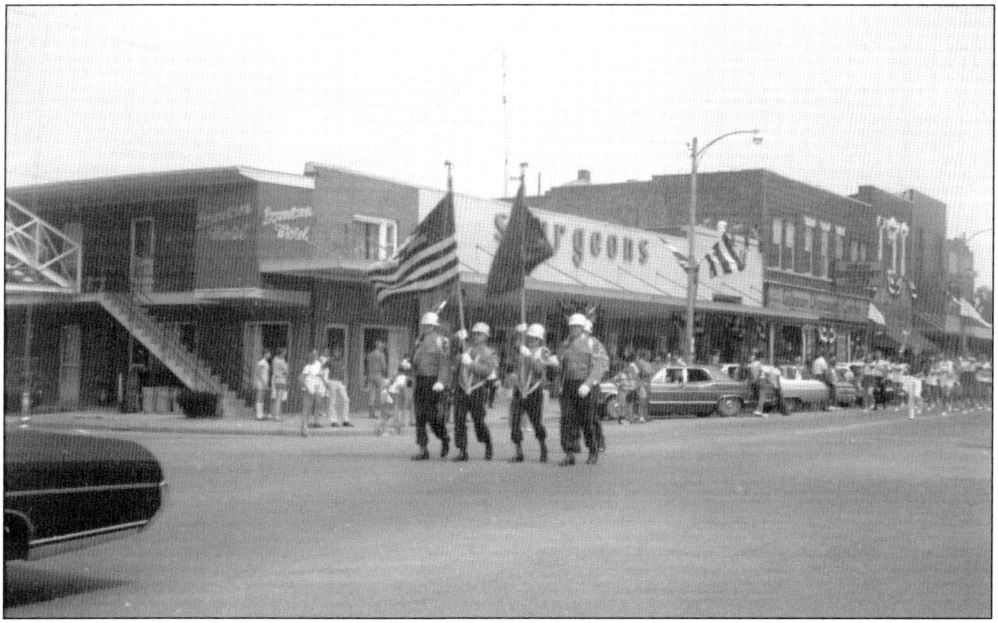

This 1971 Hoopeston centennial parade shows Spurgeons, which was later lost to a fire; Gibson Discount building, now an empty lot; the Paper House, now the Little Lorraine Theatre; Shur Fit; and Lester's Drug Store. (Courtesy of Scott Baer.)

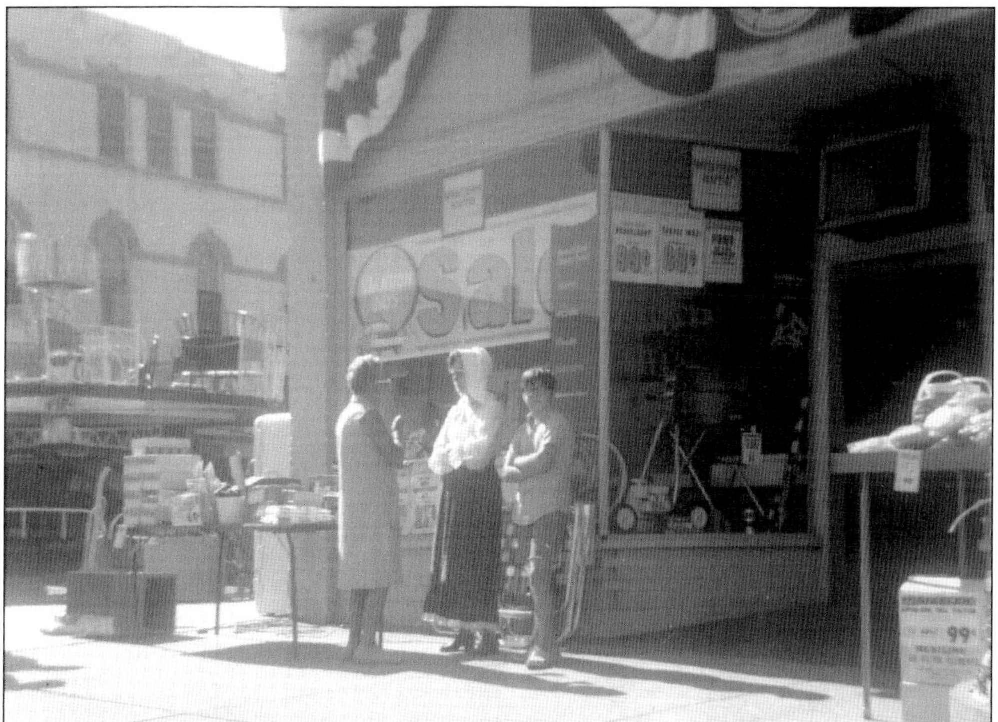

Downtown Hoopeston held a street sale during the centennial on East Main Street. This 1971 photograph shows items for sale in front of Western Auto on the southwest corner of Main Street. (Courtesy of Scott Baer.)

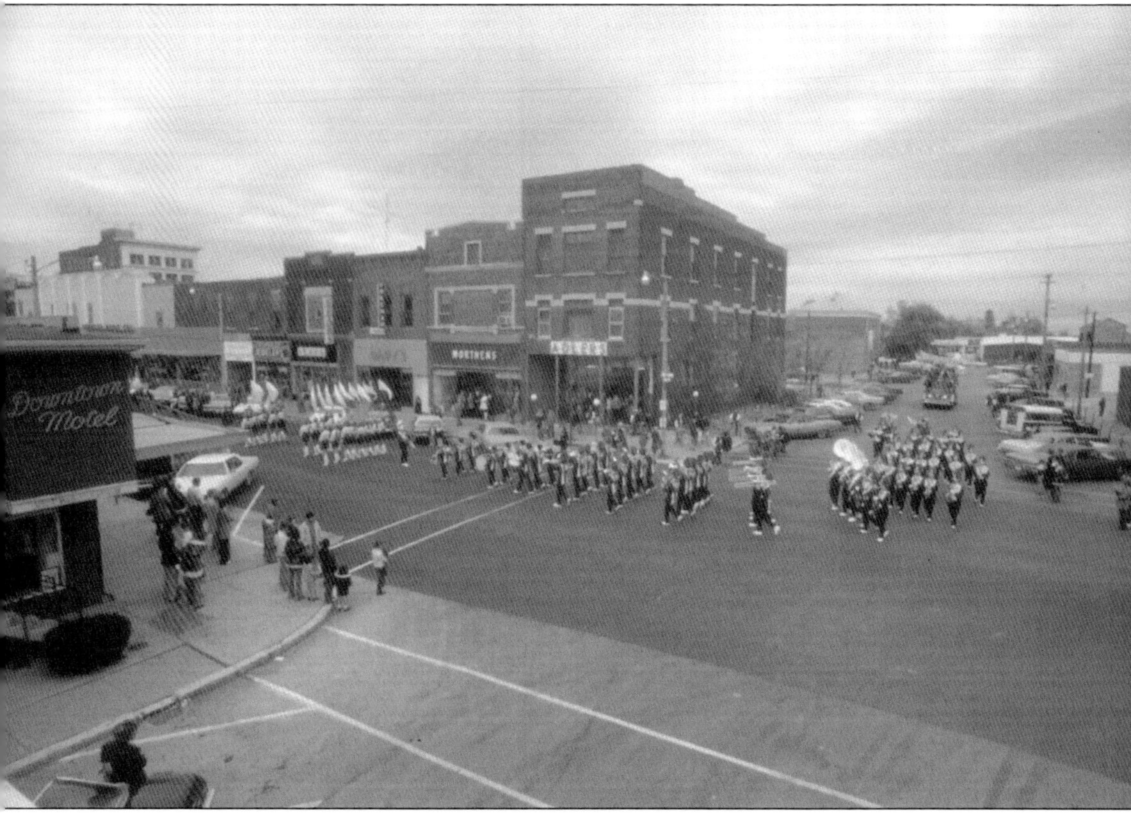

Hoopeston's marching band is shown traveling down Bank Street to Main Street during the 1971 homecoming parade in this photograph taken from the Downtown Motel walkway across South Bank Street. Businesses shown from right to left are Adlers, Worthens, Garys, Sears, Fronville Jewelers, Thrashers Shoe Store, and Schultz Brothers Company. (Courtesy of Scott Baer.)

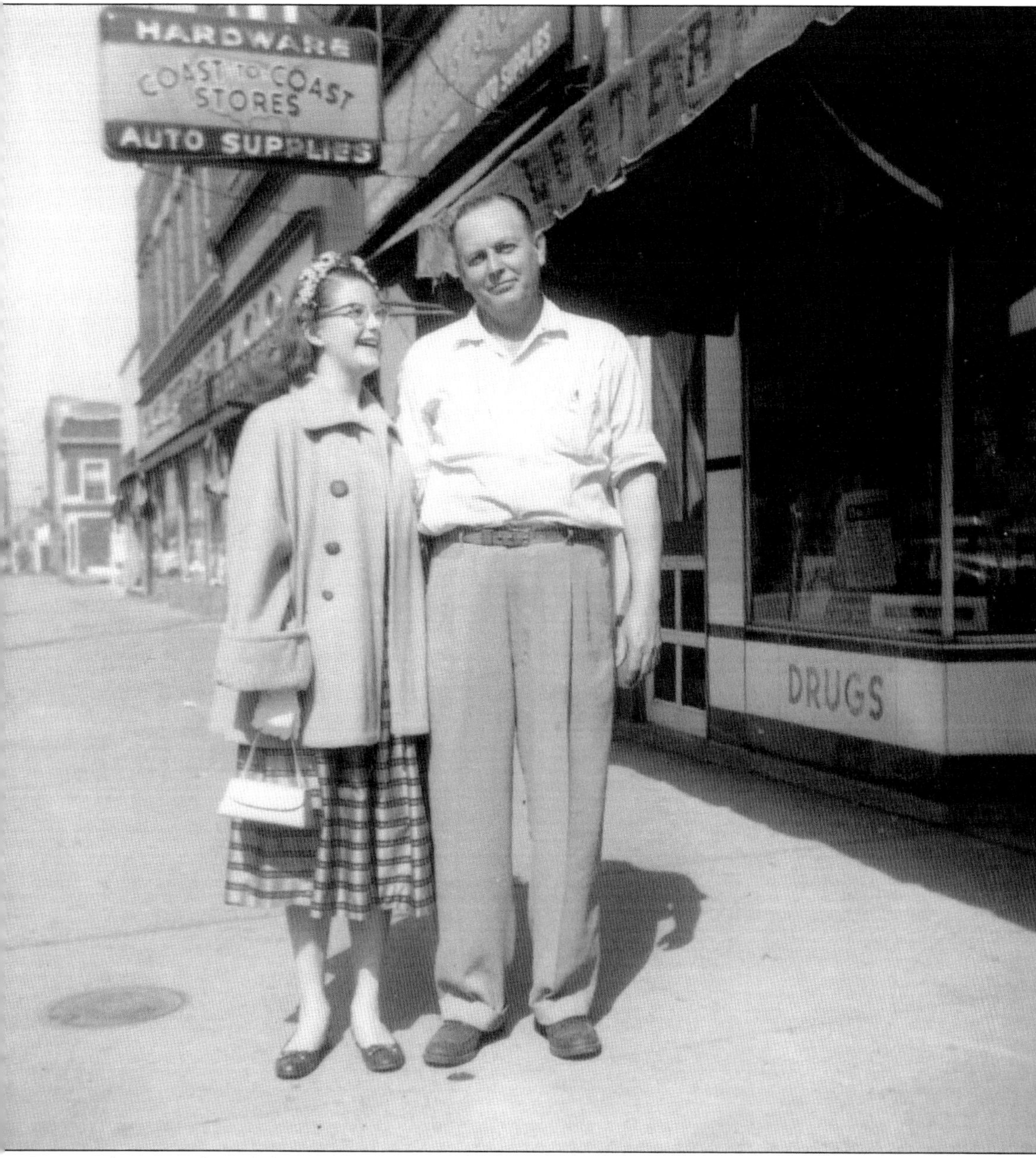

Jean Carlson stands with her father, Web Carlson, in front of Lester's Drug Store in the 200 block of East Main Street. Part of the Coast to Coast sign and G.C. Murphy's Co. department store are seen in the background.

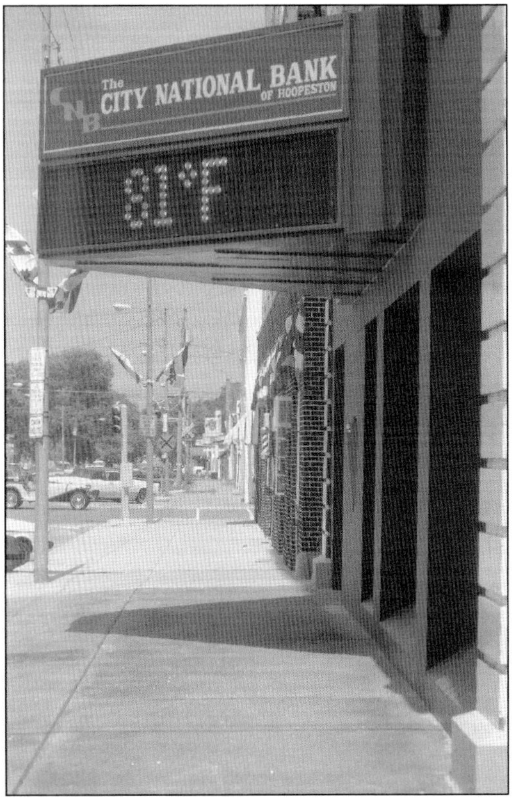

The sign for the City National Bank in the Willdon Building, pictured in August 1978, shows a temperature of 81 degrees. The National Sweetcorn Festival banners were up in preparation for the annual event. (Courtesy of Scott Baer.)

The Lorraine Theatre was a big part of downtown business in 1984. Customers came from miles around, some as far as Chicago, to see a movie in the Lorraine. (Courtesy of Scott Baer.)

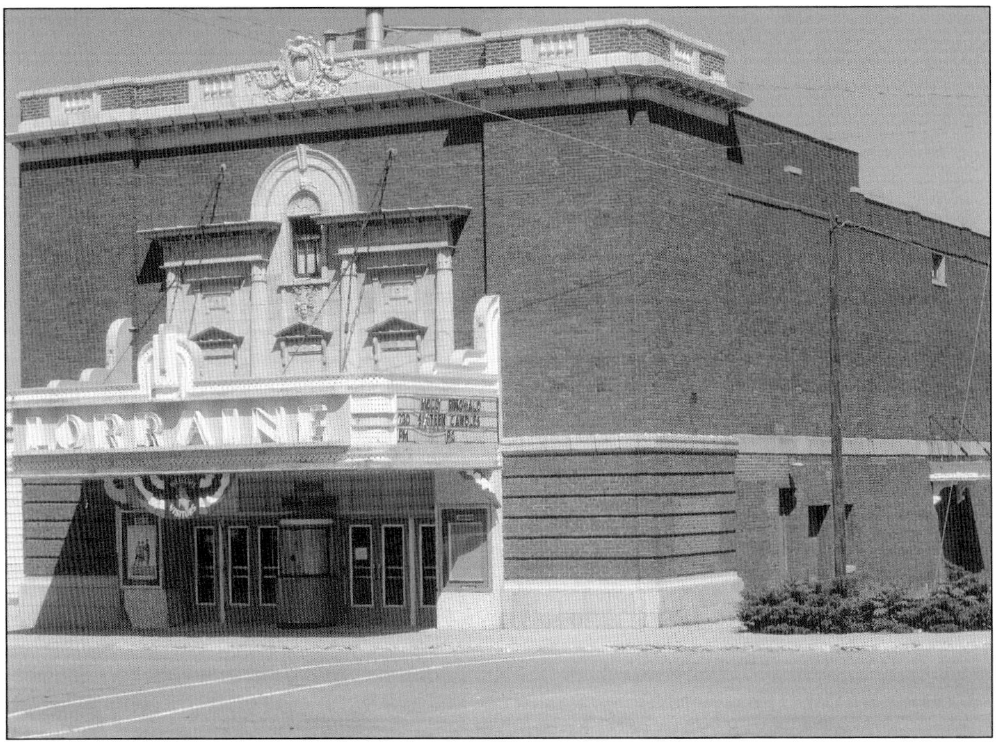

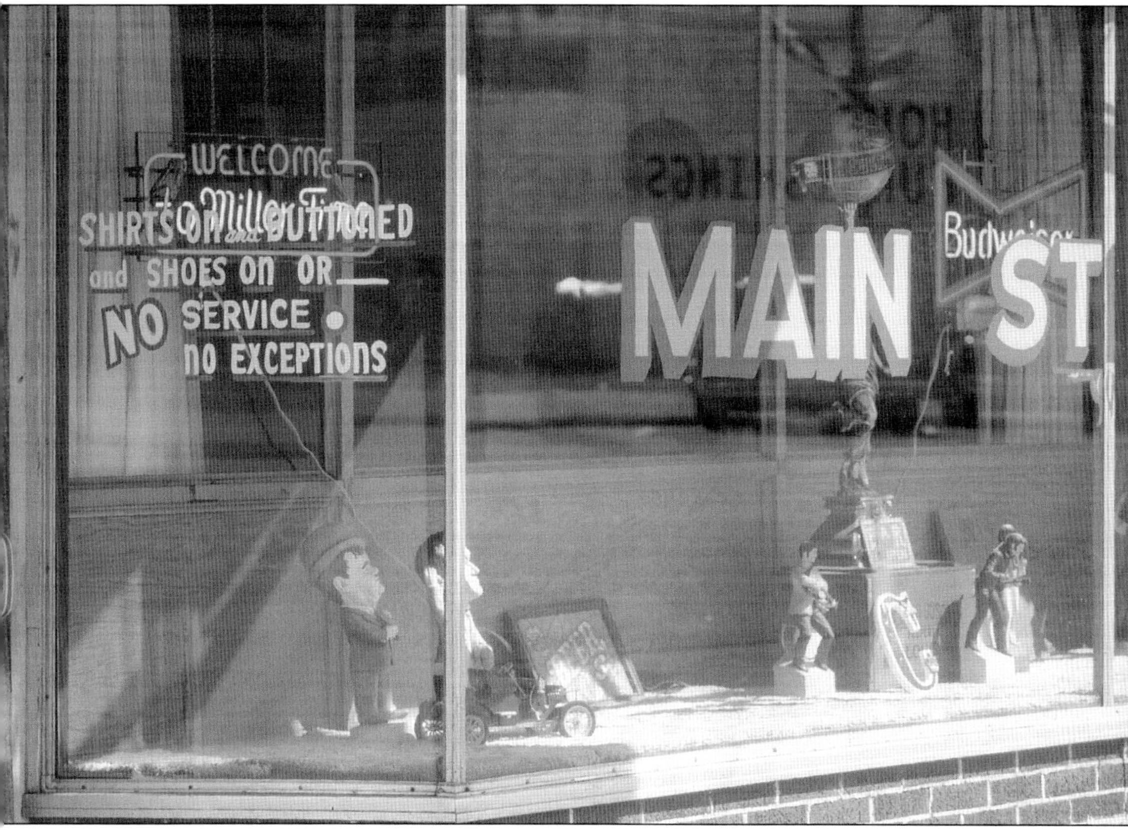

Main Street Inn Tavern, 306 East Main Street, was under the ownership of Jim and Rosalie Drollinger in 1984. It had its early beginning in 1948 as Coleman's Main Street Inn. In 1973, Jack Gregory bought it, and the Drollingers purchased it in 1982 and owned it until 1992. (Courtesy of Scott Baer.)

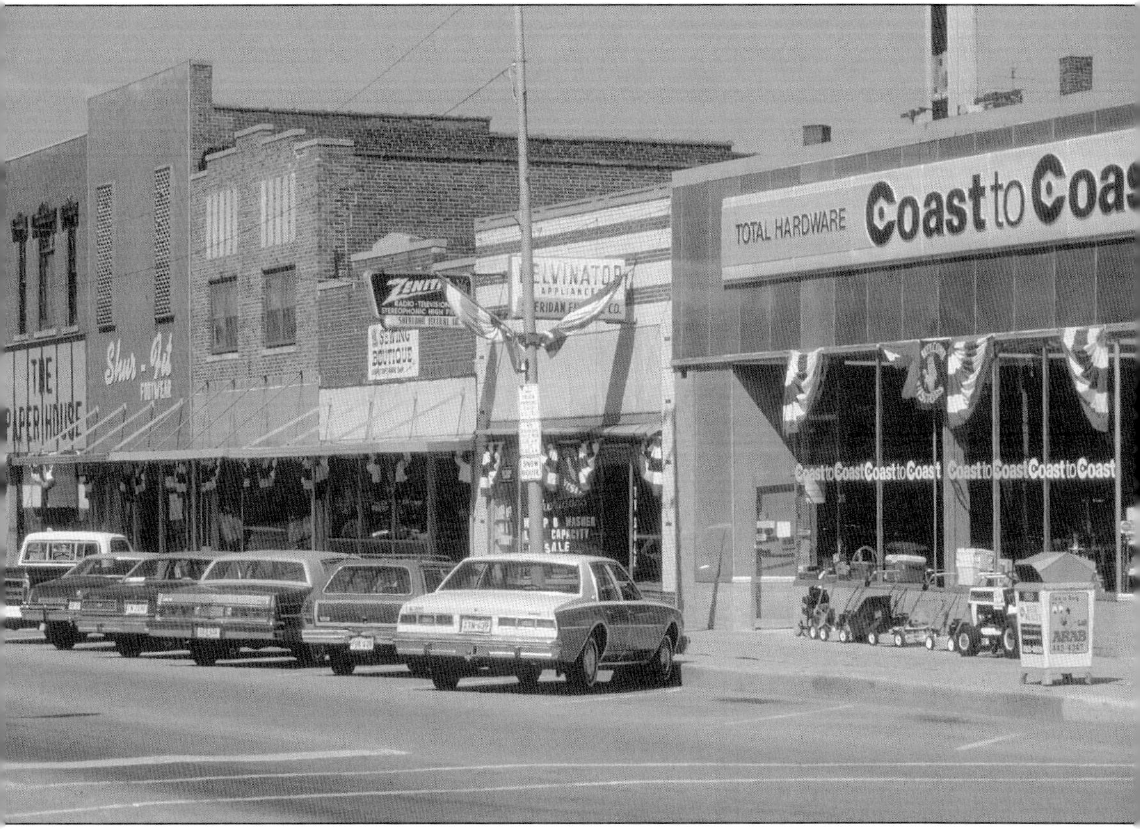

This 1984 photograph of the 200 block of East Main Street gives a view of the businesses on the north side of the block. They are Coast to Coast hardware, Sheridan's, the Sewing Boutique, Lester's Drug Store, Shur-Fit Footwear, and the Paperhouse. (Courtesy of Scott Baer.)

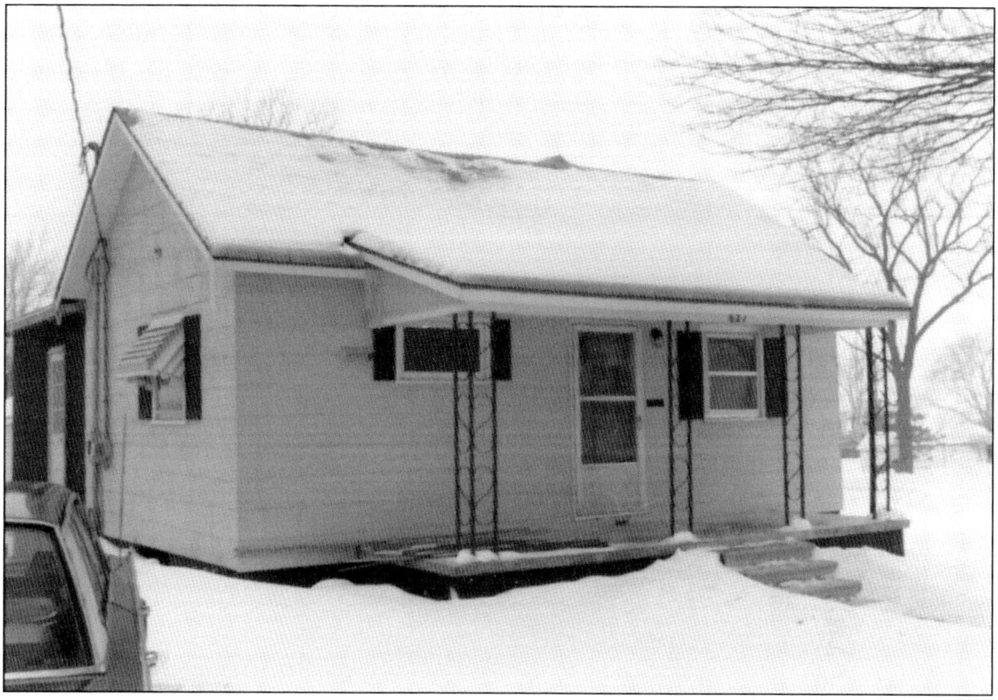

The original WHPO radio station's first broadcast was in 1979. The station was still located on the corner of 627 North Market in 1984. It moved to its Route 1 location in 2003. (Courtesy of Scott Baer.)

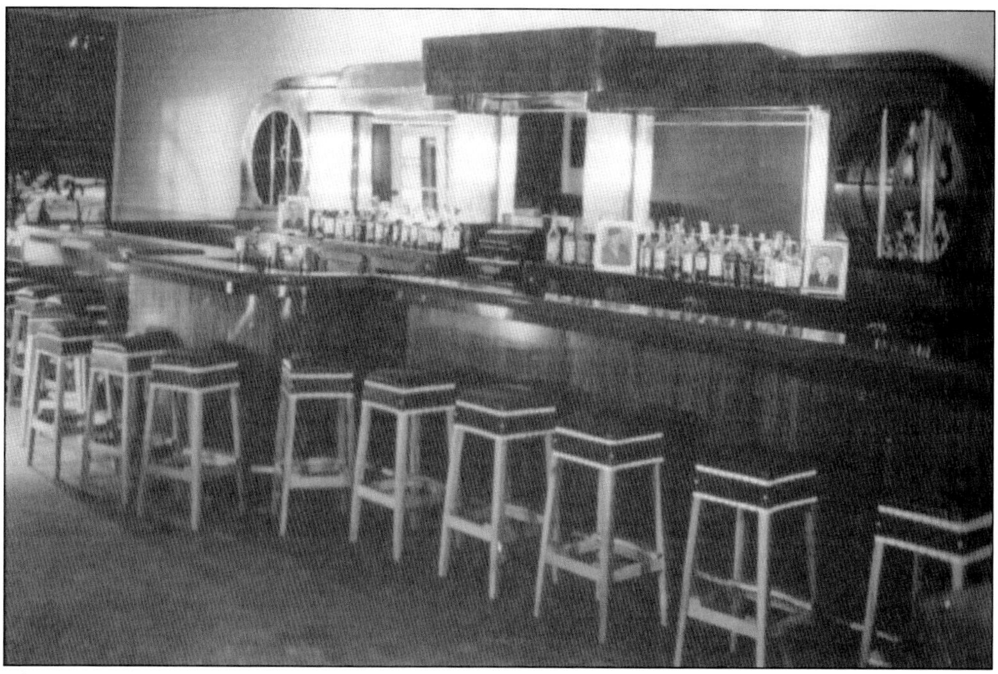

This view of E.V. Gray's Tavern shows photographs of the owners, Jack, Bill, and Lowell Gray, on the back counters. Gray's was located at 104 North Market Street from 1934 to 1946. (Courtesy of Hoopeston Historical Society.)

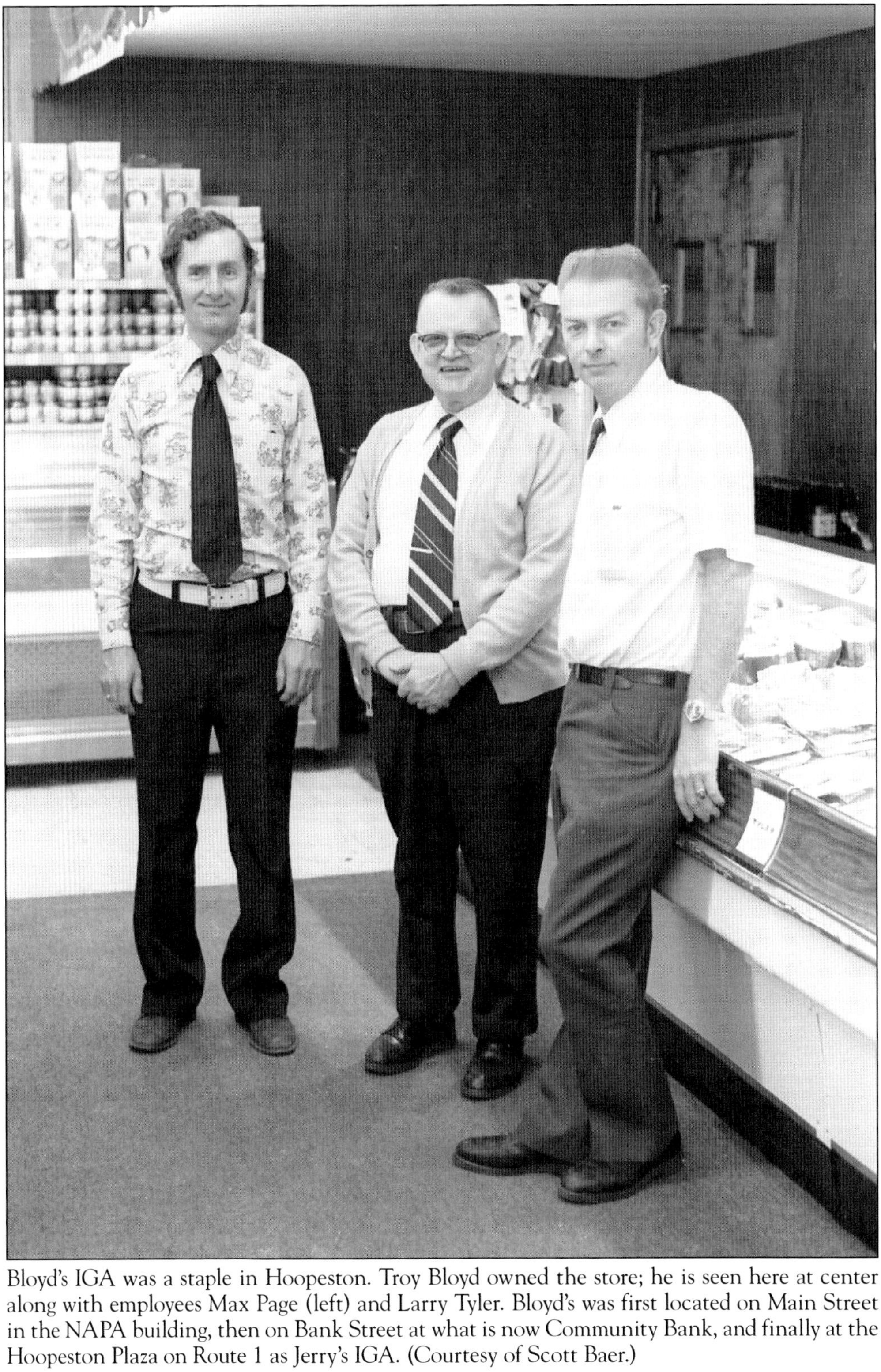

Bloyd's IGA was a staple in Hoopeston. Troy Bloyd owned the store; he is seen here at center along with employees Max Page (left) and Larry Tyler. Bloyd's was first located on Main Street in the NAPA building, then on Bank Street at what is now Community Bank, and finally at the Hoopeston Plaza on Route 1 as Jerry's IGA. (Courtesy of Scott Baer.)

Two

Hoopeston City Buildings

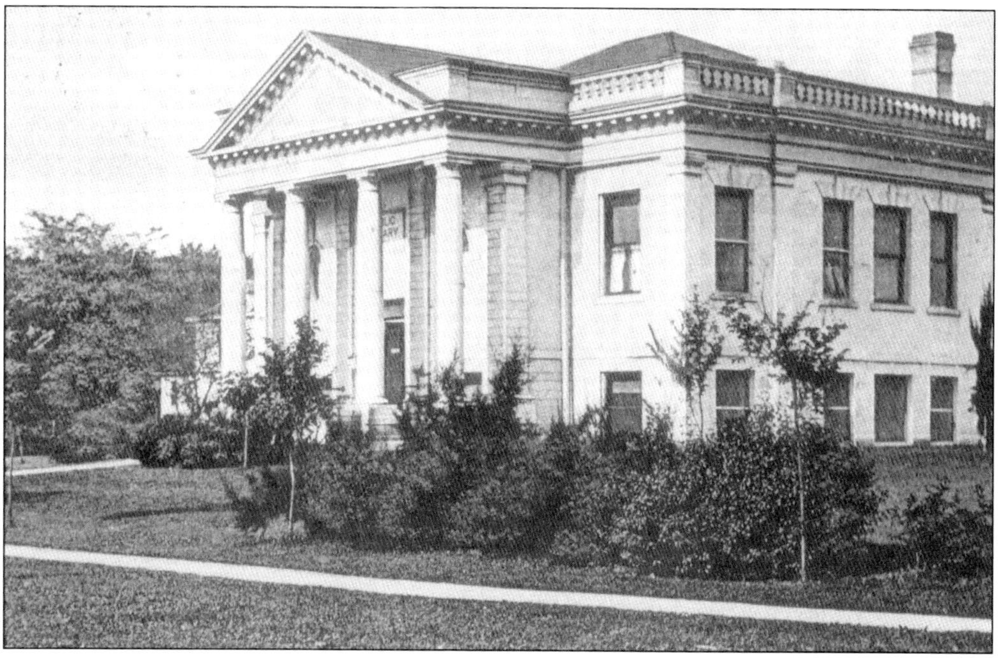

The Hoopeston Public Library, founded by Mary Hartwell Catherwood, opened its doors on November 23, 1898. Catherine Stites was the first librarian. The first community library was located in the municipal building (city hall). In 1905, a permanent library was built at 110 North Fourth Street on land donated by Alba Honeywell and funded by Andrew Carnegie at a cost of $12,500. It featured a semicircular oak circulation desk, which is still in use today.

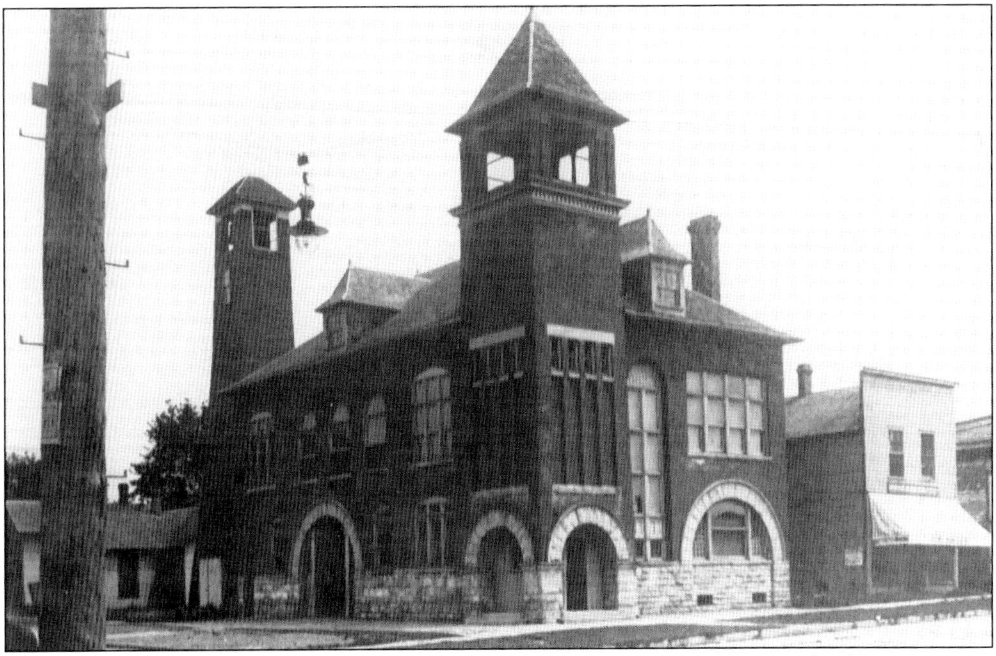

The original city hall and fire department, built by William Silver in 1897 for $5,600, was at Davis Street/Seminary Avenue and North Market Street. It housed the city hall, fire department, community library, council chambers, police department, and steel jail cells. After a fire in 1926, city hall moved to the Commercial Club basement on the northwest corner of South Market and Penn Streets. The Hoopeston Fire Department remains on Seminary Avenue. The city hall and police department moved July 30, 1994, to 301 West Main Street.

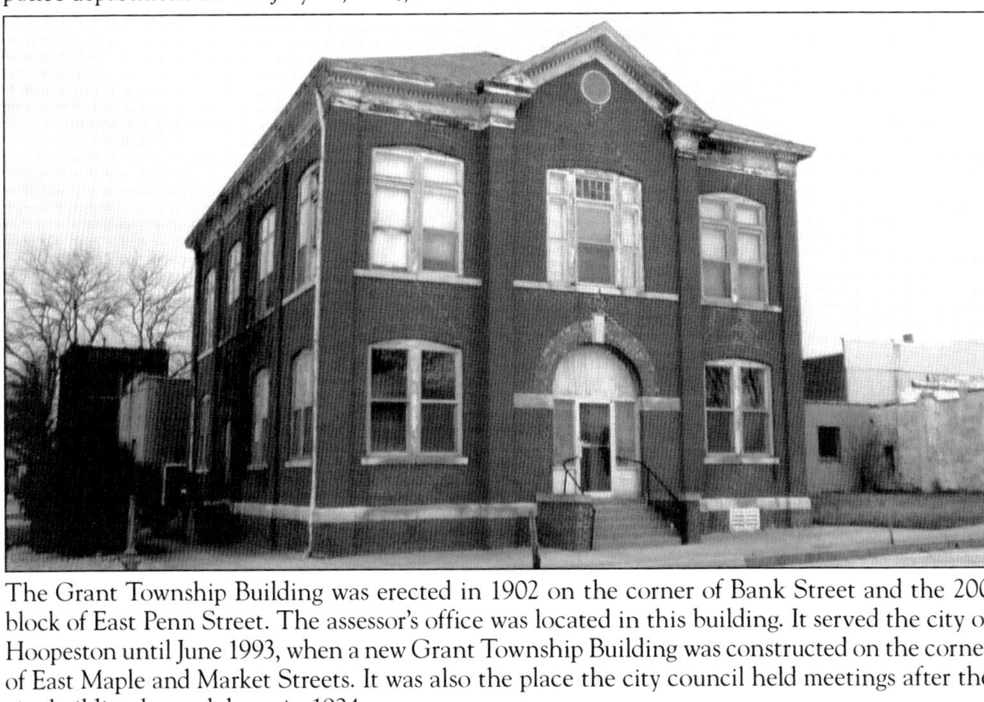

The Grant Township Building was erected in 1902 on the corner of Bank Street and the 200 block of East Penn Street. The assessor's office was located in this building. It served the city of Hoopeston until June 1993, when a new Grant Township Building was constructed on the corner of East Maple and Market Streets. It was also the place the city council held meetings after the city building burned down in 1924.

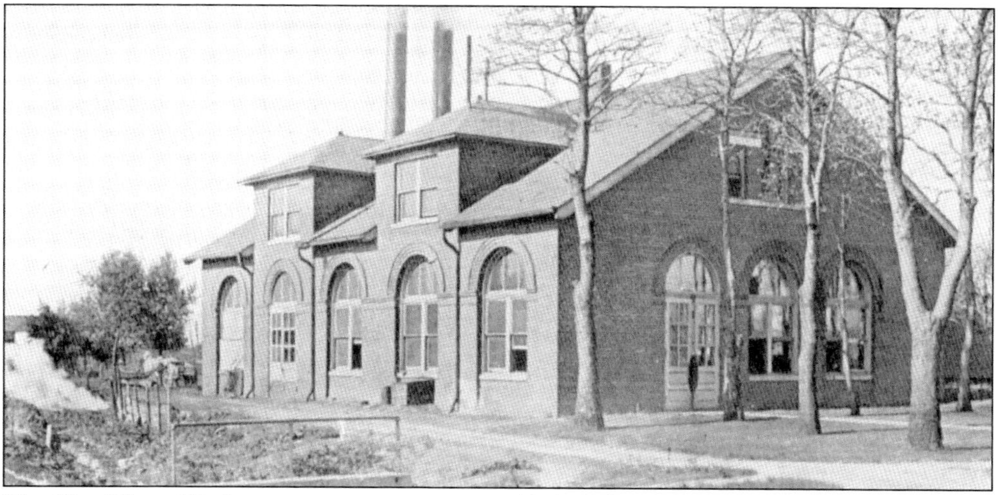

The City Water Works pumping station was established during I.E. Merritt's term as mayor of Hoopeston (1913–1917). Subsequent mayors William Moore and John A. Heaton improved on the wells that supplied water to the city, increasing the capacity with an additional well, a new reservoir, and the use of two pressure pumps.

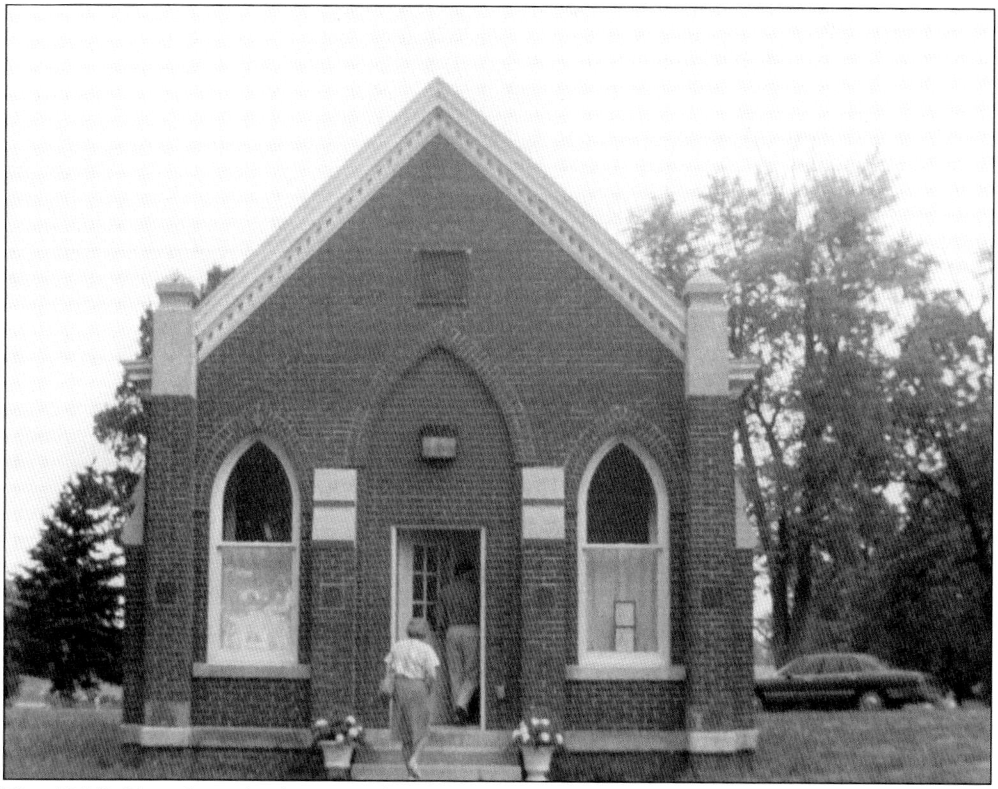

Floral Hill Chapel was built in 1889 by William Silver, ancestor of the current owners of Silver Bros. Construction. John Greer donated the initial $2,000 toward the building of the chapel, which was first used as a receiving vault for bodies until burial could take place. During winter months, the ground was extremely hard to dig by hand. Bodies were stored in the vault until the ground was soft enough to dig a grave.

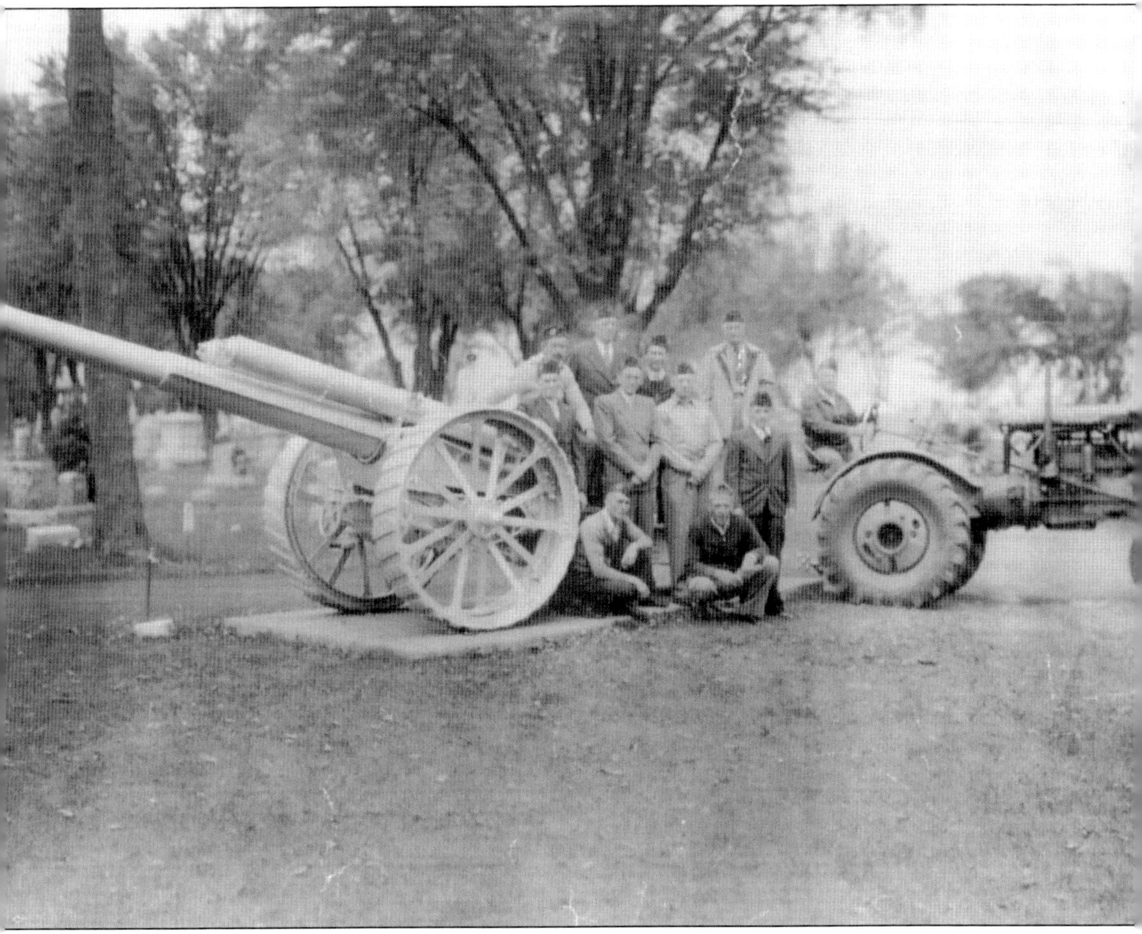

The Floral Hill British Artillery field piece, built in 1918 in England, was located just inside the entrance to Floral Hill Cemetery. Ira Owen Kreager American Legion Post 384 obtained the World War I weapon from the Rock Island Arsenal. A dedication service was held Monday, November 11, 1935, at the cemetery. During World War II, Hoopeston received a letter in October 1942 from the Rock Island Arsenal stating they had to dispose of the field piece. A nationwide appeal for scrap steel was made, and the artillery piece was melted down for steel needed in the war effort.

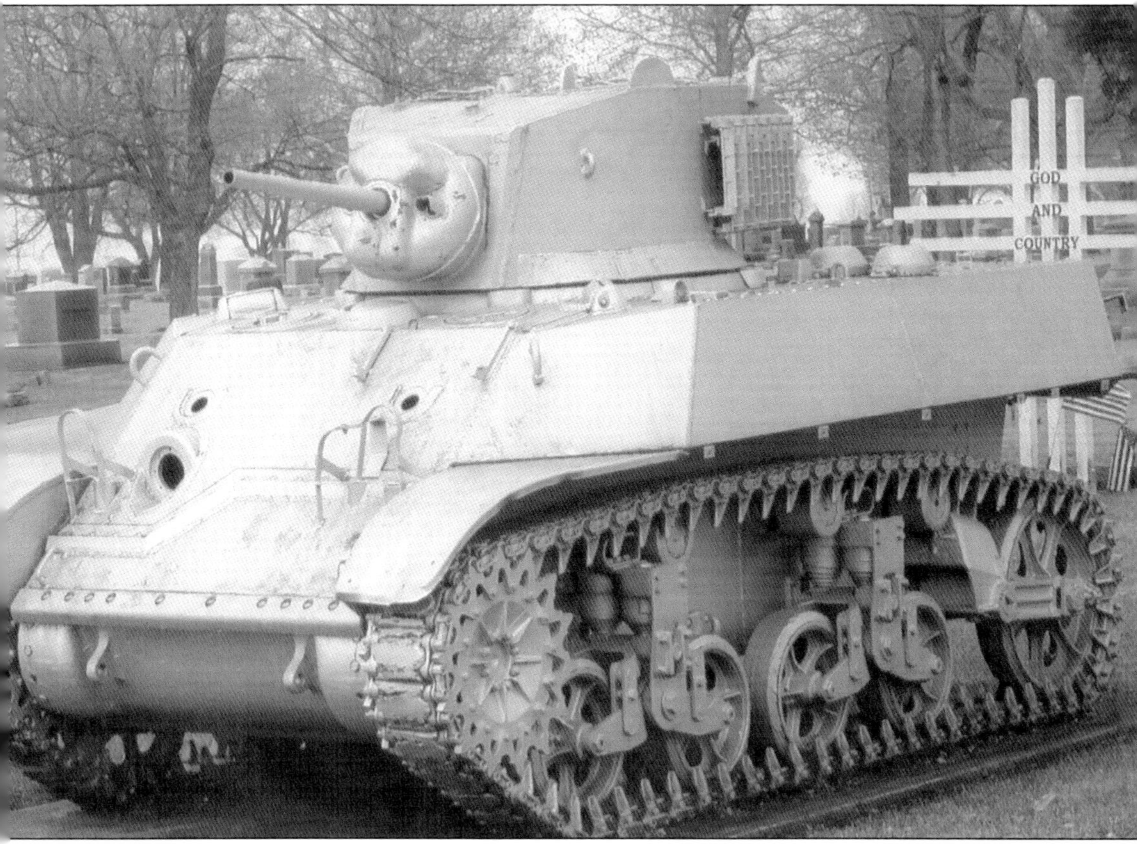

The Floral Hill World War II Army tank was obtained by Ira Owen Kreager American Legion Post 384 from the Rock Island Arsenal to replace the artillery field piece melted down during World War II. It was placed near the entrance of Floral Hill Cemetery on a new concrete slab in January 1947. Two Hoopeston men, Ira Owen Kreager and Buddy Egnew, killed in action in World War II, are commemorated near the tank. Their bodies were not brought home. (Courtesy of Jordan Crook.)

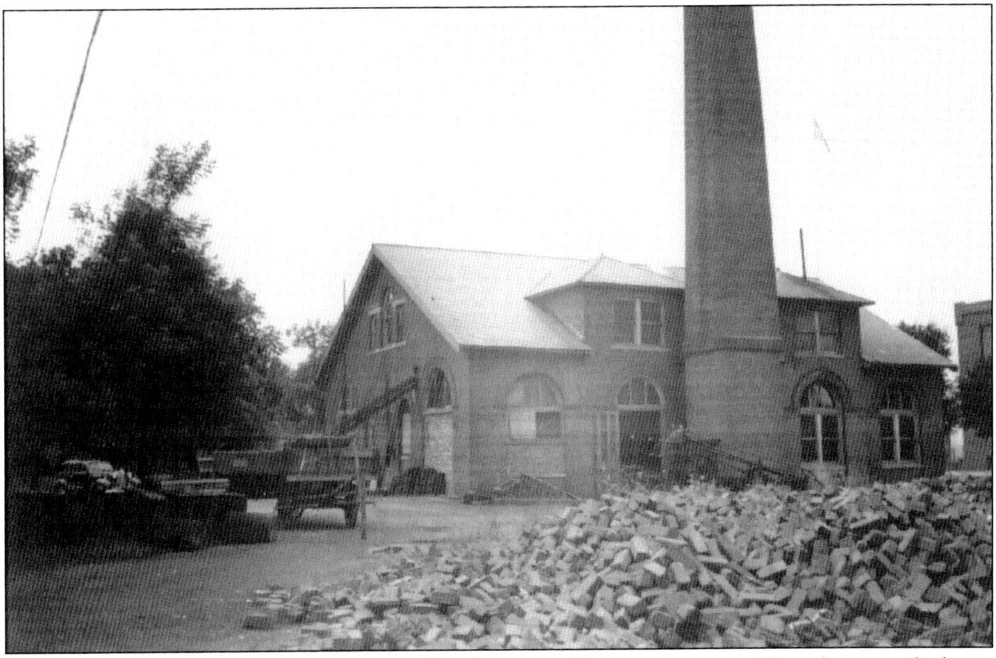

The Hoopeston Water Works was updated as the city of Hoopeston grew. This photograph shows the water works in 1938, probably the year before the water tower was built. (Courtesy of Steve Baker, Hoopeston Water Department.)

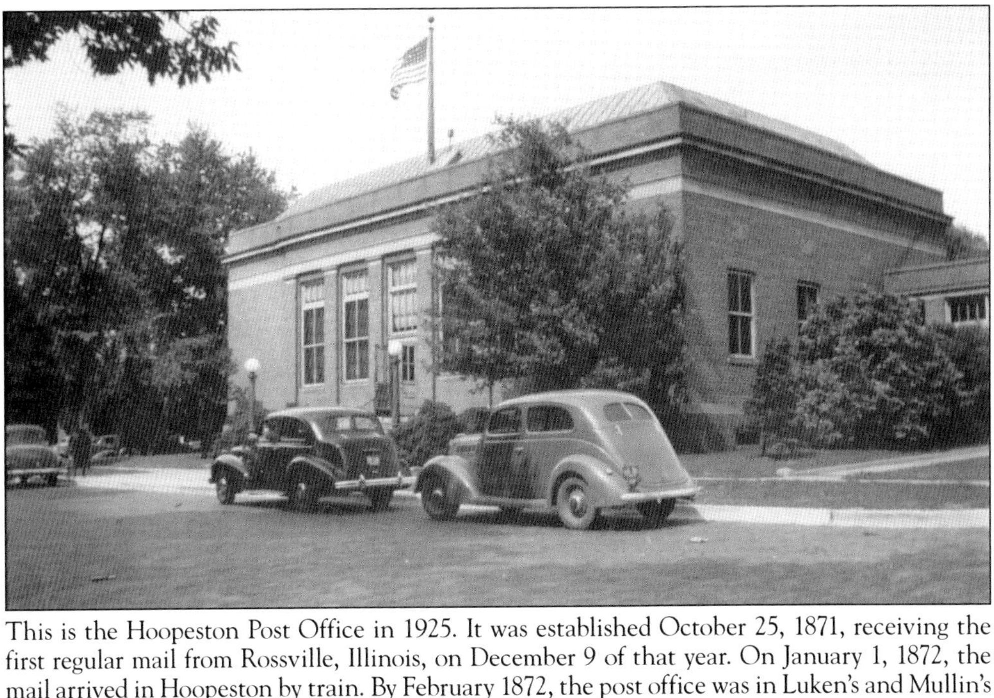

This is the Hoopeston Post Office in 1925. It was established October 25, 1871, receiving the first regular mail from Rossville, Illinois, on December 9 of that year. On January 1, 1872, the mail arrived in Hoopeston by train. By February 1872, the post office was in Luken's and Mullin's store on the corner of Main and Bank Streets. The present building, 314 South Market Street, was built and completed in 1918 at a cost of $10,000.

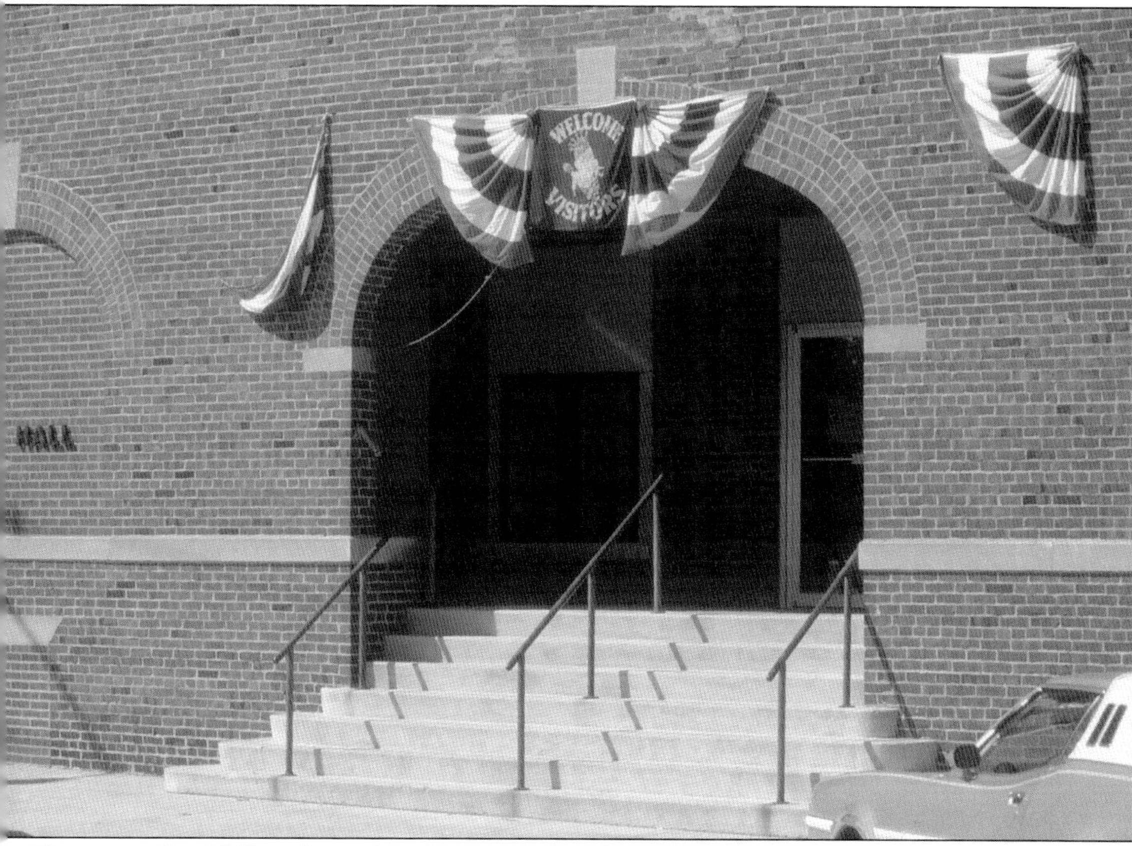

Hoopeston City Hall was located on the corner of Market and Penn Streets in 1984. The police station was downstairs in the basement, and the courthouse and council were on the first floor of the building. (Courtesy of Scott Baer.)

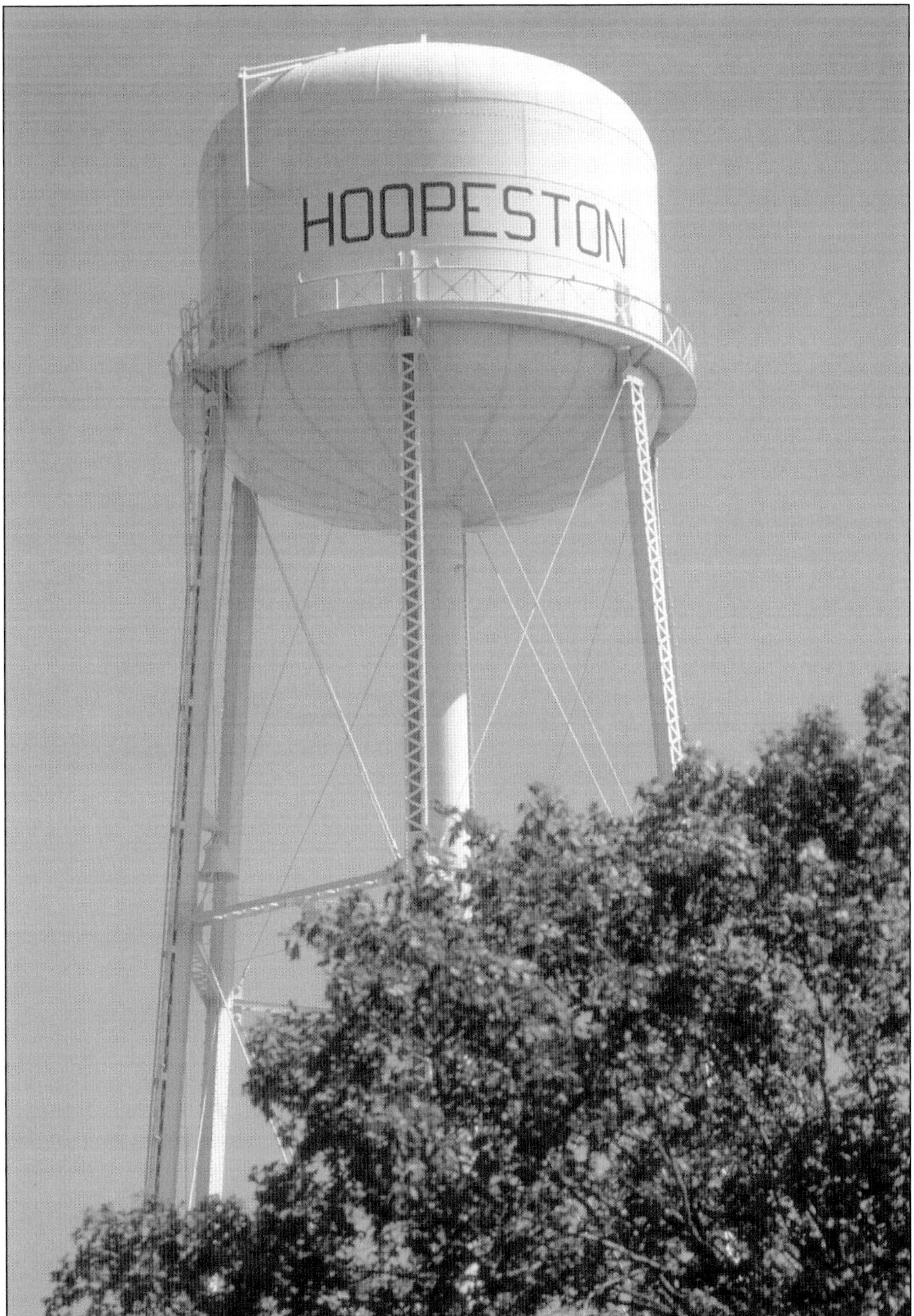

The water tower was built after 1938 to increase the pressure of water to residents' homes and to replace the one built about 1888, which stood in the middle of East Main Street at Fourth Street. (Courtesy of Scott Baer.)

Three

HOOPESTON ENTERTAINMENT

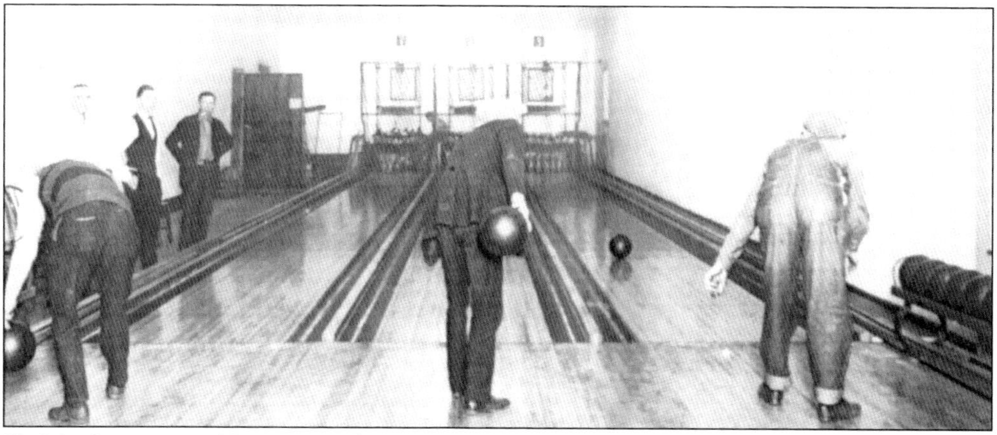

Pla-Mor Lanes served Hoopeston for 81 years, beginning at 310 East Main as Smith's Bowling & Billiard Hall from 1923 to 1930. In 1930, it was Dawson & Son Bowling; it was renamed Frame's Pla-Mor Lanes Bowling Alley in 1942, and Adkins Pla-Mor Bowling Alley in 1944. William Childers added a lunch counter in 1953 before Bob and Ray Chesnut bought it. Pla-Mor Lanes moved to a new building on West Orange Street in 1957 but was destroyed by fire in April 1990. Kenny Morris was the owner.

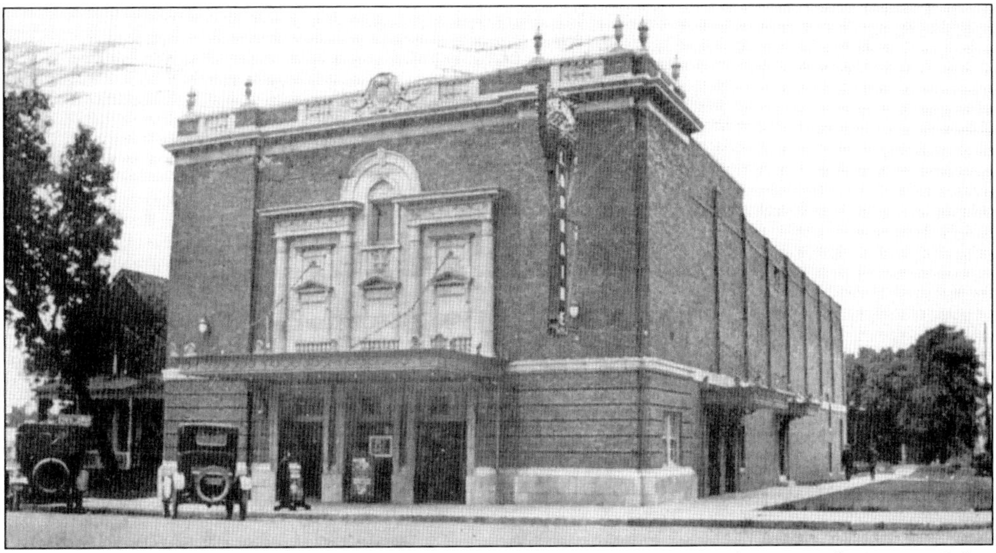

The Lorraine Theatre was built in 1921 by Elijah J. Boorde and opened on March 6, 1922. John Rosslyn Boorde, the son of Elijah Boorde, was the first manager of the Lorraine. According to the newspapers in 1922, the construction cost of the theater was close to $100,000. In front of the building was a huge sign with the words "Theater" and "Lorraine" that glowed at night with multicolored lights. The theater held 800 seats. (Courtesy of the Save the Lorraine Foundation.)

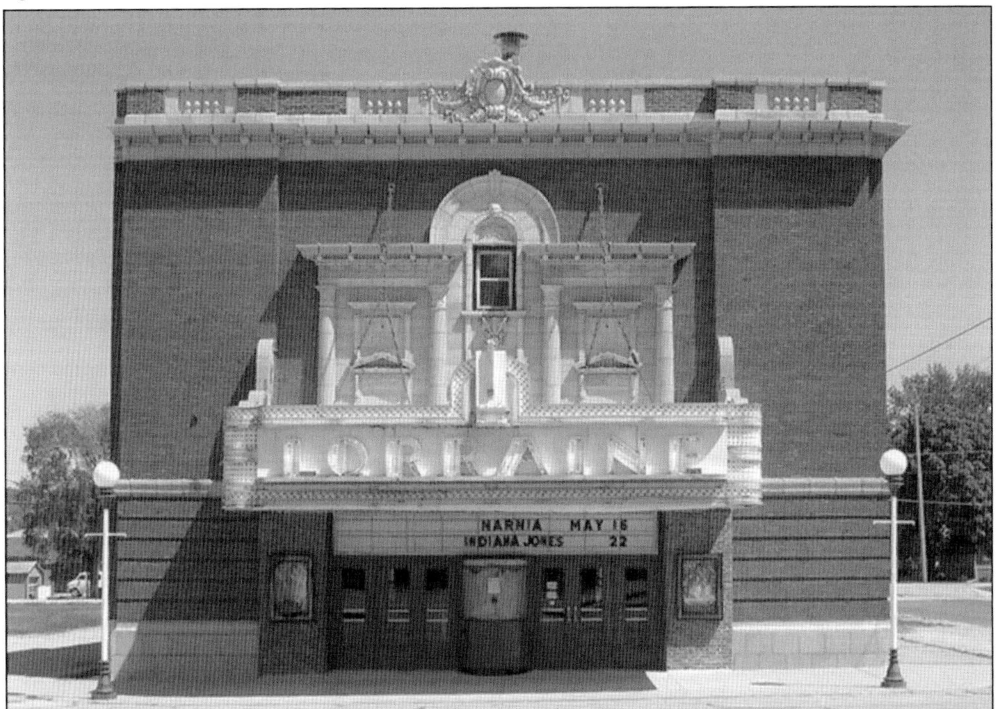

The Lorraine Theatre, owned by Greg Boardman from 1987 to 2007, had two old-fashioned lights installed on either side of the front of the building. These lights were donated by the Hoopeston Historical Society, as shown in this 1989 photograph. (Courtesy of the Save the Lorraine Foundation.)

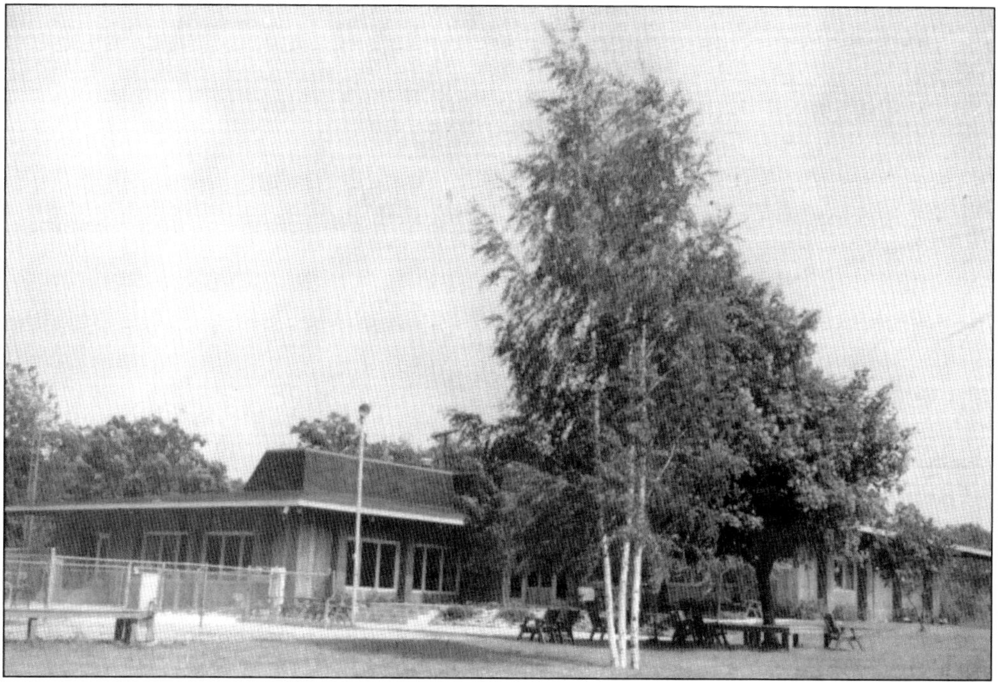

A group of Hoopeston and Rossville golf enthusiasts invested in the new golf course, drew up a constitution and bylaws, and received a certificate of incorporation for the Hubbard Trail Country Club on September 16, 1925. The directors were listed as E.F. Trego, Harold Crays, and George Schumann. Dr. R.G. Kline was elected the first president; George Lester, first vice president; and George Schumann, first secretary-treasurer.

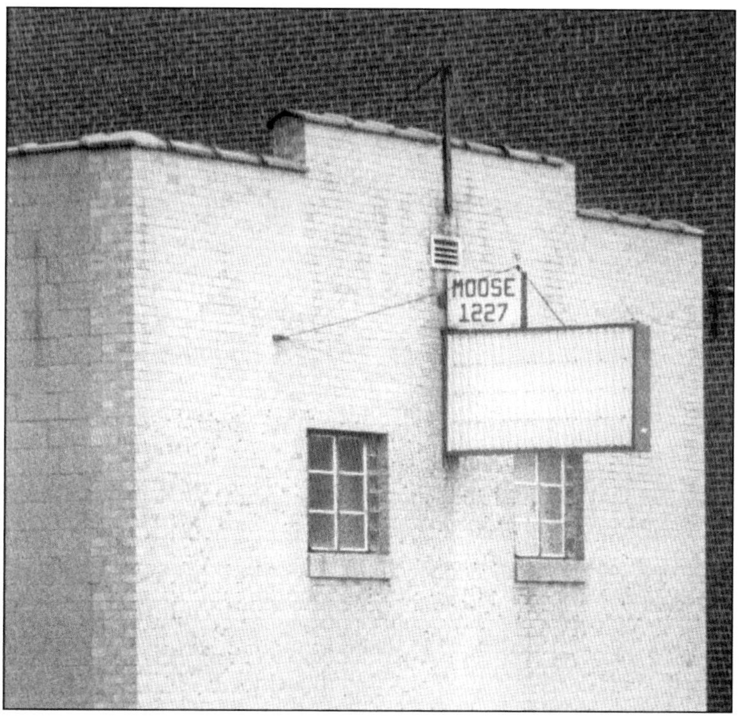

The Moose lodge, formed in the early 1920s, was originally located on East Main Street in Hoopeston. It boasted of being the scene of social activities and dances in 1925. It eventually moved to Bank Street and closed in the 1990s. (Courtesy of the Hoopeston Public Library.)

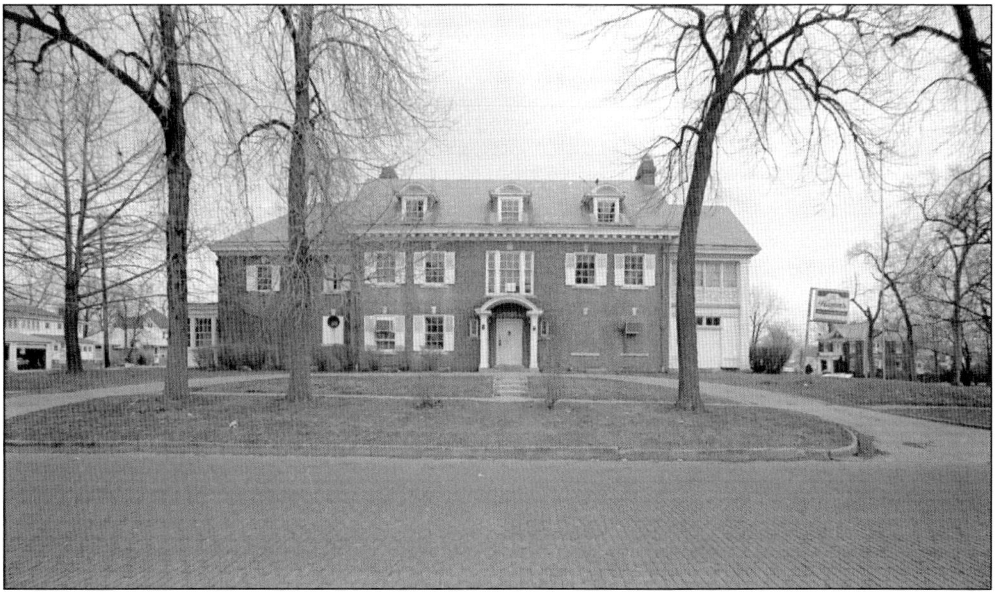

Ira Owen Kreager American Legion Post 384 organized October 28, 1918, and moved into its first home at 114 1/2 East Main Street, where City Chef is today. The Legion Auxiliary was formed in 1921. Later, the post moved to 205 East Penn Street, home of the First Apostolic Church today. It moved again in December 1948, this time to the William McFerren home at 501 East Penn Street. The site burned in February 1979, and a modern, one-story building was erected in that location. (Courtesy of Scott Baer.)

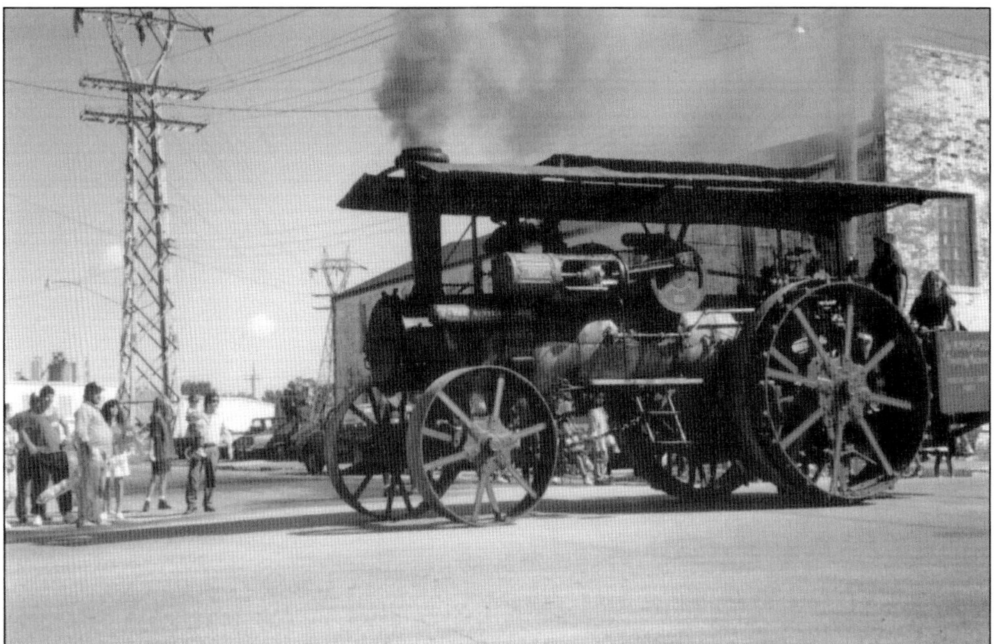

This Hoopeston Steam Engine in the Sweetcorn Festival parade in the 1990s was taken at First Avenue and West Main Street. In the background is Stokely USA, and to the right is the R.A. Carlson building. (Courtesy of Nancy Thorn.)

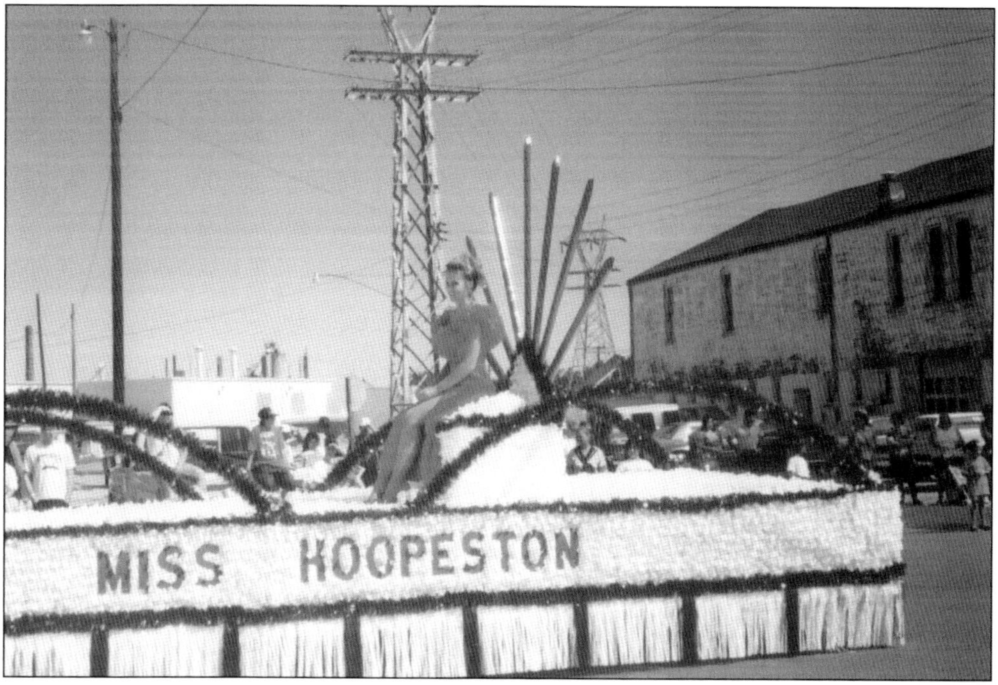

Miss Hoopeston sits on a float in this 1990s photograph. Miss Hoopeston is chosen each fall by members of the Hoopeston Jaycees from graduates of Hoopeston High School. The Miss Hoopeston winner is announced officially in January. (Courtesy of Nancy Thorn.)

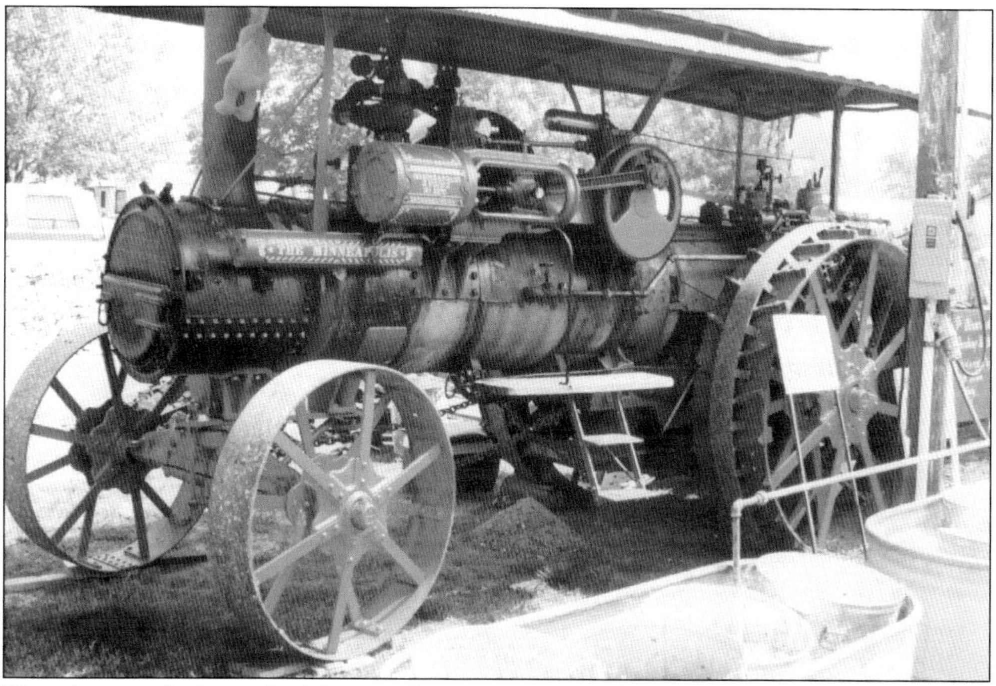

This photograph shows the Minneapolis steam engine, which is used to cook sweet corn on Saturday, Sunday, and Monday at the Hoopeston National Sweetcorn Festival in McFerren Park. Free sweet corn is given away all three days to visitors.

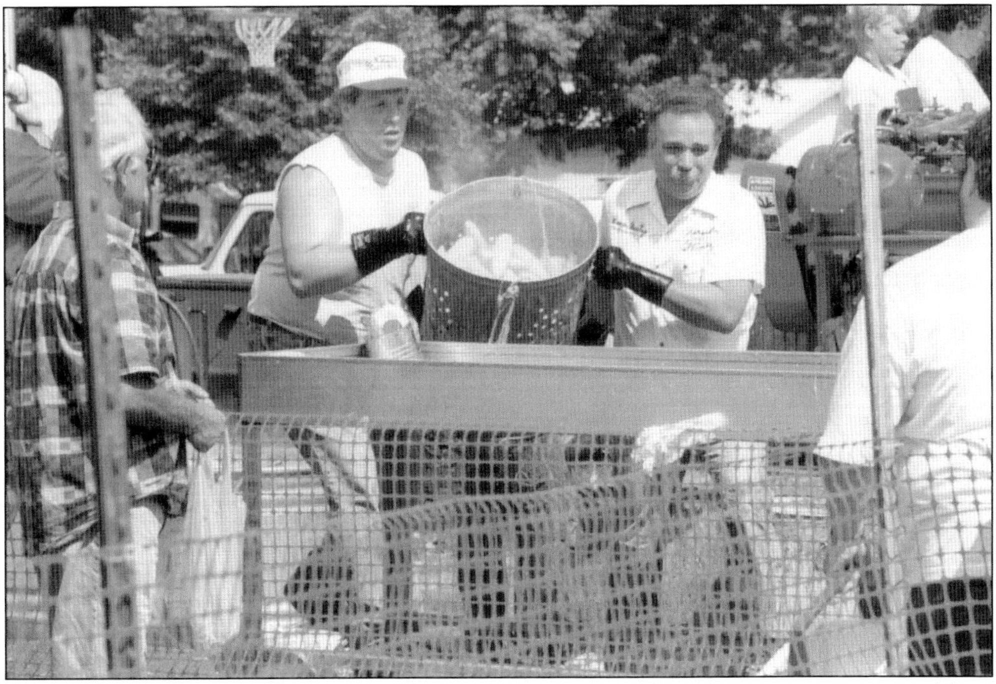

Two members of the Jaycees, Brian Williams and Roger Beaty, dump hot sweet corn on a table in 1992 to be given to the people standing in line. Each person can receive six ears each time they go through the line. (Courtesy of Stephen and Holly Eyrich.)

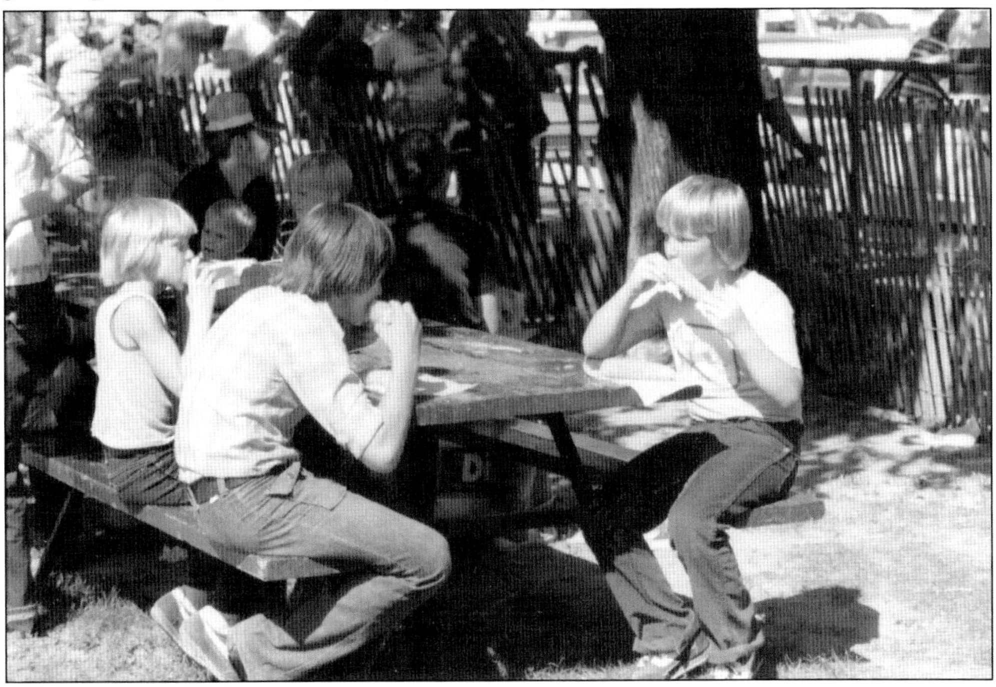

This family of young men is taking a break from the carnival rides and other events for some free sweet corn at the Hoopeston National Sweetcorn Festival. (Courtesy of Stephen and Holly Eyrich.)

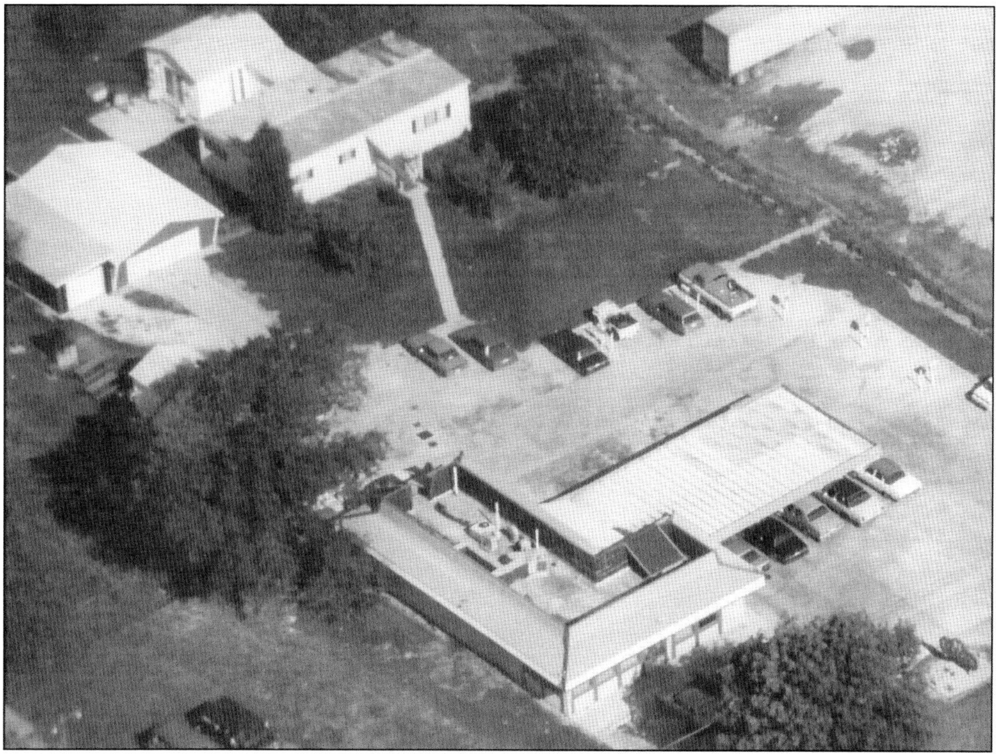

This aerial view shows the A&W root beer stand in the 1960s. The home and garage behind the business is the home of the owners. Customers could drive in, sit in their cars to order, or go inside the building to order and eat. (Courtesy of Scott Baer.)

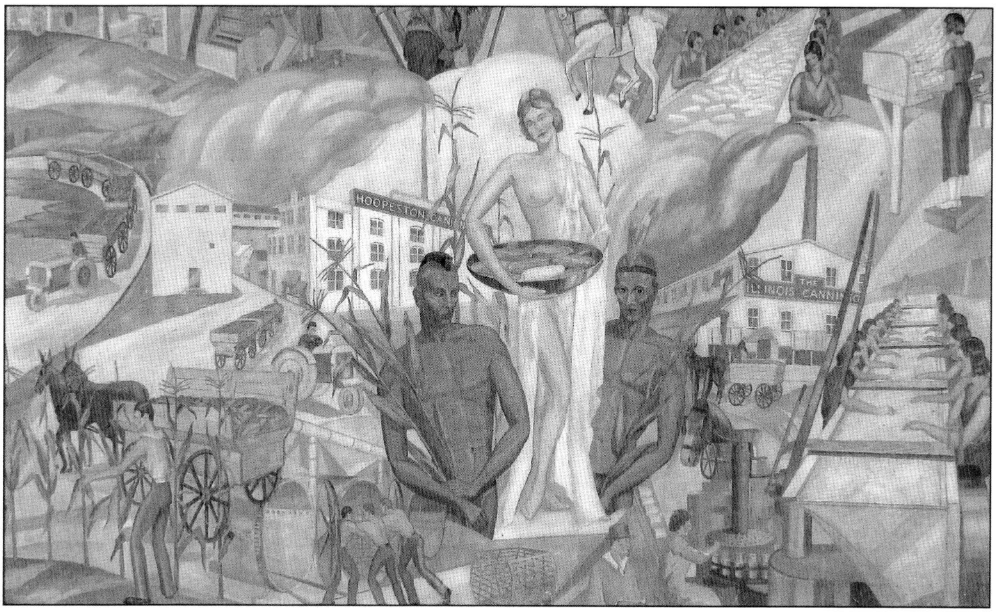

This painting depicts Hoopeston's growth from 1871 and resides in the Lorraine Theatre. The painting was a gift of Alex Claussen, who remodeled the Lorraine Theatre in 1937. (Courtesy of the Save the Lorraine Foundation.)

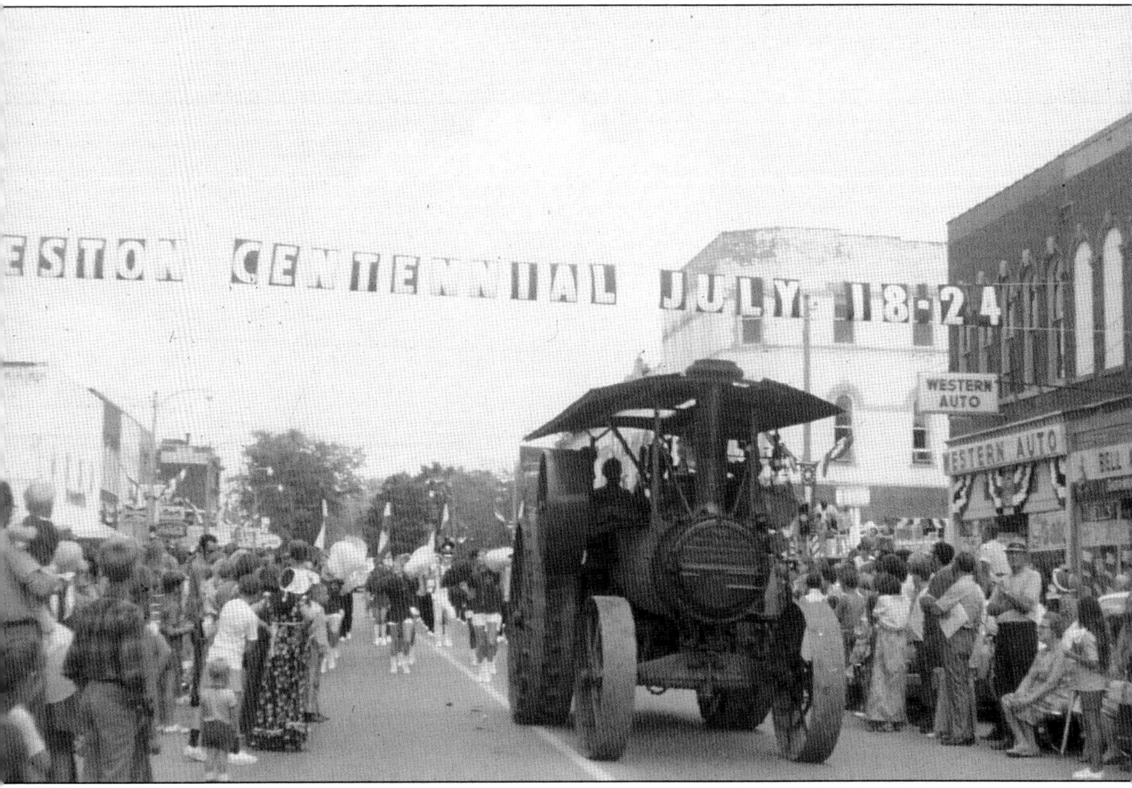

Hoopeston celebrated 100 years as a town on July 18–24, 1971, as the banner across the 200 block of East Main Street shows. The celebration began with a parade, with the steam engine leading the way. Many residents dressed the part, as is shown by some of the onlookers. (Courtesy of Scott Baer.)

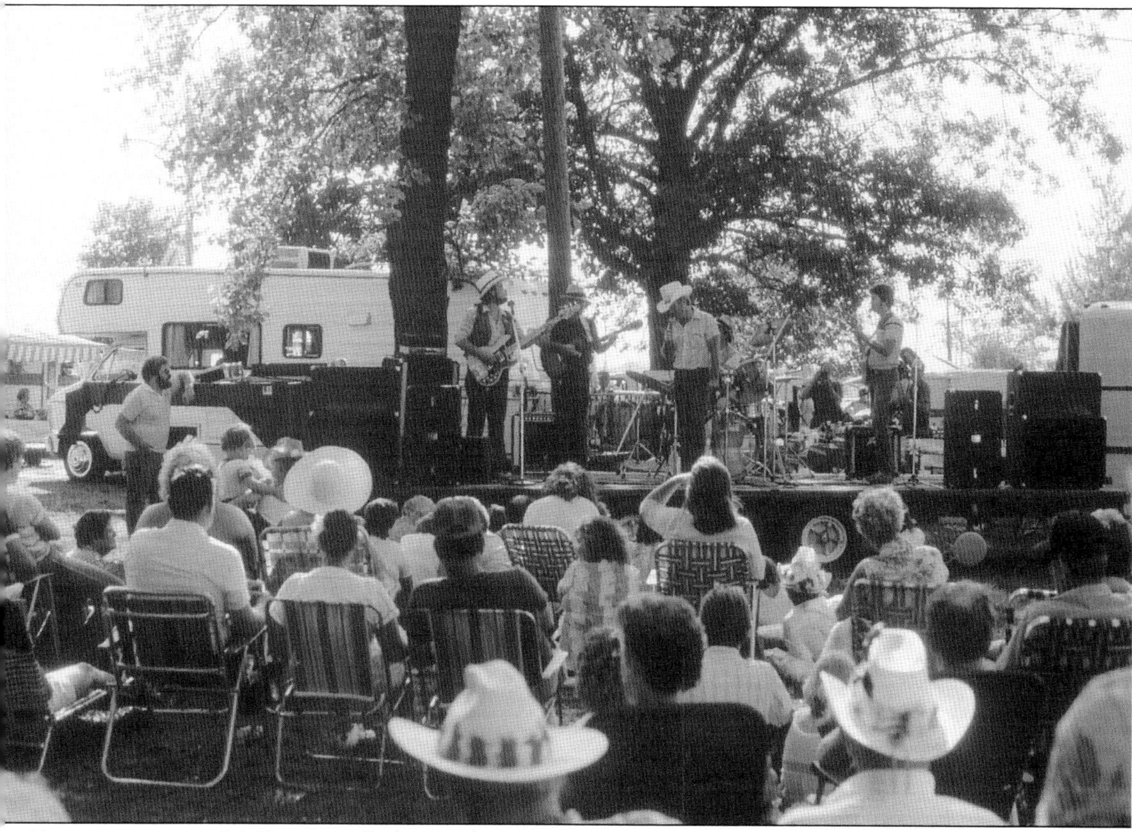

Entertainment in McFerren Park during the Sweetcorn Festival was a must, and country-and-western singers were a highlight. The crowd in this 1984 photograph is enjoying the music. (Courtesy of Scott Baer.)

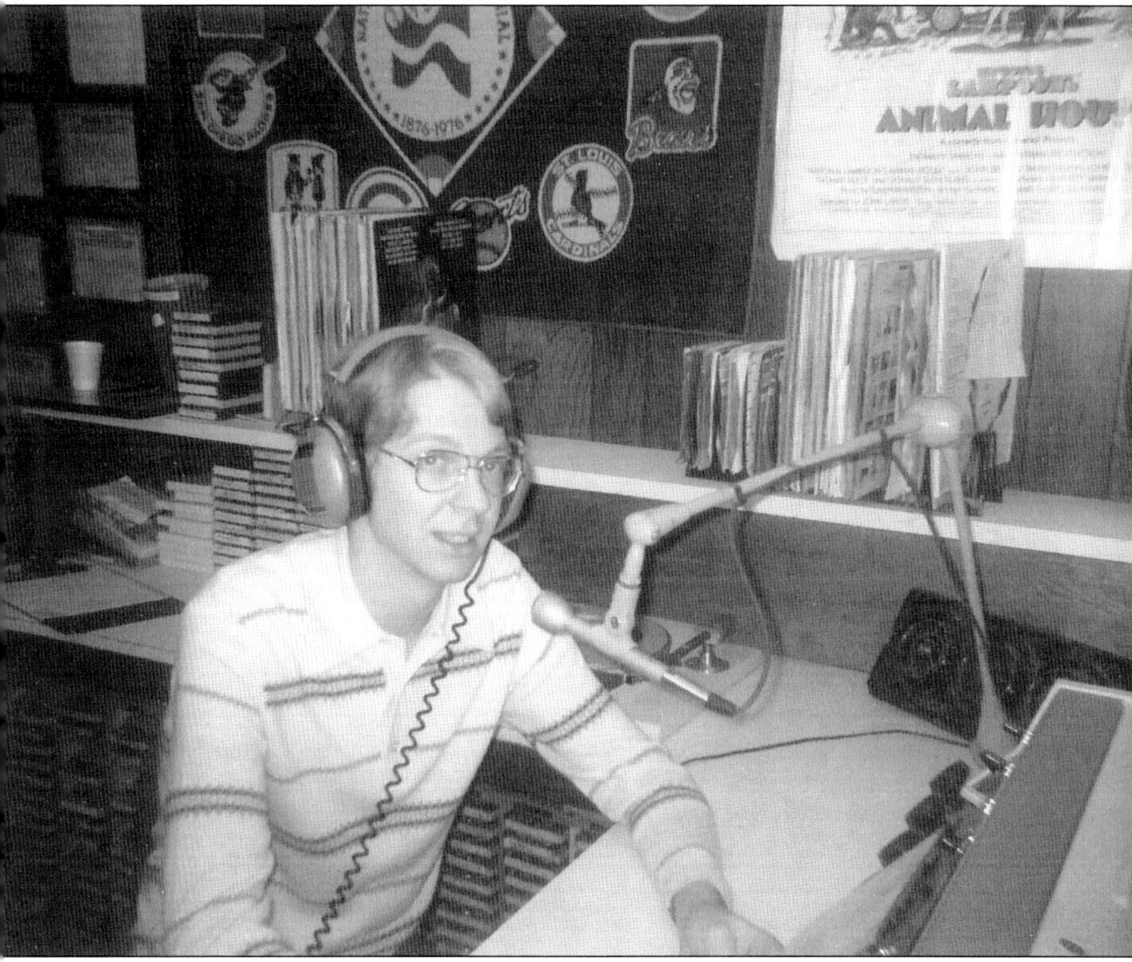

Scott Baer, one of the earliest DJs at WHPO, is shown in the studio in this 1979 photograph. Some of the earliest radio personalities were Walter J. Tater Jr., Dan Daugherty, Ed Morrissey, Gary McCullough, Dave Stawick, Tony Fidanzo, Ken Johnson, Don Shields, Chrissie Manion, Rick Greenlee, Joey Gagnon, Ann Singleton, and Phil Blobaum. (Courtesy of Scott Baer.)

Four

Hoopeston Schools

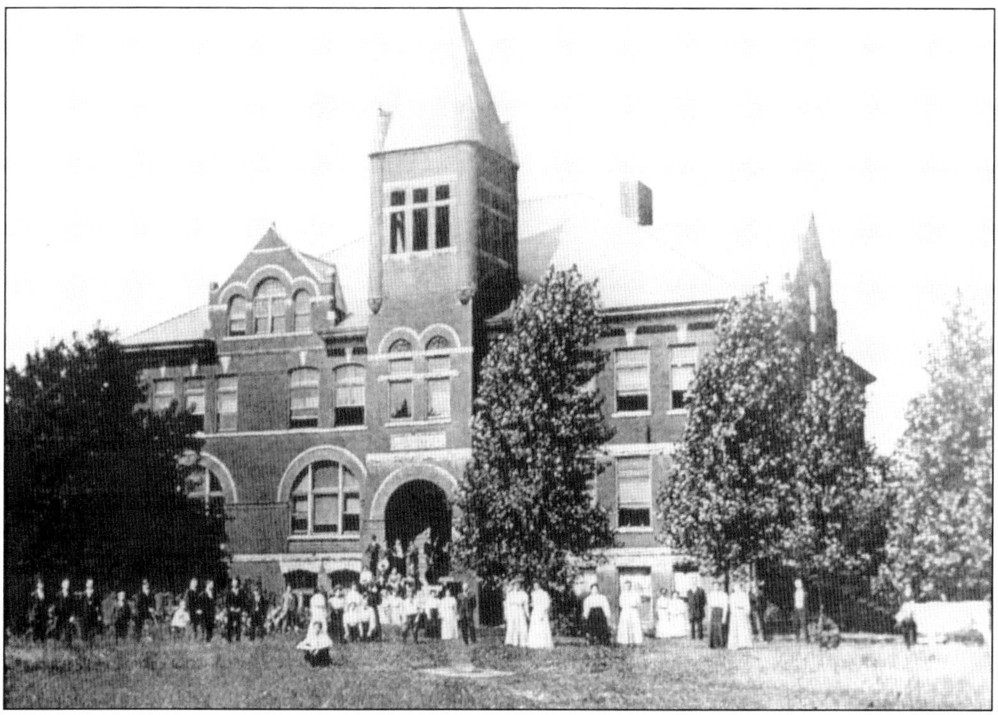

John Greer College was founded in 1891 when Hoopeston resident John Greer endowed $50,000 to build a college as "a heritage to all young people who are ambitious to rise in the world." The college, located in the 600 block of West Penn Street, had an auditorium seating capacity of 700. The first president was Prof. J.M. Clary. The college was dissolved in 1926 and torn down March 6, 1969.

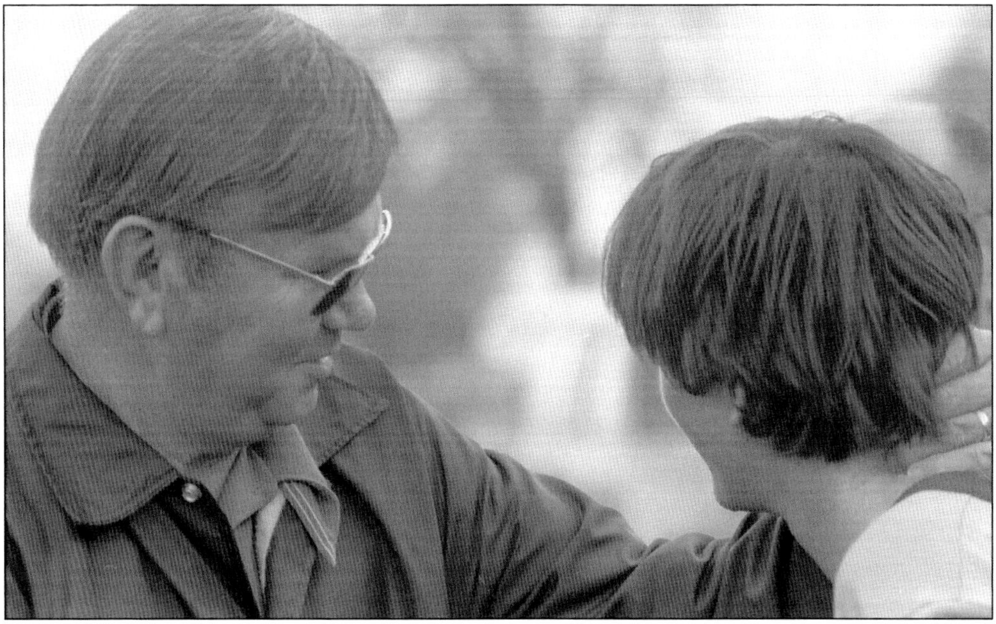

Coach Dick Hobbs, shown in this 1974 photograph, created the mascot known as "Jerky" in 1965. The original Cornjerker name was coined by Bob Poisall, a sports writer for the *Commercial-News* in the 1920s when Glenn Brasel was coach. Many of the players had to help their families jerk corn during harvest, and the buses had to wait for the players to finish. In irritation, Poisall called them a bunch of "cornjerkers." Brasel thought it was an appropriate name. (Courtesy of Scott Baer.)

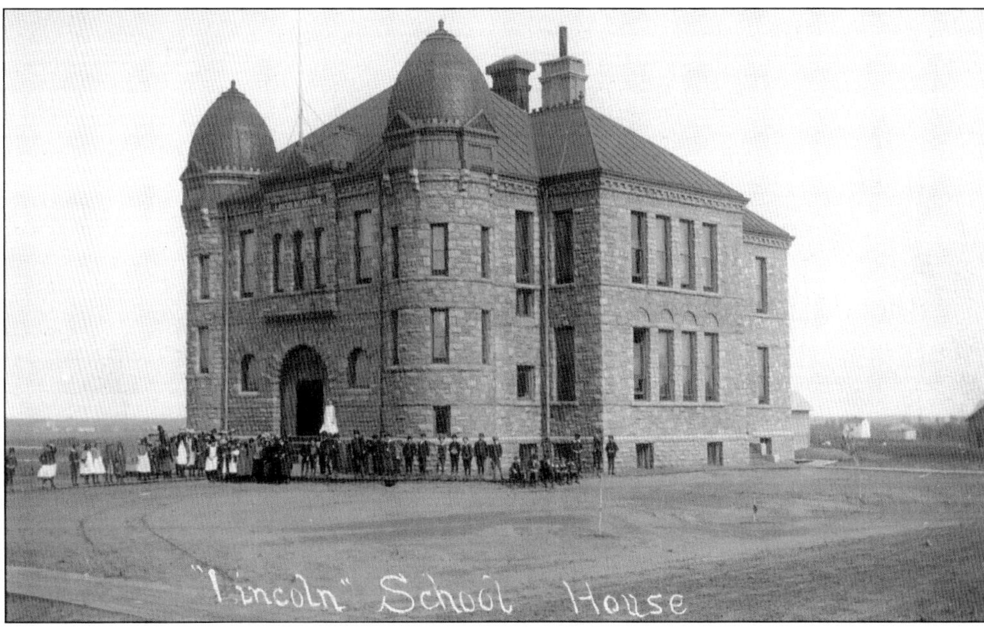

Lincoln Grade School changed over the years from its early beginning in 1874. This photograph shows the school as it looked in 1890. Lincoln was closed in 1969 when students were sent to the newly built John Greer Grade School on West Penn Street. (Courtesy of Hoopeston Public Library.)

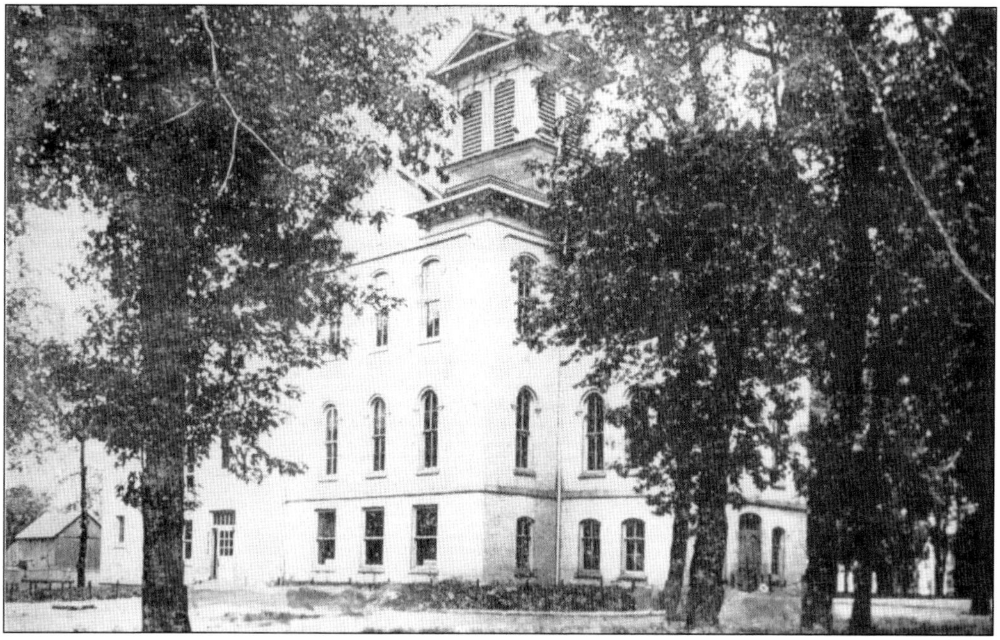

Holy Angel Catholic School, pictured in 1907, became Honeywell Grade School. Honeywell was rebuilt in 1927 by Jerry Warner and crew in the 500 block of East Honeywell Avenue, housing grades one through eight. In 1956, seventh and eighth graders were sent to John Greer Junior High School. Honeywell became a grade center in 1982, housing kindergarten, third-, and fourth-grade students.

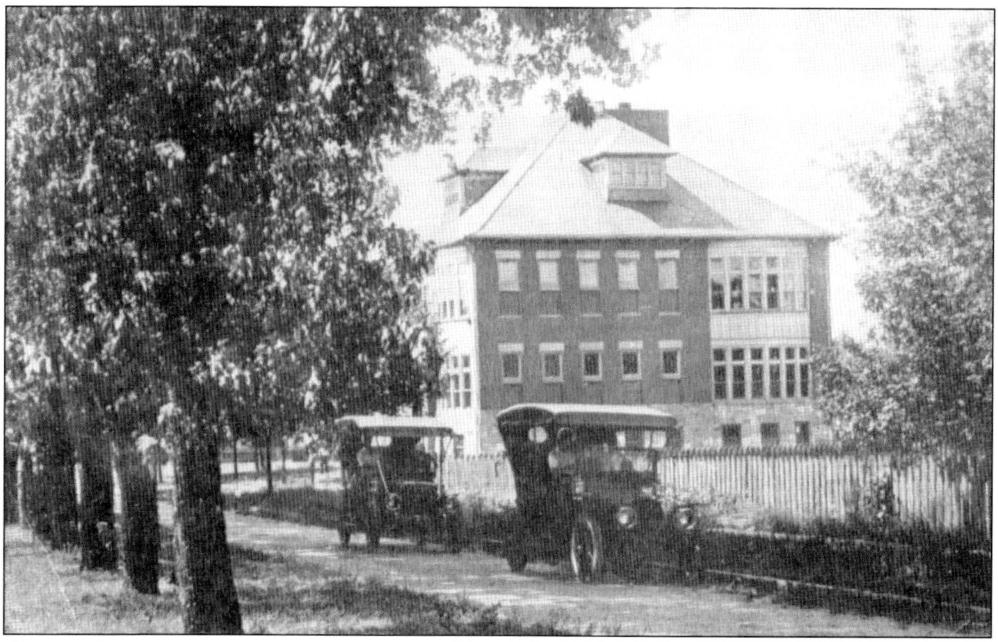

The first high school was opened in 1873–1874 on Seminary Avenue. It moved in 1897 to South Fourth and Maple Streets and, at that time, was called Maple High School. It later relocated to John Greer College in 1914, combining with the college until the college dissolved in 1926. A new gymnasium was added in 1927, with the first basketball games being played in December 1927.

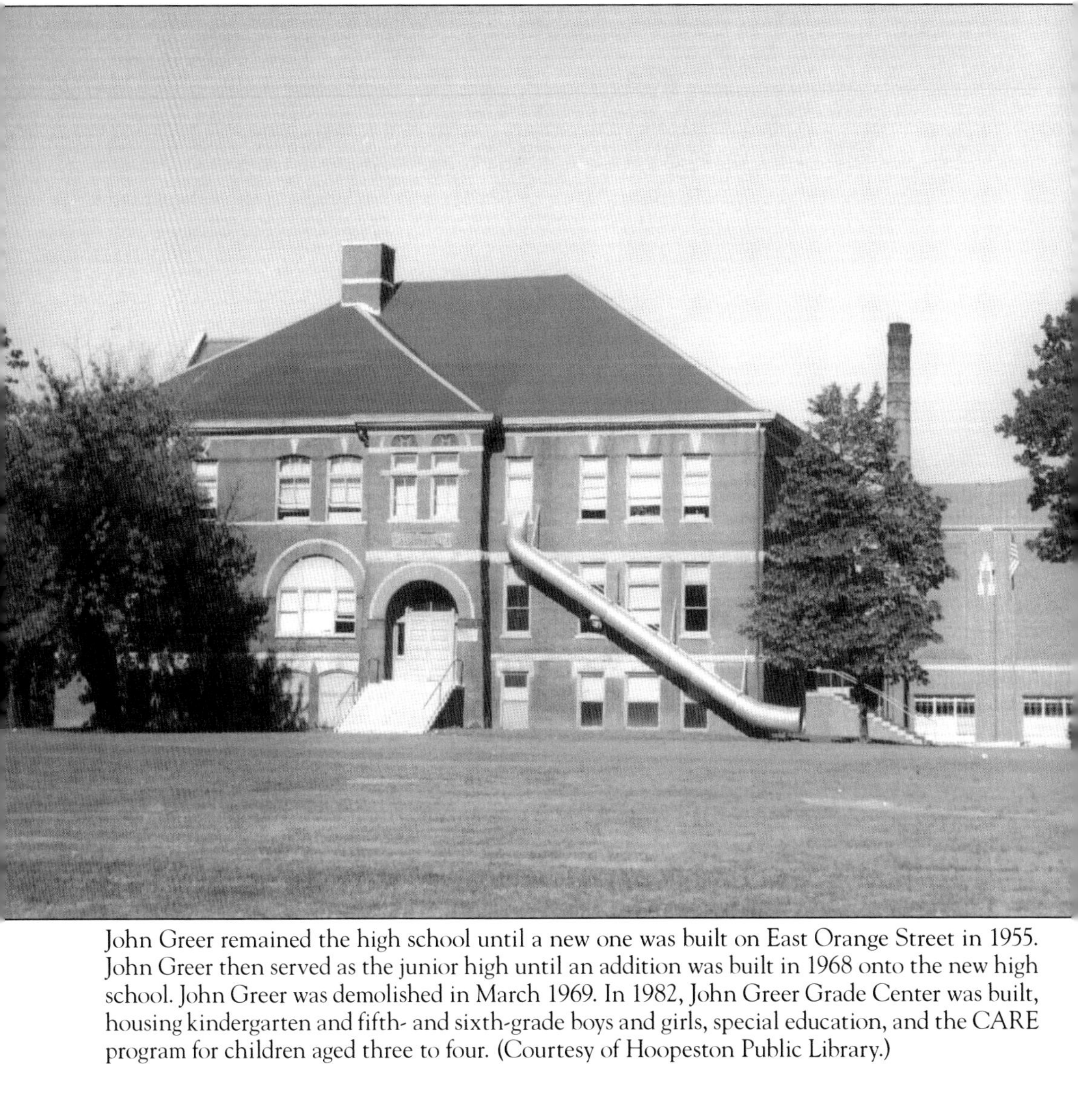

John Greer remained the high school until a new one was built on East Orange Street in 1955. John Greer then served as the junior high until an addition was built in 1968 onto the new high school. John Greer was demolished in March 1969. In 1982, John Greer Grade Center was built, housing kindergarten and fifth- and sixth-grade boys and girls, special education, and the CARE program for children aged three to four. (Courtesy of Hoopeston Public Library.)

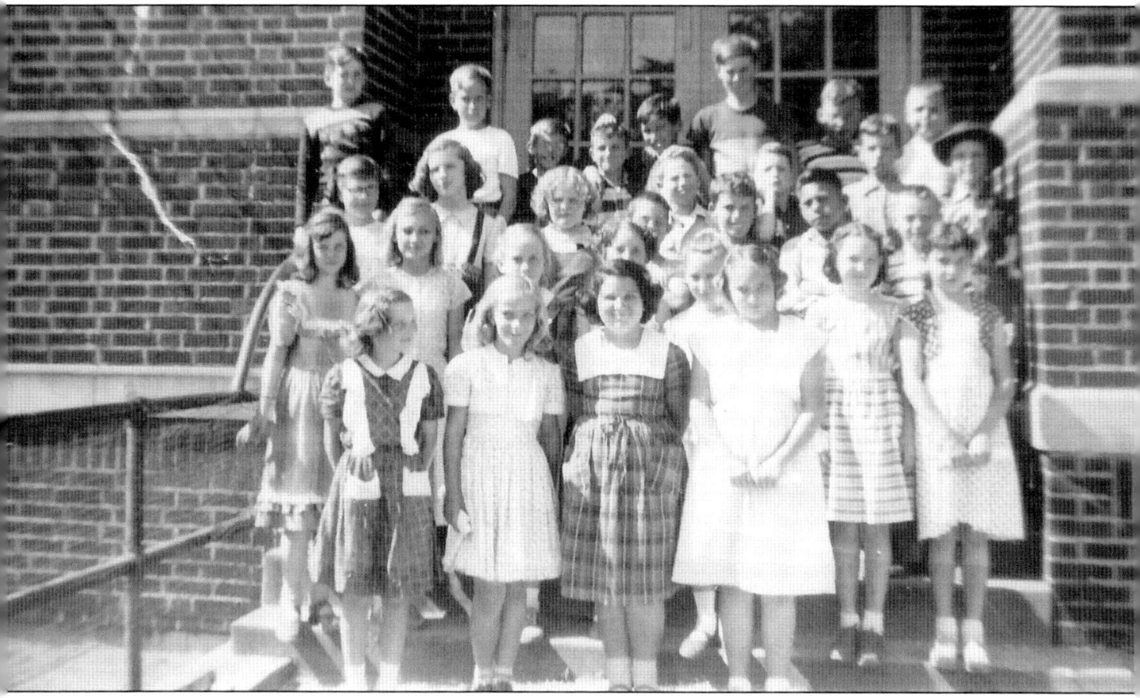

This Honeywell Grade School photograph shows students in 1952. They are, from left to right, (first row) Karen Wells, Linda Tincher, Sherry Devore, and Nancy Johnson; (second row) Sandy Cox, Susan Cleveland, Sally Blakey, Gloria March, Darlene Lane, Judy Rayls, and Artie Mae Justice; (third row) Susie Mitchell, Sharon Stark, Margie Casner, Terry Edwards, David Yanders, unidentified, and Terry Forshier; (fourth row) unidentified (with hand on his head) Mike Jessup, Dennis Noyes (tongue stuck out), and unidentified; (fifth row) Jack Boyer, unidentified, John Musson, Danny Kelley, unidentified, Theo Clyaborn, Joe Roberts, and Edward Rund. (Courtesy of John Musson.)

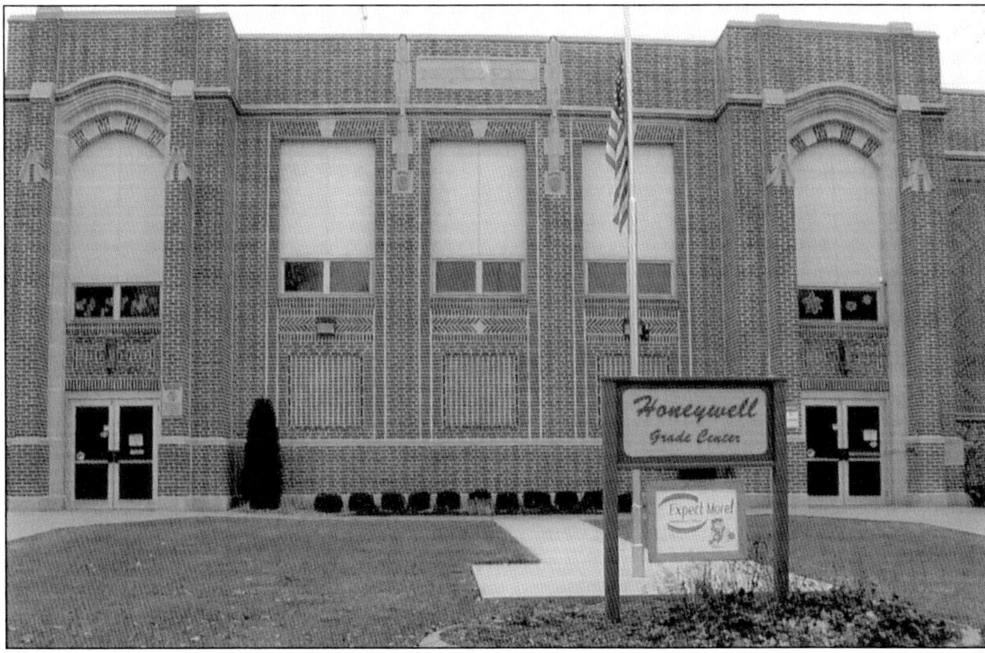

Honeywell Grade School is shown in this 1950s photograph. It housed students from first to eighth grades until seventh and eighth grade students were sent to John Greer Junior High School in 1956. In 1982, it became a grade center for students in kindergarten and third and fourth grades. (Courtesy of Jordan Crook.)

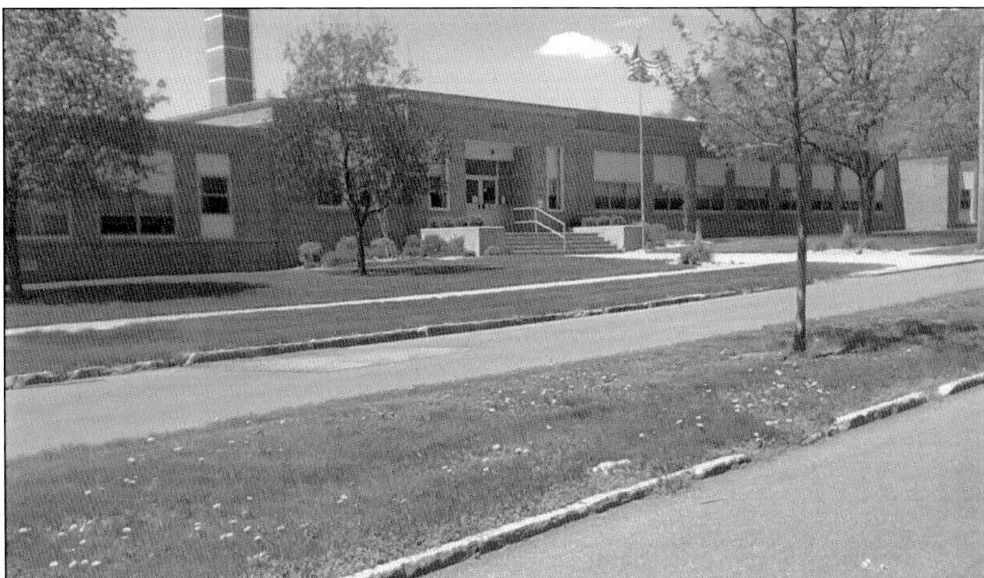

Maple Grade School (first through sixth grades) held its first classes in 1927. Housed in the old Maple High School until a fire in 1944, it was rebuilt in 1949 as a one-level facility. It then housed grades one though eight until 1956, when seventh and eighth grades were sent to junior high. In 1982, the school became a grade center. Additions were made in 1967 and again in 1994. The extra space was to accommodate all the CARE, at-risk, and early childhood children, as well as kindergarten through second grade.

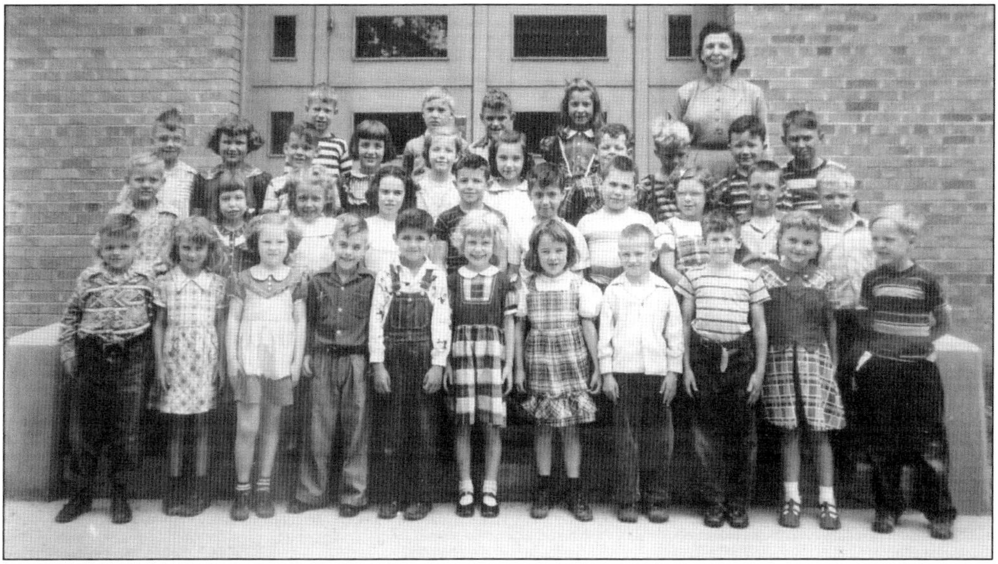

This photograph shows Maple Grade School first grade students in 1951. Pictured are, from left to right (first row) three unidentified, John Musson, Art Musk, Becky Swanick, two unidentified, Mike Milburn, unidentified, and Jim McAnally; (second row) two unidentified, Sandy Erickson, Kay Whitehouse, Randy Chesnut, Dave Crews, Dick Vines, Susie Mitchell, Jerald Strickler, and Jim Reece; (third row) Ronnie Reed, Linda Gooch, two unidentified, Mary Boylan, Linda Potts, Bob Braden, Dick Lawson, and unidentified; (fourth row) two unidentified, Eddie Lee, unidentified, and teacher Minnie Foster. (Courtesy of John Musson.)

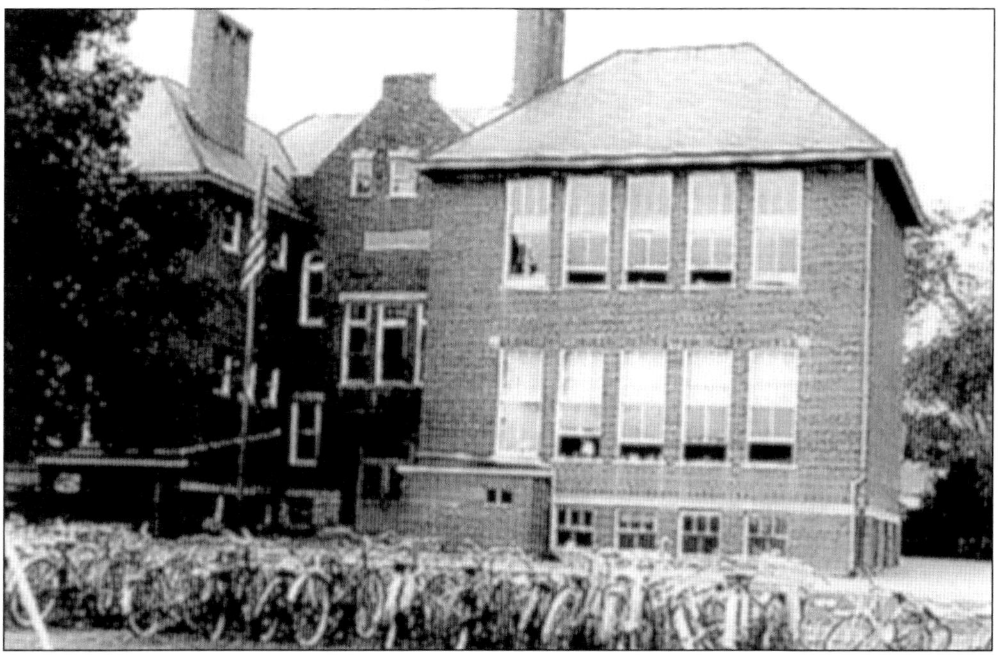

Lincoln Grade School, located on the northwest corner of Washington Street and First Avenue, was first built around 1874. It housed kindergarten through eighth grade until 1956, when seventh and eighth graders and freshmen went to John Greer Junior High. Lincoln was closed in 1969 and later demolished.

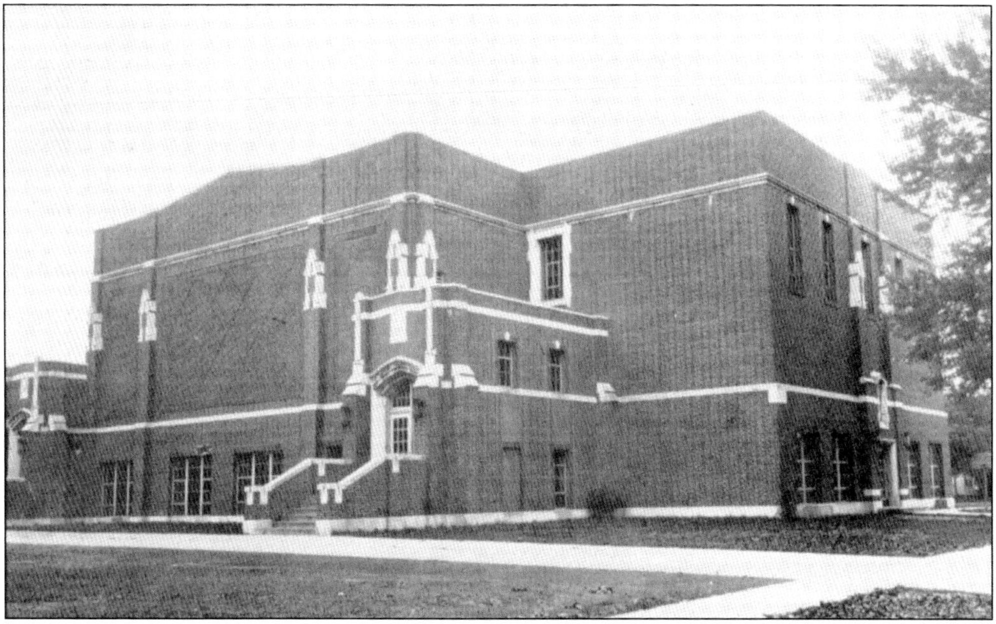

John Greer gymnasium was built in 1927 and was attached to John Greer High School with a tunnel. When the old John Greer was demolished in 1969, the new John Greer Grade School was built around the gymnasium and is still in use today. The tunnel was sealed.

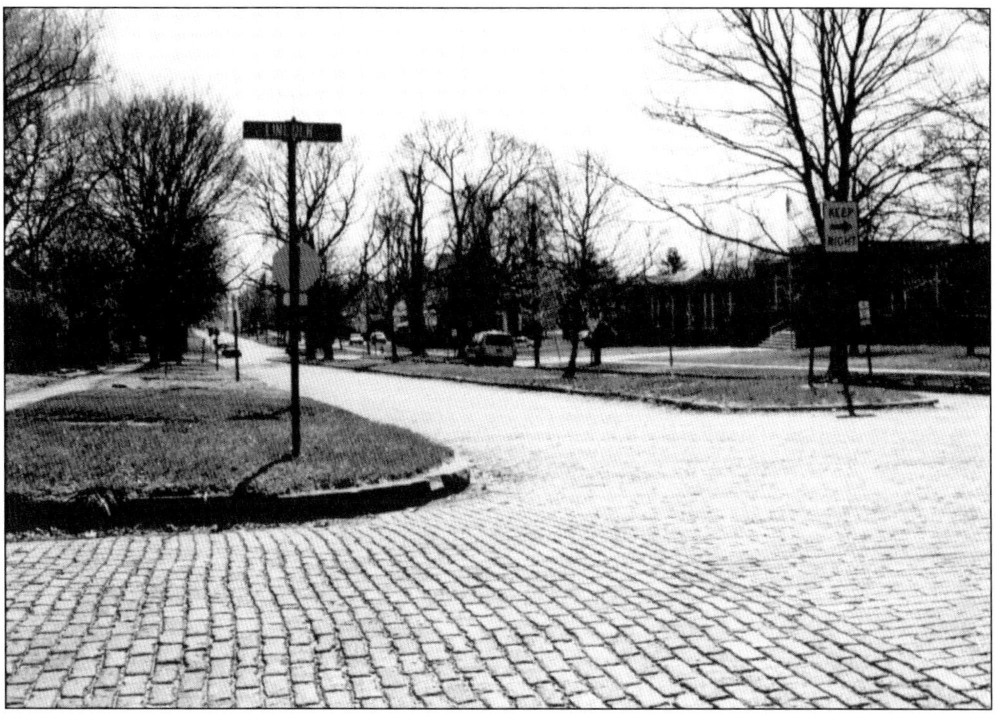

Fourth Street on the east side of Maple Grade School at one time was covered with bricks. The City brought men from the prison at Danville to clean the bricks; in fact, most of Hoopeston's city streets were brick.

Five

Hoopeston Parks

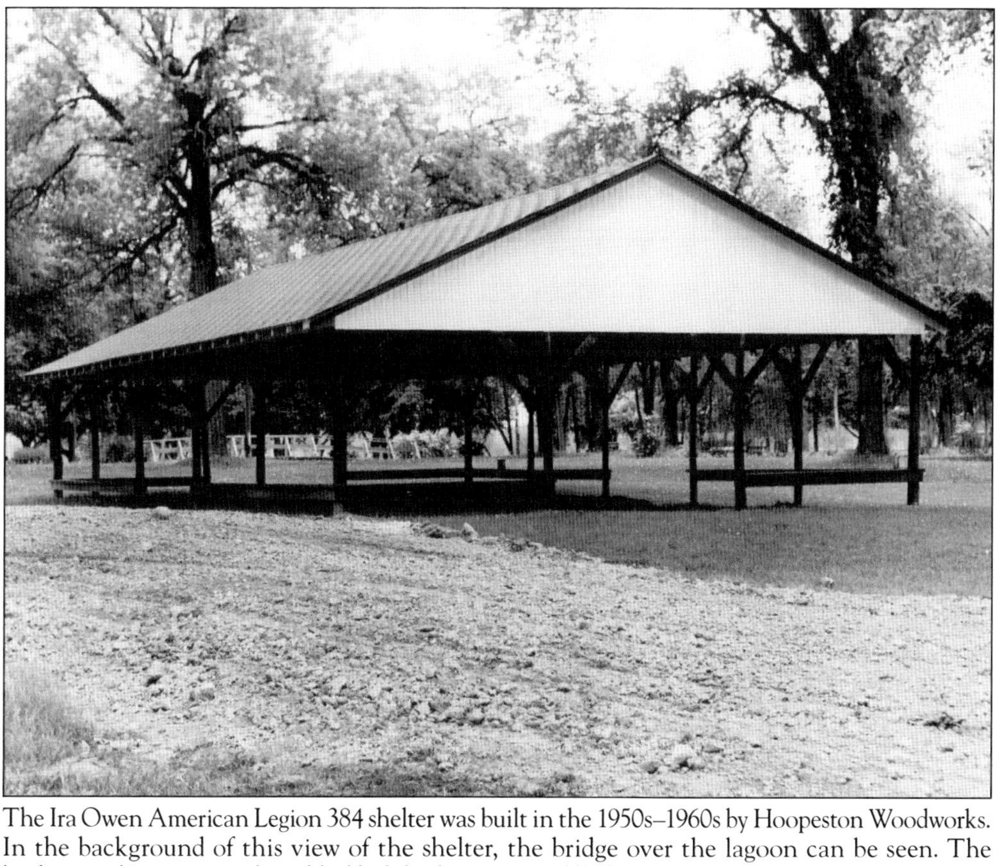

The Ira Owen American Legion 384 shelter was built in the 1950s–1960s by Hoopeston Woodworks. In the background of this view of the shelter, the bridge over the lagoon can be seen. The bridge was later removed, and half of the lagoon was filled in with dirt. (Courtesy of Scott and Traci Brown.)

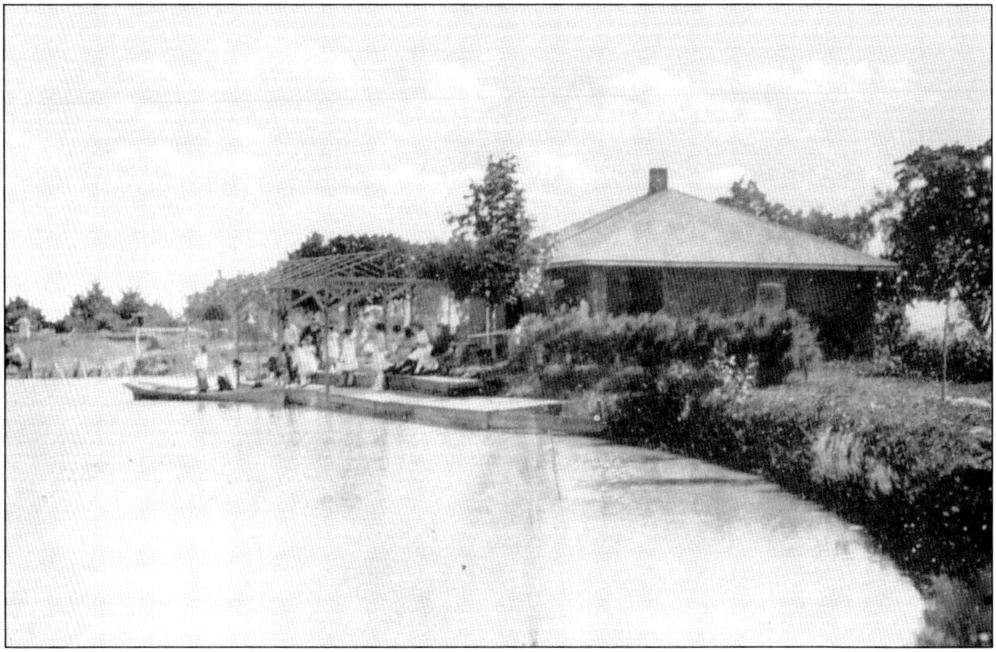

The boathouse was located on the McFerren Park lagoon on an island in the center. A bridge over the lagoon led to the boathouse, where couples and others could rent boats for an afternoon of leisure.

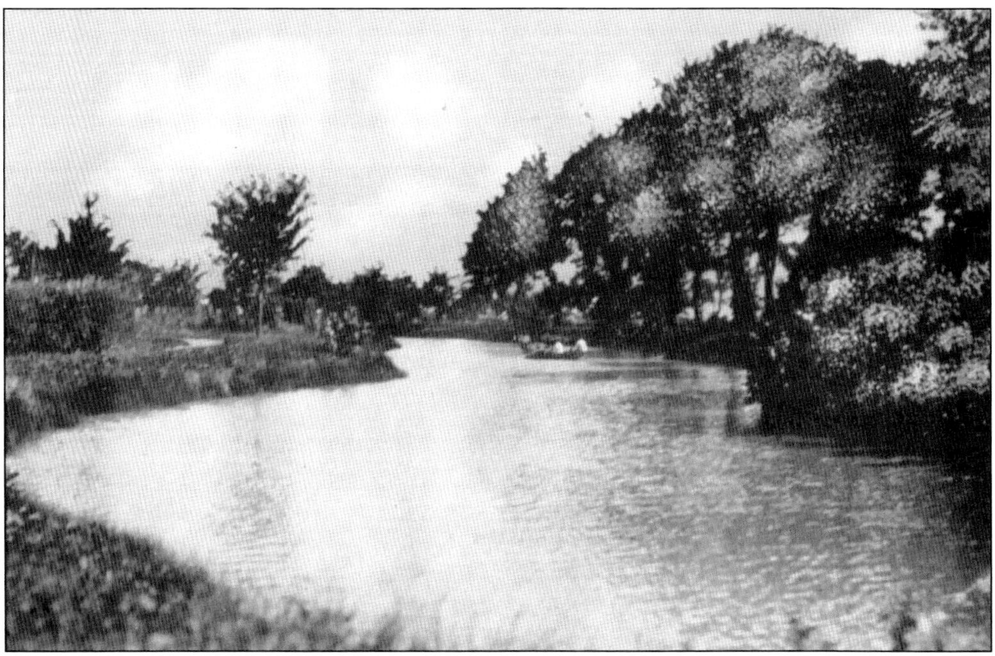

McFerren Park Lagoon in the early 1900s, as seen in this photograph, was a popular place to go boating with a lady friend. The winters were so cold the lagoon froze over, so ice skating was a popular sport in the winter.

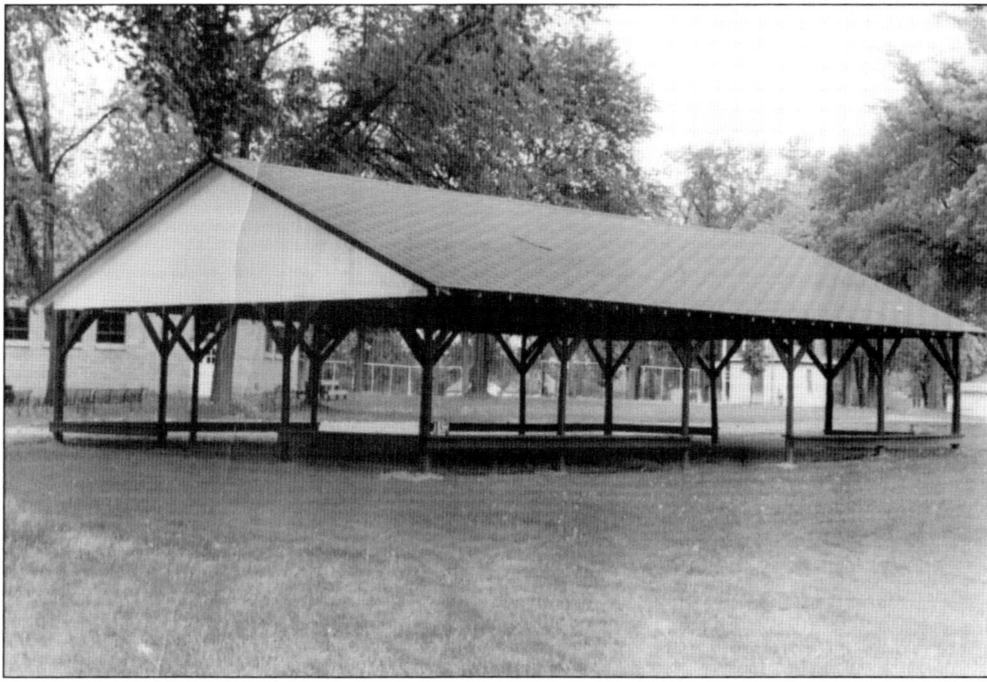

This view of the Ira Owen American Legion 384 shelter shows the Civic Center in the background on the left. The building at right is the park office. (Courtesy of Scott and Traci Brown.)

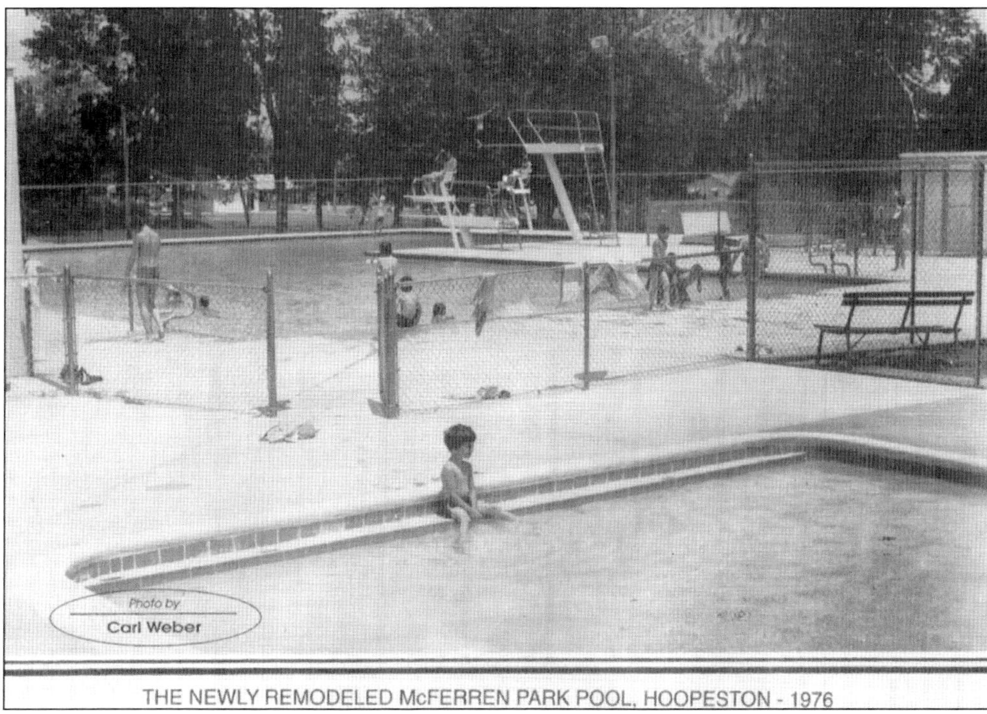

McFerren Park pool was remodeled in 1976 to include a separate baby pool for younger children. A fence and gate separated the children's pool from the deeper one reserved for the older children and adults. High and low diving boards were added during the remodel.

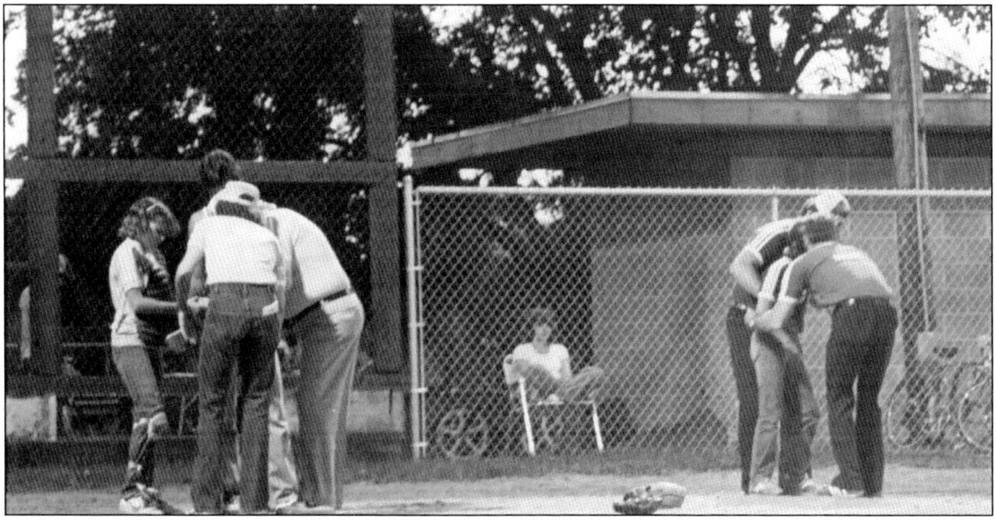

Union Park, a gift of Alba Honeywell, sits beside Sixth Street between McNeil and Wyman Avenues. It is the home of the Hoopeston Girls' Softball Association, which had its start in April 1974. Judy Blalock Green, its first president, began the organization to give young girls a sport of their own. This 1981 photograph shows opposing coaches talking to their team members.

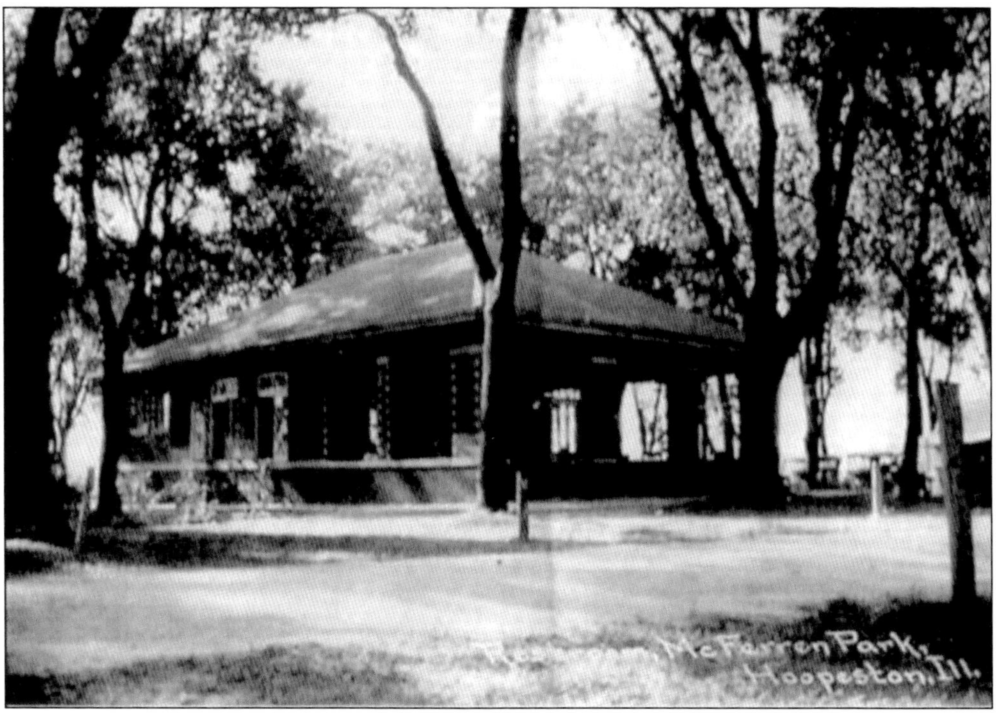

The original McFerren Park restroom and shelter, located north of the civic center and pictured here in the 1940s, is now the location of the Jaycee park shelter.

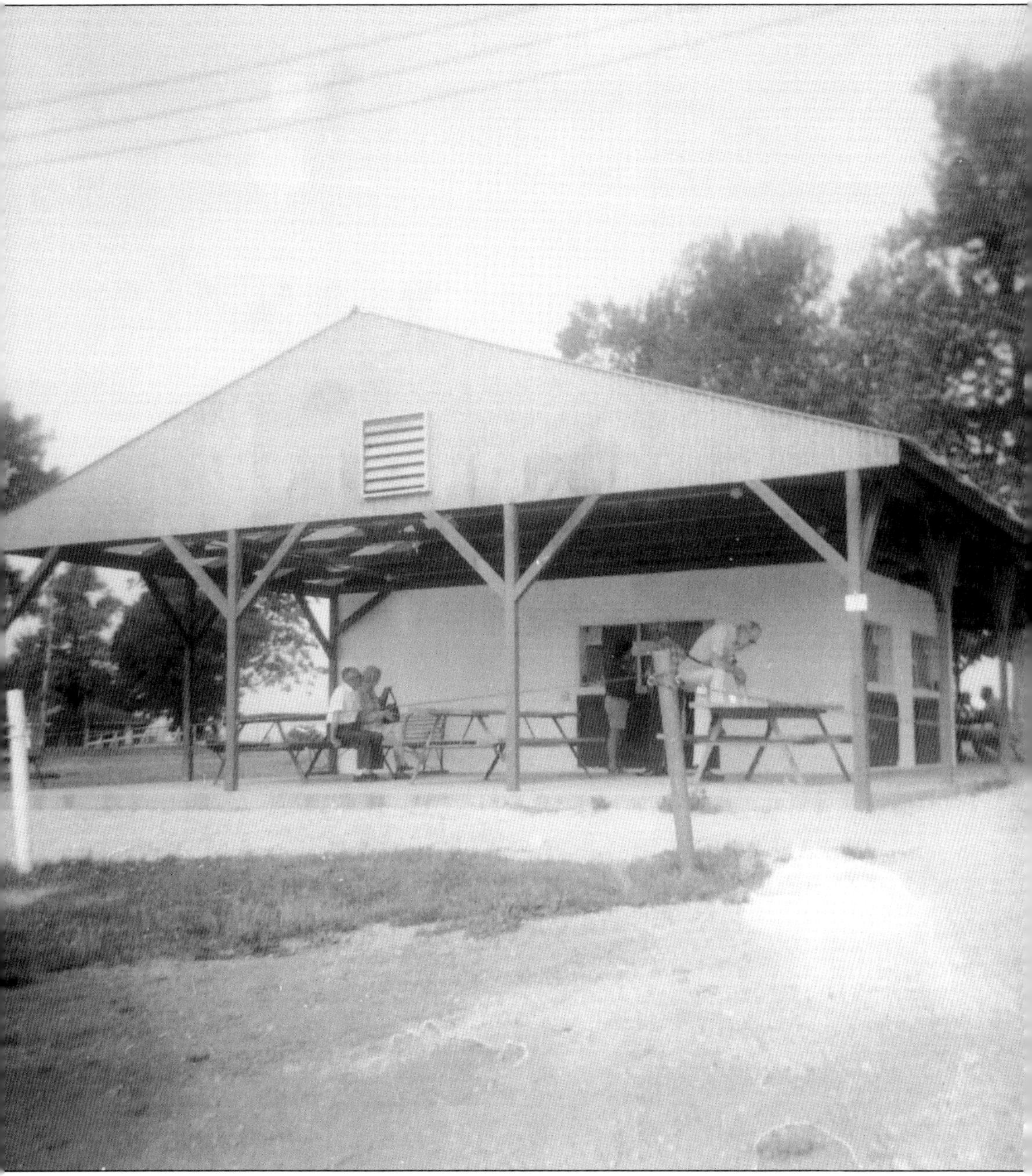

The Lions' Club shelter, seen in this 1971 photograph, sold food items during the week. It is now open during the National Sweetcorn Festival, catering to the many fairgoers who trek into Hoopeston over Labor Day weekend. (Courtesy of Scott Baer.)

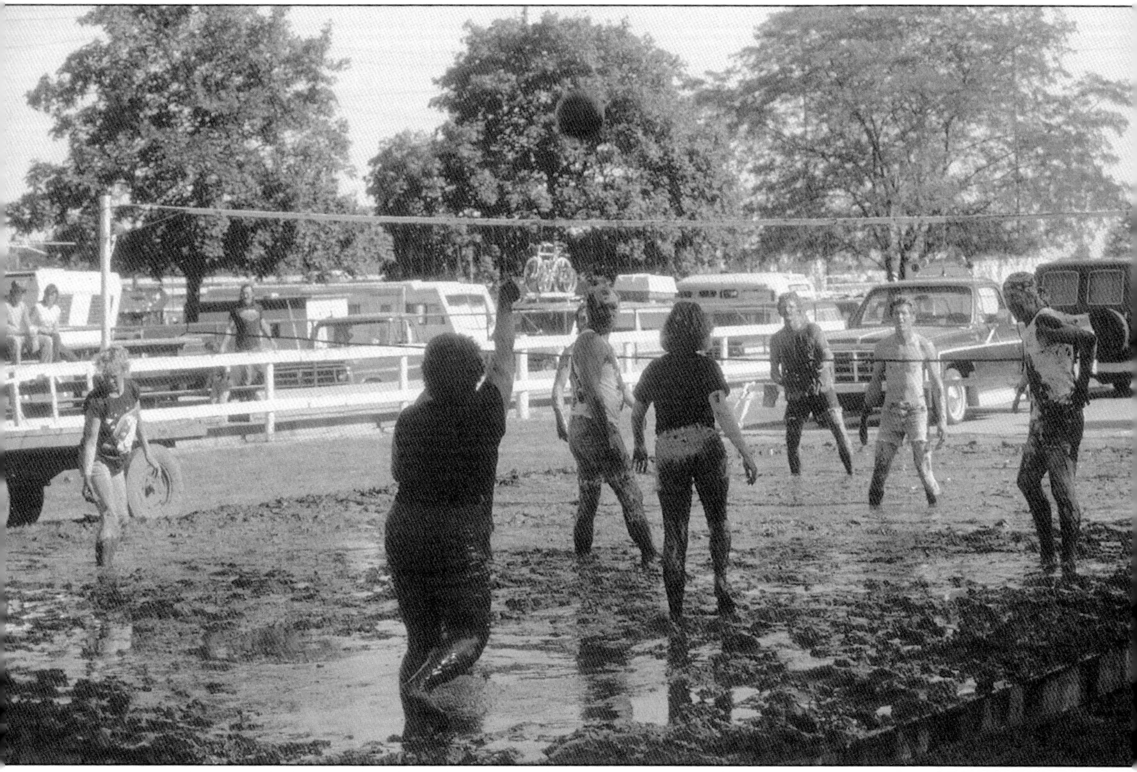

One of the highlights at the 1984 National Sweetcorn Festival was the mud volleyball tournament held on the east side of the park. There were six to eight teams that participated in the game. (Courtesy of Scott Baer.)

Six

HOOPESTON CHURCHES

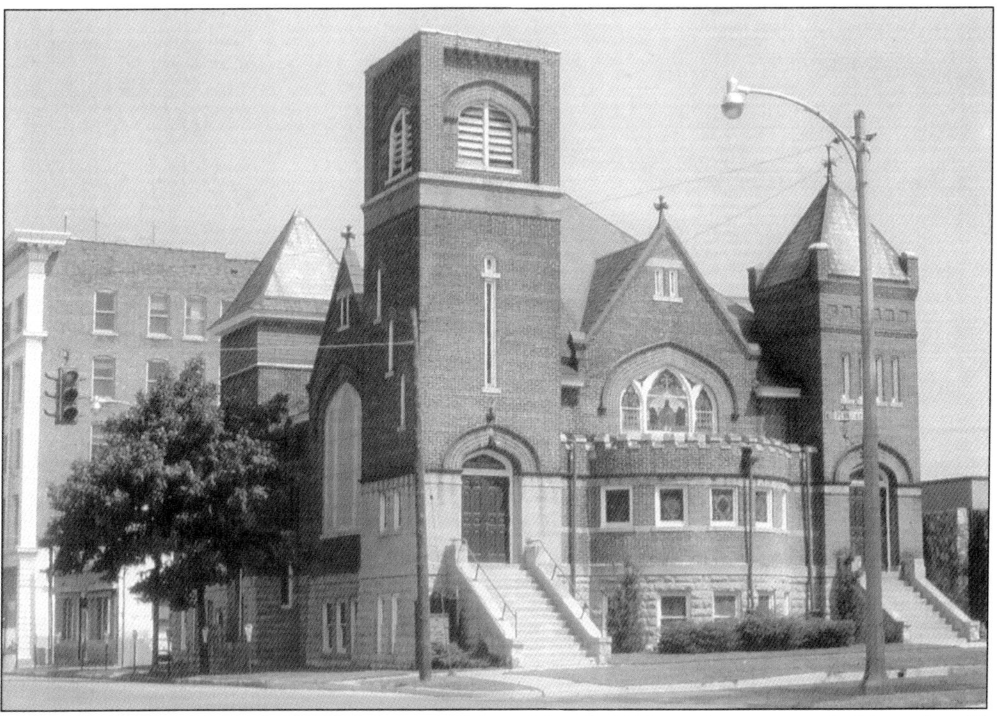

The First Presbyterian Church was organized on May 3, 1872, with meetings held in the old Hibbard House, which stood at the corner of Penn Street and Second Avenue. In 1881, a new frame church was erected at the corner of Penn and Market Streets. The church was replaced with a brick and stone building at a cost of $20,000 in 1900. It was later torn down for a parking lot. (Courtesy of Scott Baer.)

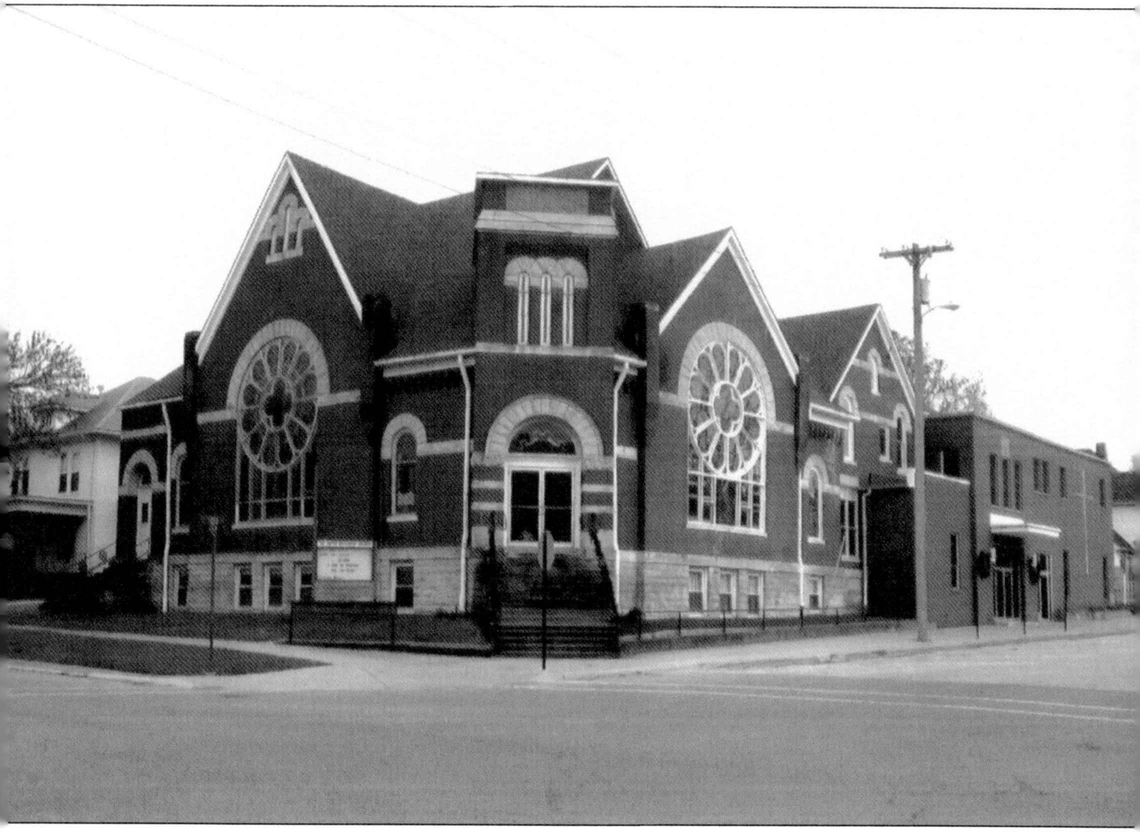

The first Methodist church in Hoopeston was the Methodist Episcopal Church in 1873. A new church was built in 1874 on the corner of Main and Third Streets that served the congregation until the present church was erected in 1896. Several changes and additions over the years can be seen in this photograph of the church.

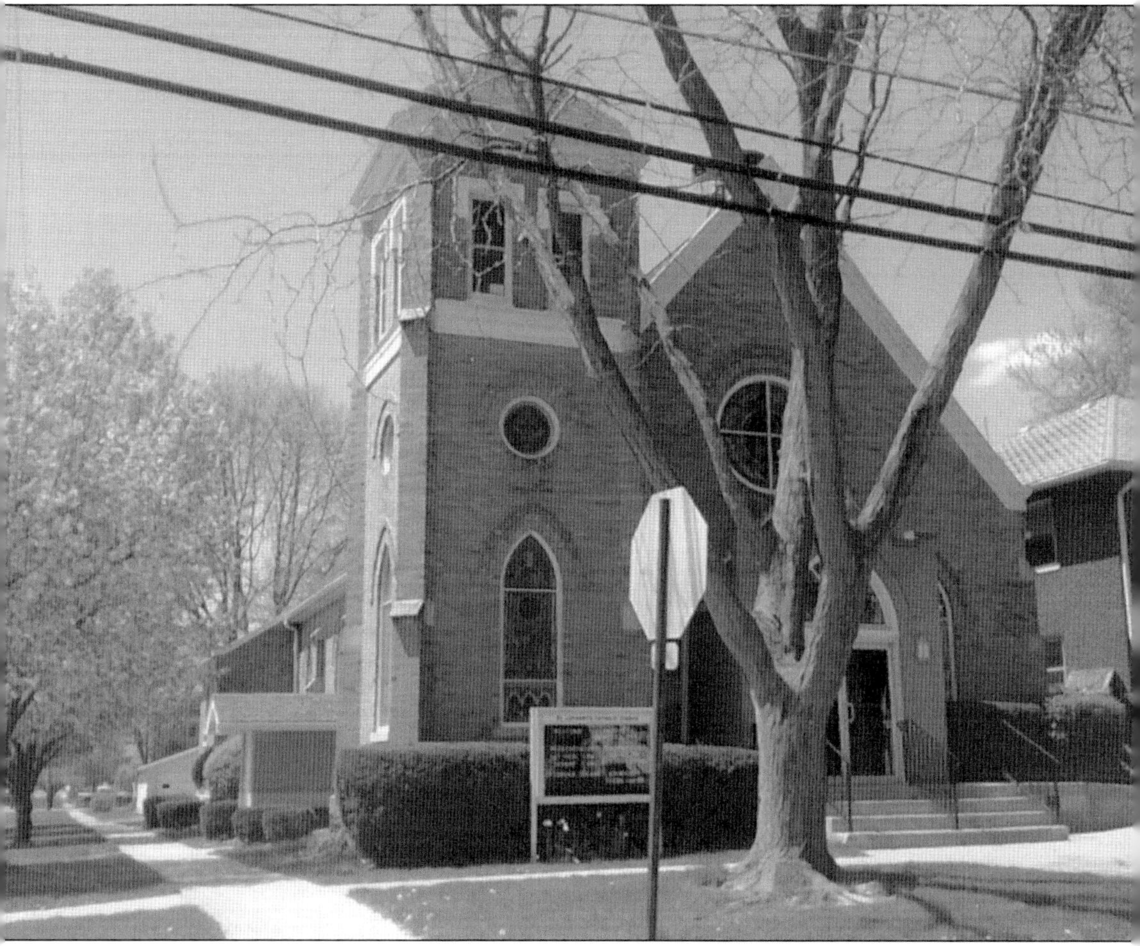

The first Catholic church, St. Anthony's, was built in 1877 on the corner of East Lincoln and South Third Streets. The present church was constructed in 1907 at a cost of $35,000.

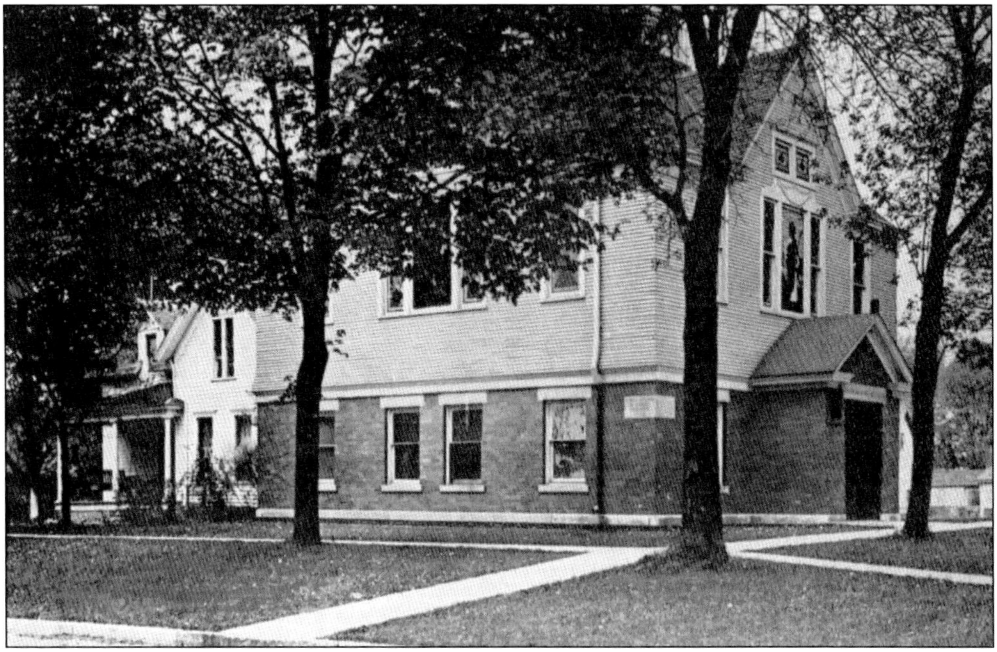

The Christian Science Society of Hoopeston was organized in September 1898 with 14 members. Early meetings were held in members' homes; they later moved to the Quakers' meetinghouse until rooms were secured in the McFerren Block. The society reorganized in 1900 as the First Church of Christ, Scientist, of Hoopeston.

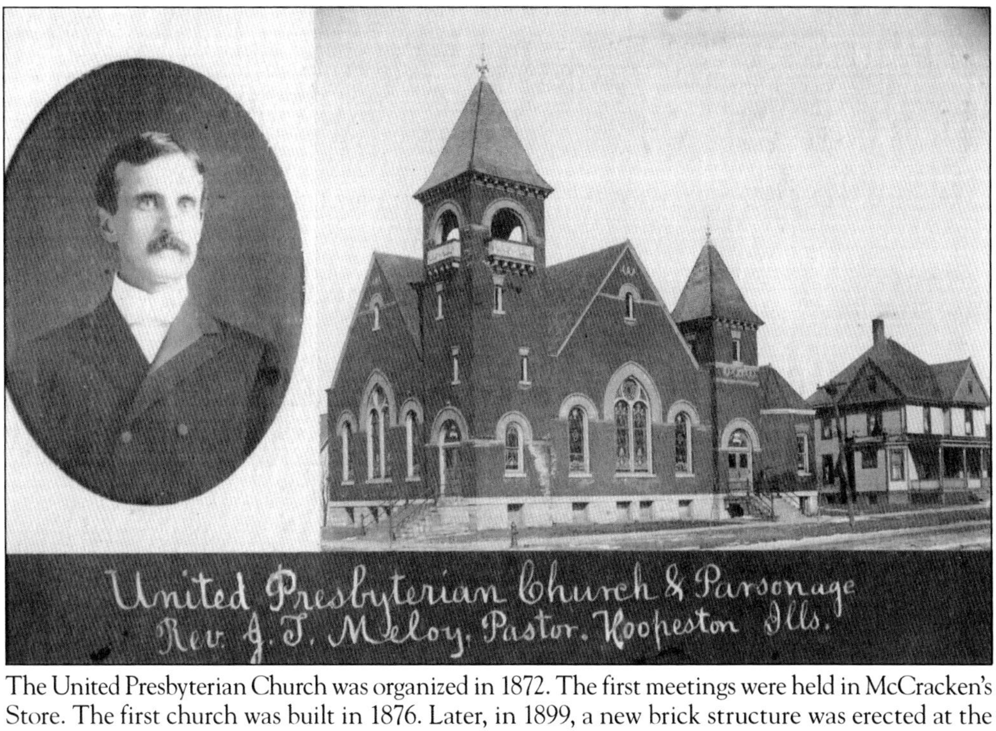

The United Presbyterian Church was organized in 1872. The first meetings were held in McCracken's Store. The first church was built in 1876. Later, in 1899, a new brick structure was erected at the corner of Market Street and Honeywell Avenue.

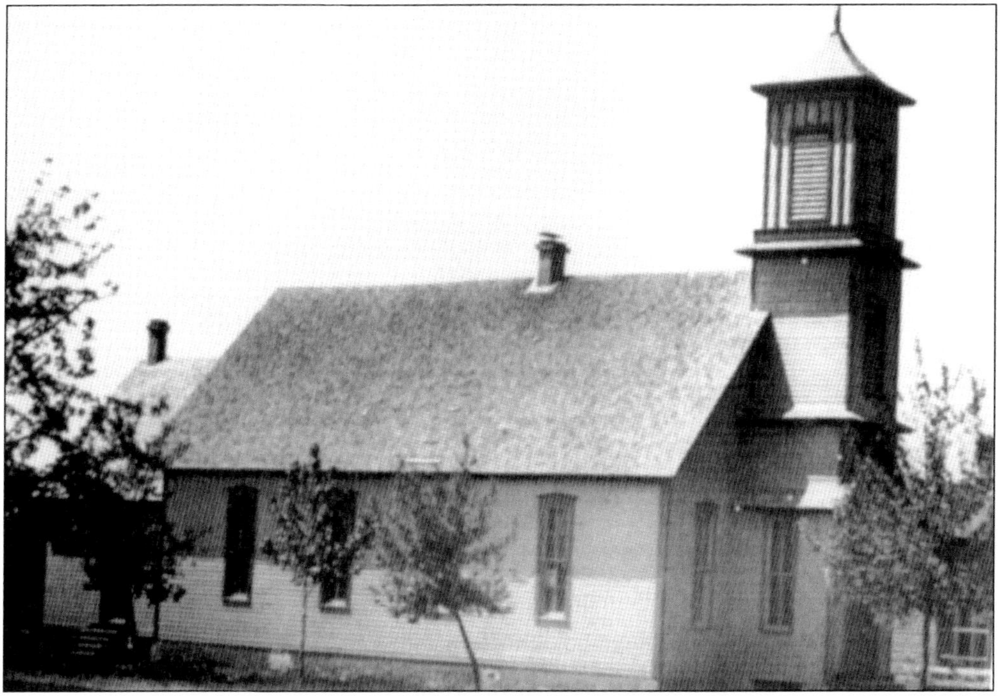

The First Baptist Church was organized in March 1873, holding its first meetings in the Franks School. Later meetings were held in stores and halls in Hoopeston until the church broke ground for a new building on September 13, 1881. The congregation raised $1,400 to build the church. This building served the members until a new brick structure was completed in 1904.

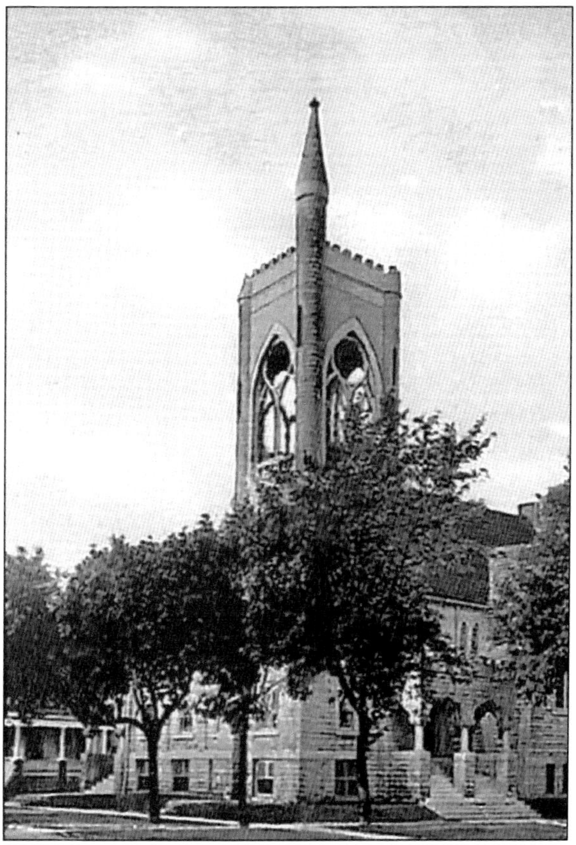

The Universalist church was erected in 1886 at the southwest corner of Market and Penn Streets. The congregation was first organized in August 1882 by Rev. T.S. Gutherie of Springfield, Ohio, before coming to Hoopeston. The church building burned in 1956, and the chimes were recovered and placed in the First Christian Church. (Courtesy of Tom Weber.)

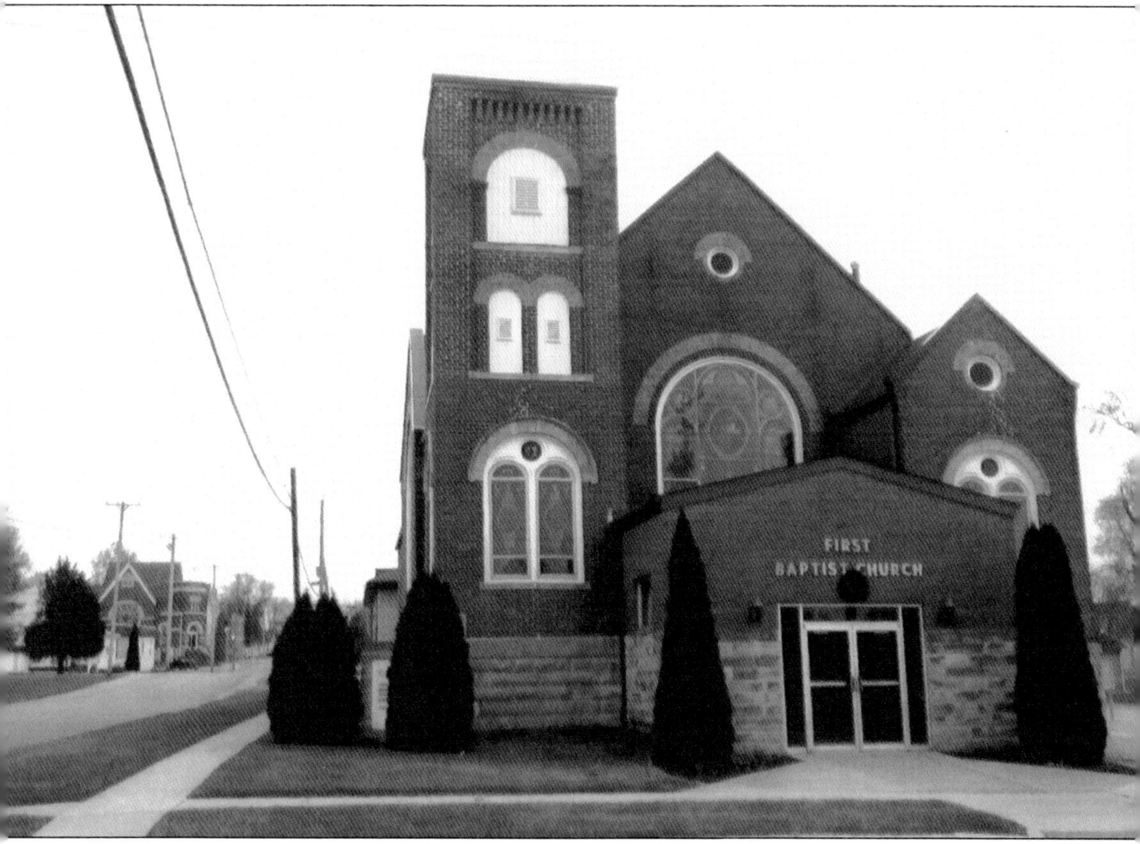

The Baptist church was organized in March 1873 and held its first meetings in a schoolhouse three miles southeast of Hoopeston. The new church in its present location on the corner of Third Street and Seminary Avenue was completed and dedicated in 1904.

Seven

HOOPESTON HOMES

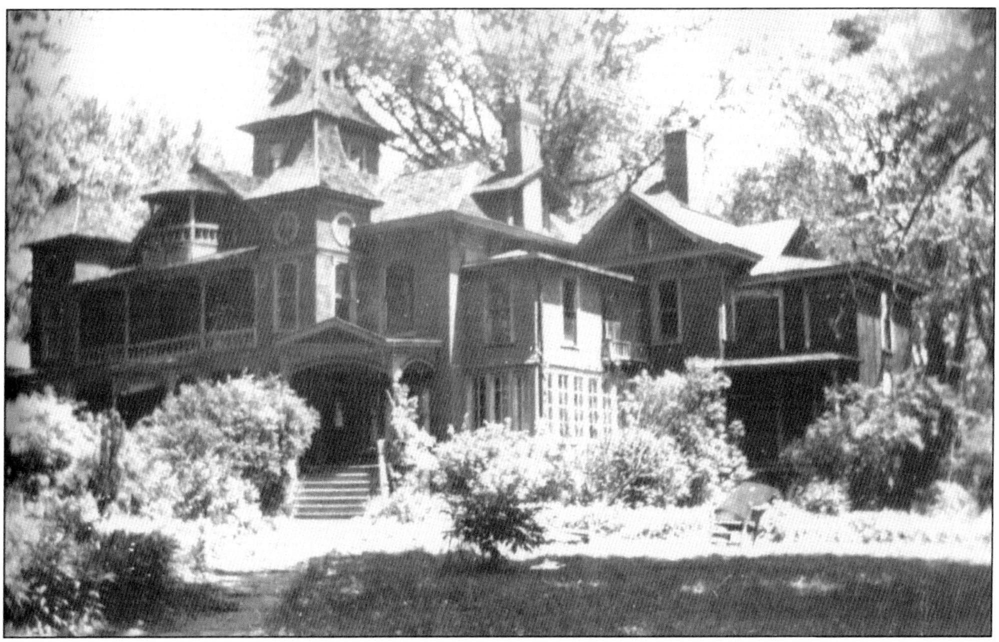

The Honeywell Mansion was first located on East Honeywell Avenue. The house was said to have had 42 rooms. When Sadie Honeywell married Dr. Earl, she had it torn down and built another home in the 400 block of East Seminary Avenue that was smaller. (Courtesy of Hoopeston Public Library.)

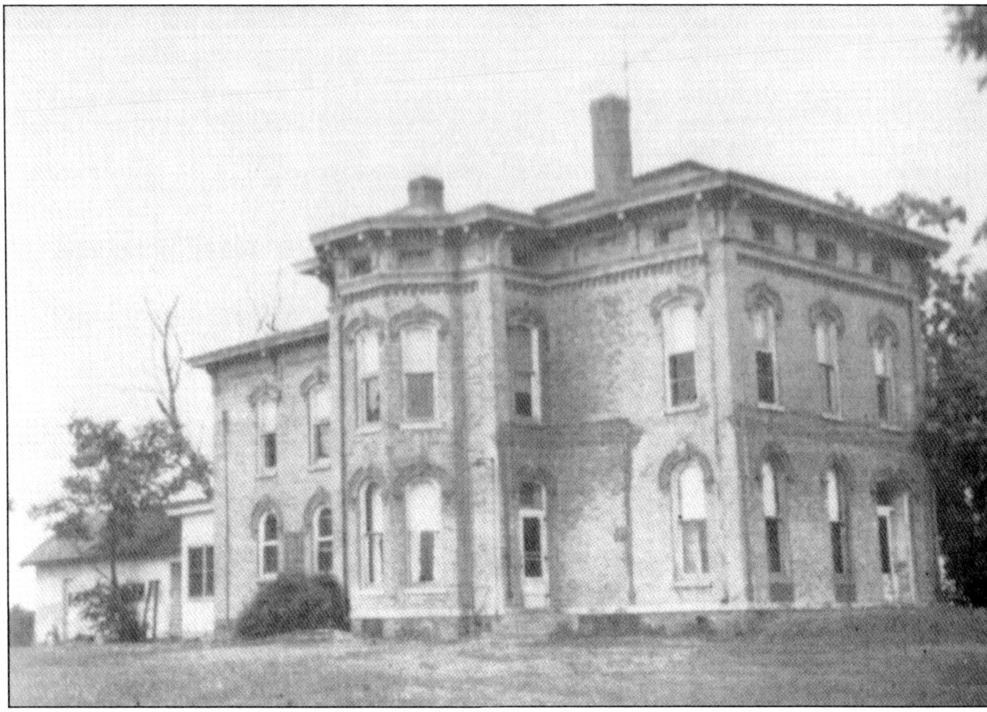

James A. Cunningham built a home one mile northwest of Hoopeston in 1880 on the site of Thomas Hoopes's cabin. It was located on the corner of Thompson and Route 1, set back from the roadway. (Courtesy of Hoopeston Public Library.)

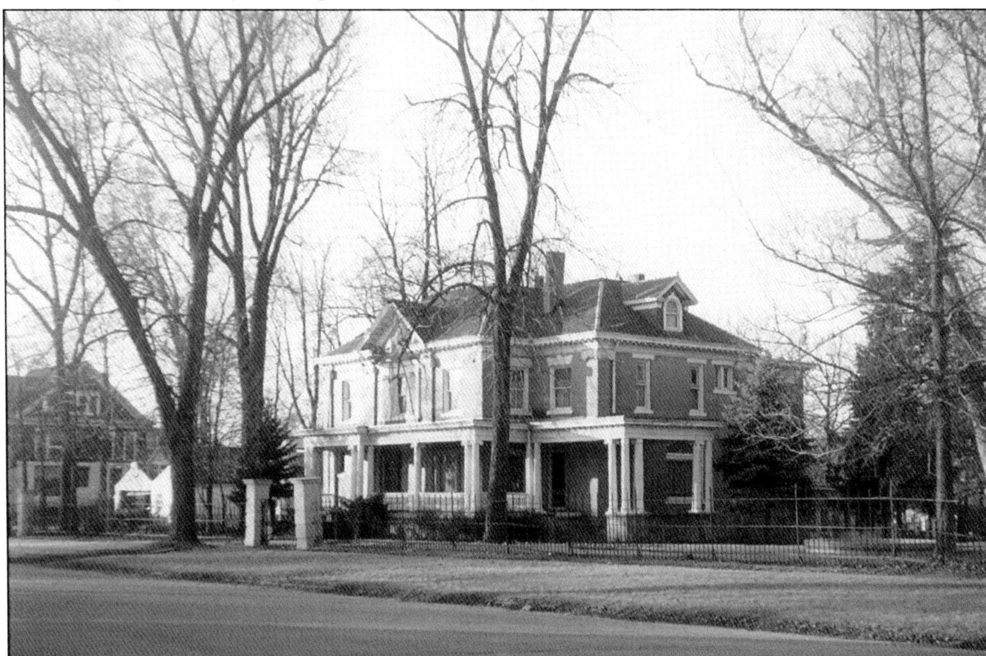

This is the Dyer Home on East Honeywell Avenue and Fifth Street, photographed in 1971. Also visible is the little fishpond at the side of the home. (Courtesy of Scott Baer.)

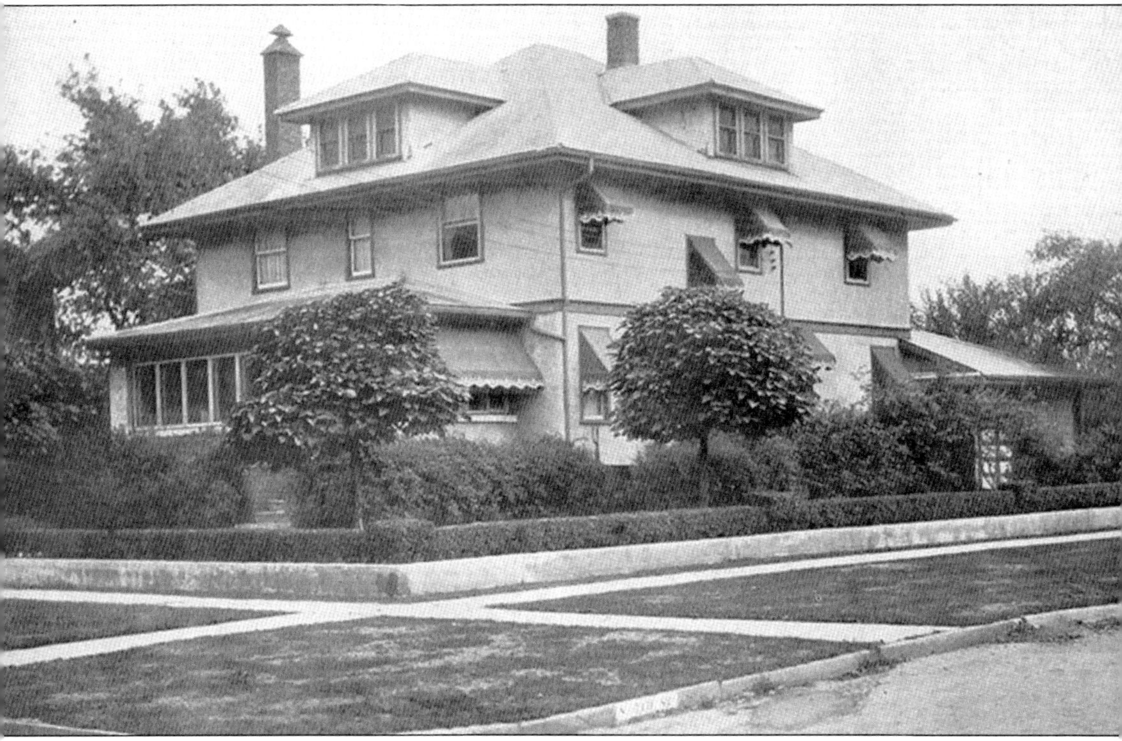

A.B. McCollum came to Hoopeston in 1925, buying the Lorraine Theatre with his partner Tracy L. Orr. He lived in the home on East Lincoln and Seventh Streets until he moved to California. McCollum was the first to bring talking movies to Hoopeston in 1930, and he did a complete remodel of the Lorraine in 1937. (Courtesy of Hoopeston Public Library.)

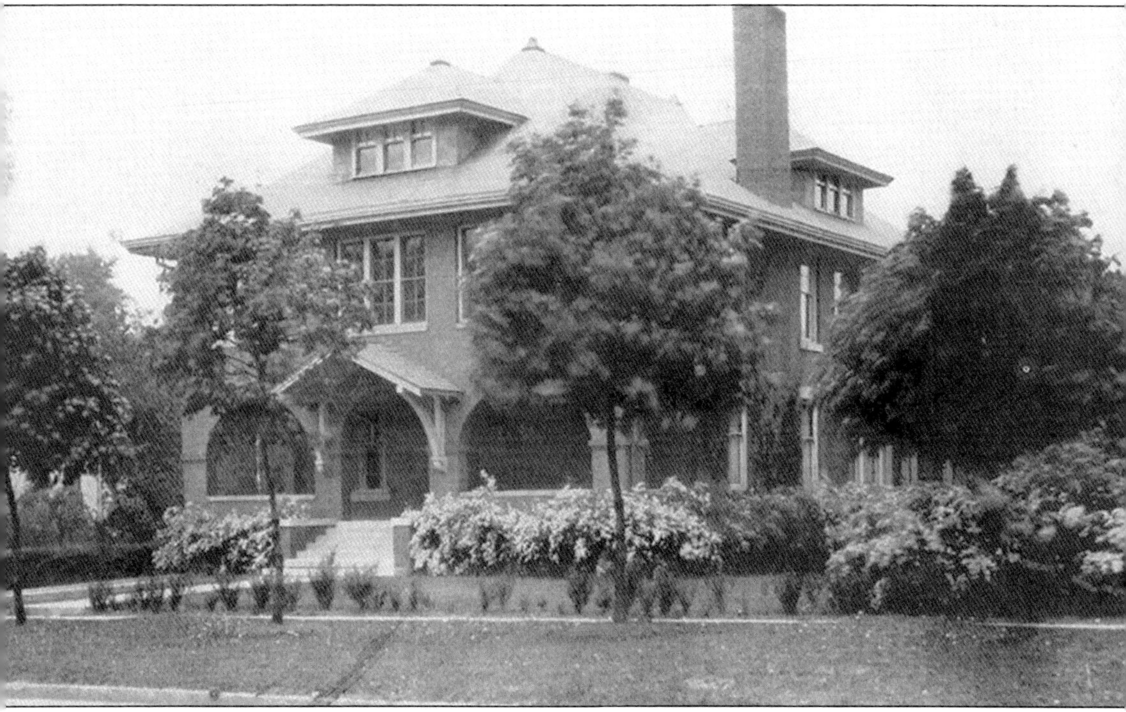

E.J. Boorde lived in this home on the north side of the 800 block of East Penn Street in the 1920s. Boorde and his son were owners of the Hoopeston Telephone Company in 1925 and built the Lorraine Theatre in 1921, opening the establishment in March 1922. (Courtesy of Hoopeston Public Library.)

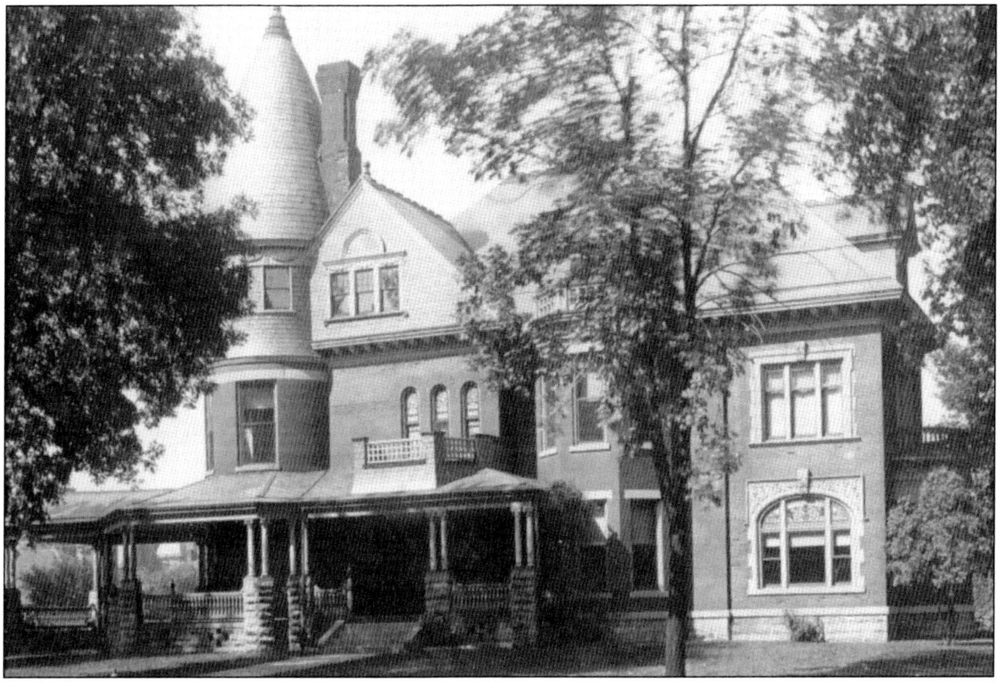

Thomas Hoopes's residence, located on the corner of Penn and Fourth Streets, was a majestic home in the late 1890s. Hoopeston derived its name from Hoopes and was built on land that he owned and donated. Hoopes is considered one of the founders of early Hoopeston.

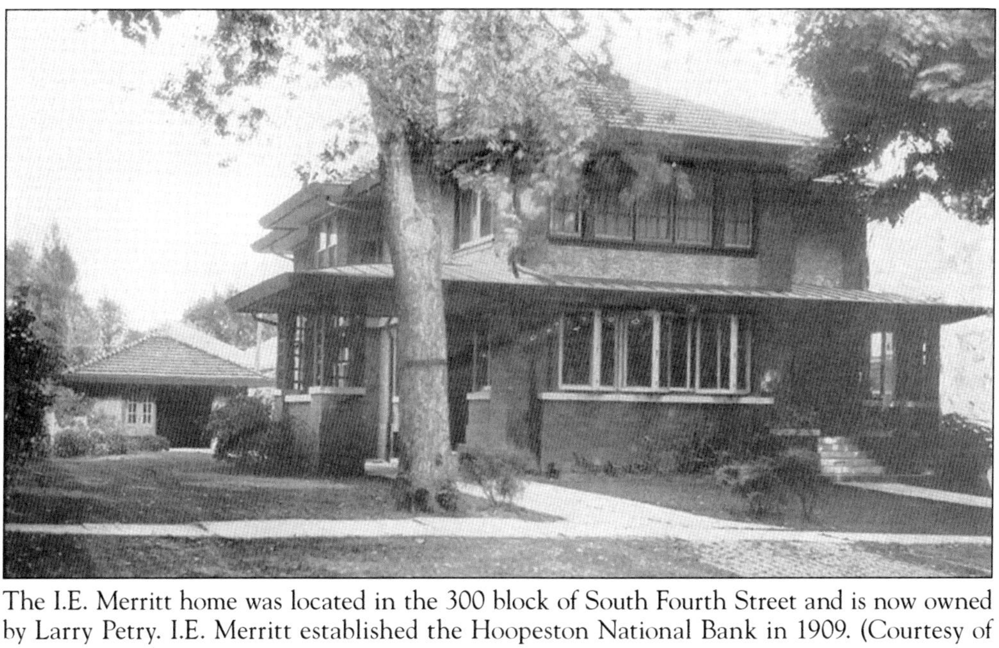

The I.E. Merritt home was located in the 300 block of South Fourth Street and is now owned by Larry Petry. I.E. Merritt established the Hoopeston National Bank in 1909. (Courtesy of Hoopeston Public Library.)

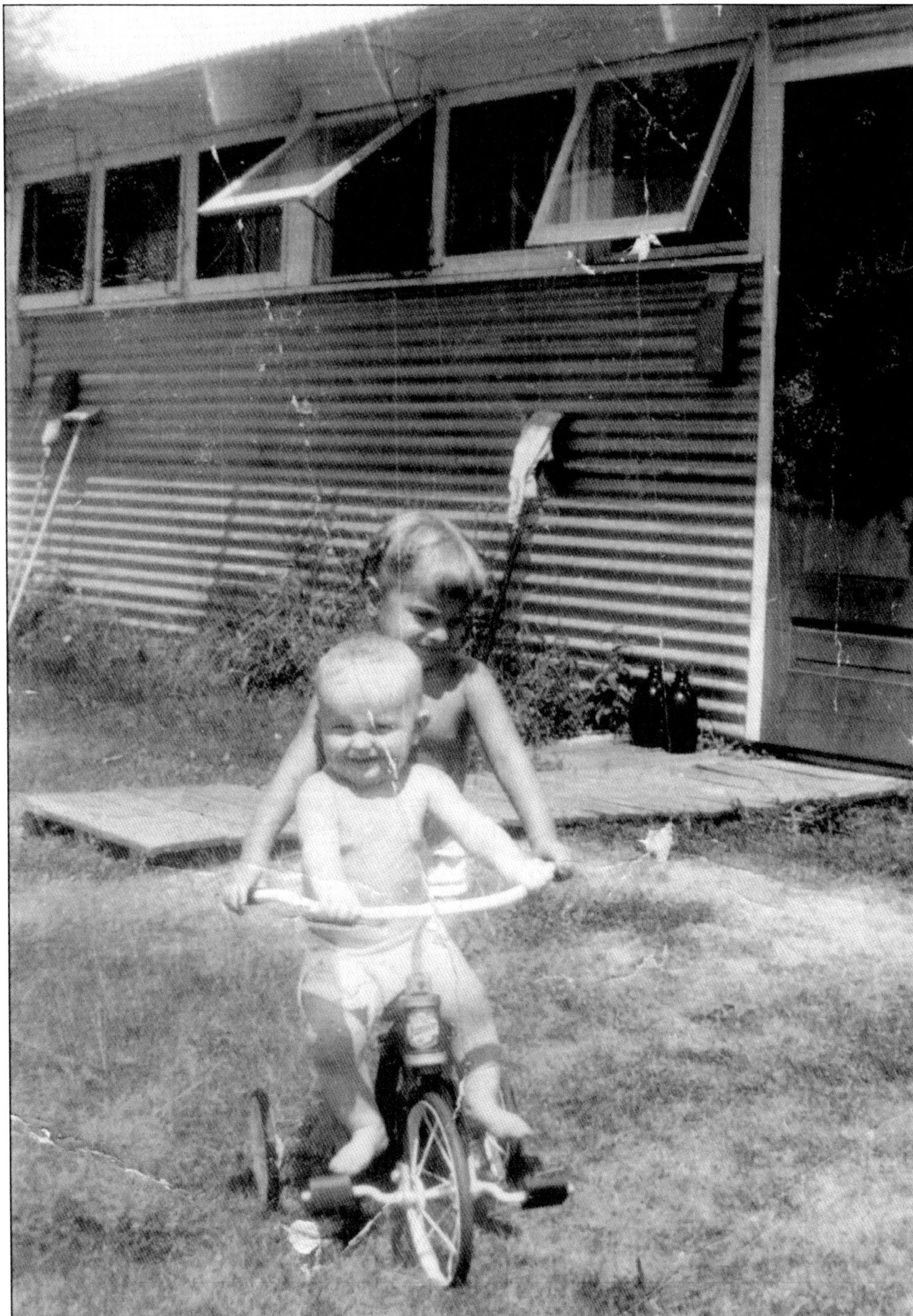

The tin houses on the corner of South First Avenue and Route 9 covered approximately two blocks. This 1957 photograph shows Gloria and Bill Gholson, children of Bill and Willia Gholson, playing in the front yard of their home. (Courtesy of Bill Gholson.)

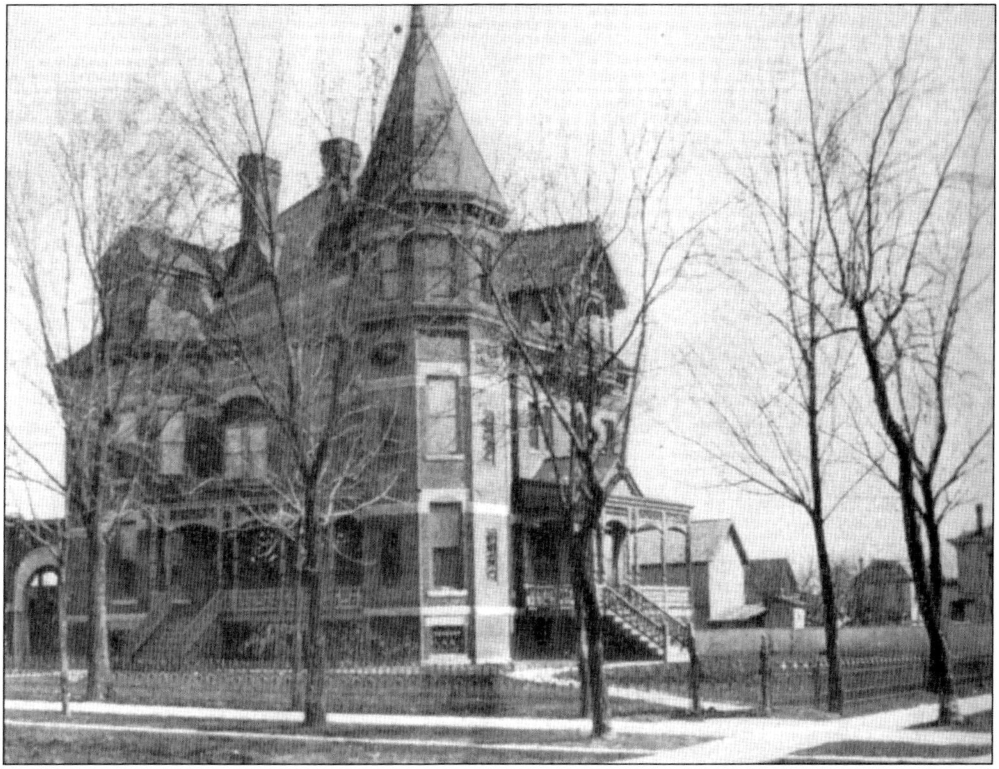

J.S. McFerren built his first home on the corner of East Penn and Third Streets. In this 1900 photograph, the home does not have the extended porch that later images show.

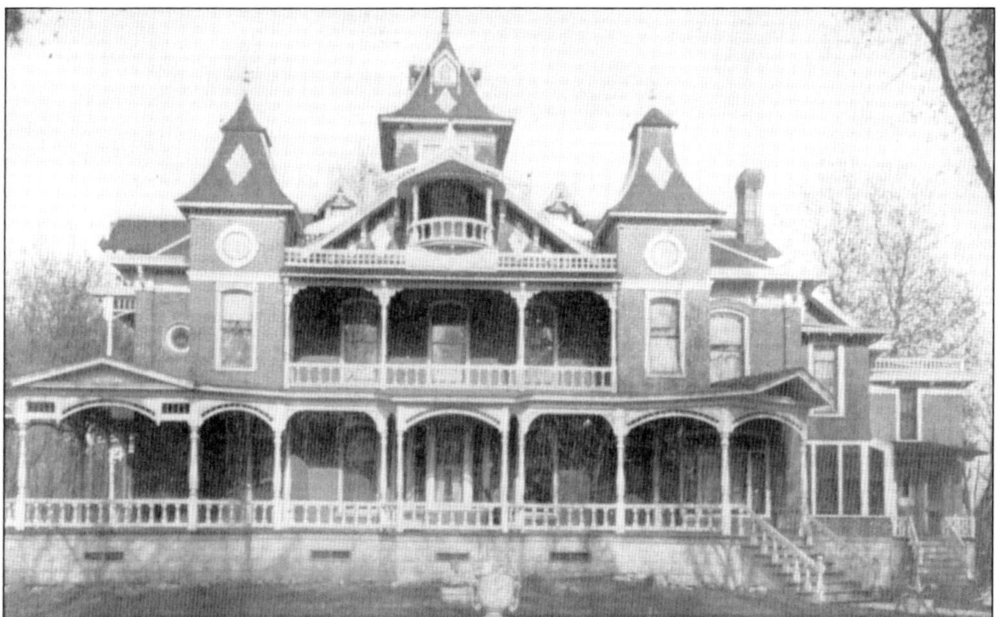

The home of Alba Honeywell was located in the 500 block of East Honeywell Avenue in the middle of the block. Honeywell served the city of Hoopeston as mayor from 1879 to 1880.

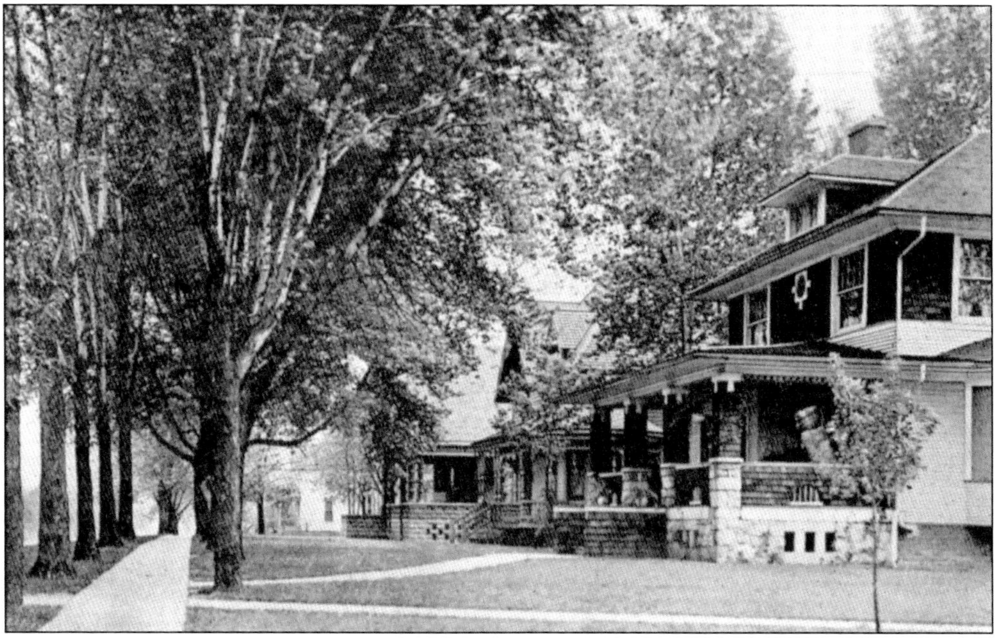

This house on the southeast corner of East Lincoln and Fourth Streets became the home of George Samaras, a native of Greece. Samaras and his son Alexander were the owners of the Ritz and were famous for their specialty candies.

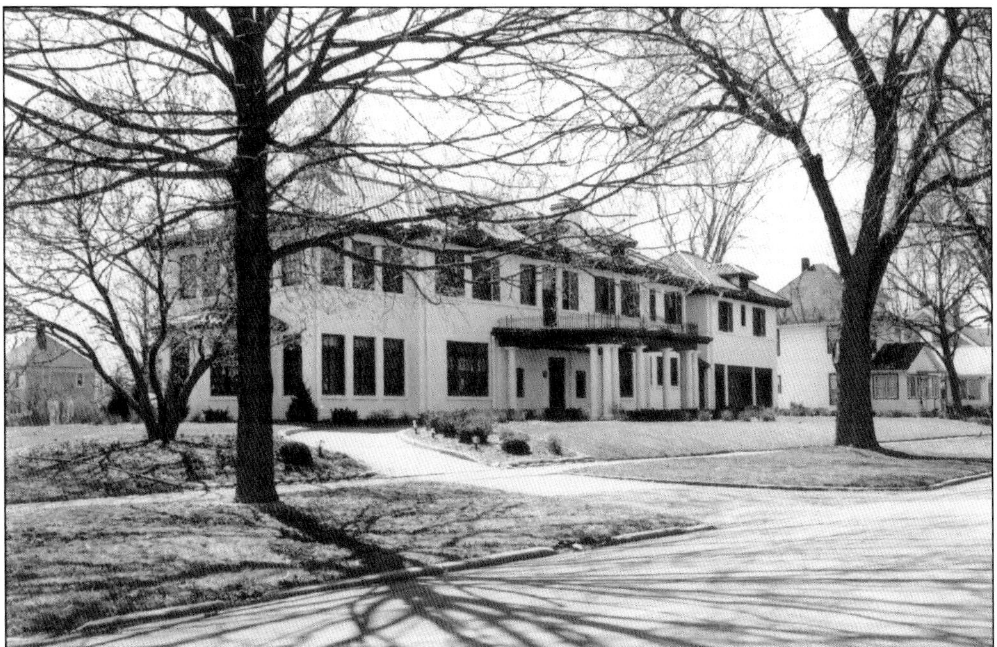

The Donald J. McFerren home was located in the 700 block of East Washington Street. He was elected mayor in 1925 and served until 1929. McFerren also became president of the First National Bank following his father's death.

Eight

German Prisoners of War

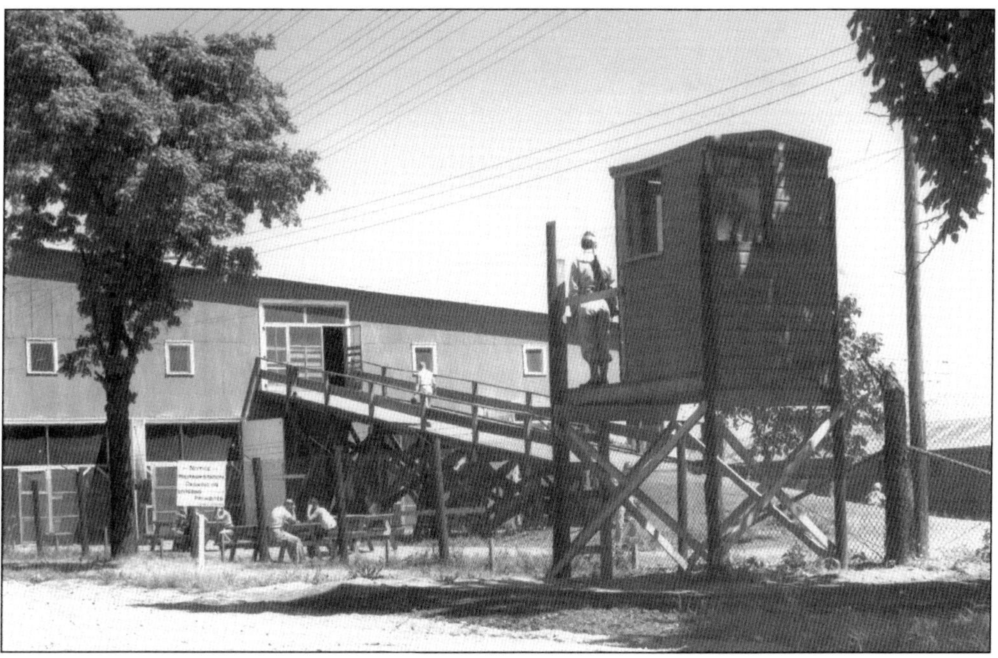

The main barracks building of the Hoopeston prisoner of war camp was situated opposite the lookout tower during the early days of the camp in 1944. This tower stood on the southwest side of the Illinois Canning Company barn on South Second Avenue. Later, one-story buildings were brought in to house the men on the south side of the camp and west of the barn. (Courtesy of the US Army Signal Corps.)

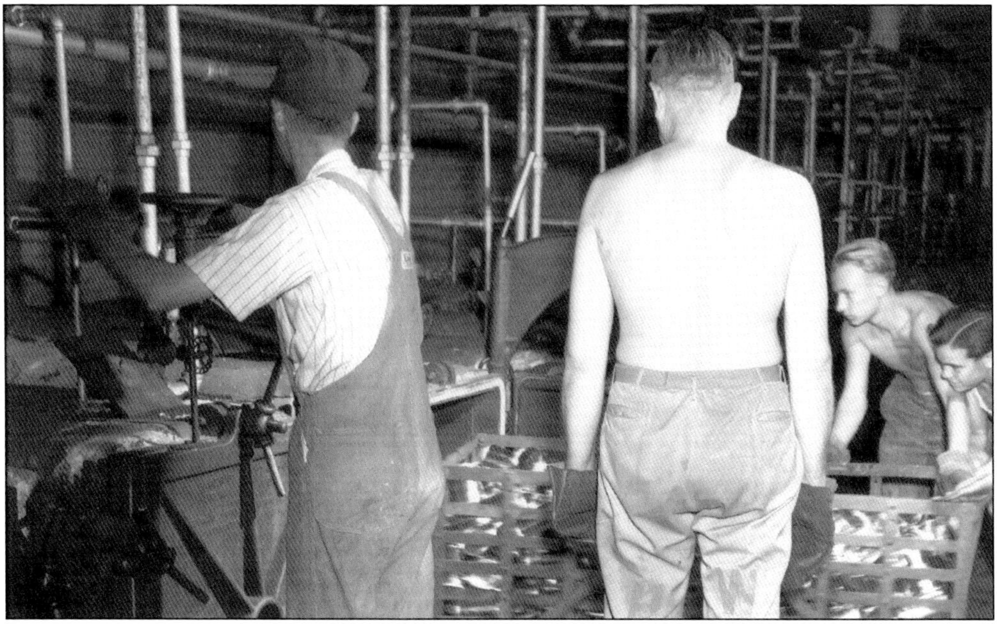

German prisoners of war are seen in this photograph pushing crates of canned corn into steam cookers at the canning factories during the harvest season of August 1944. Both the Illinois Canning Company and Stokely USA plants used the prisoners from April to November in 1944 and 1945 to alleviate the manpower shortage caused by the war. (Courtesy of the US Army Signal Corps.)

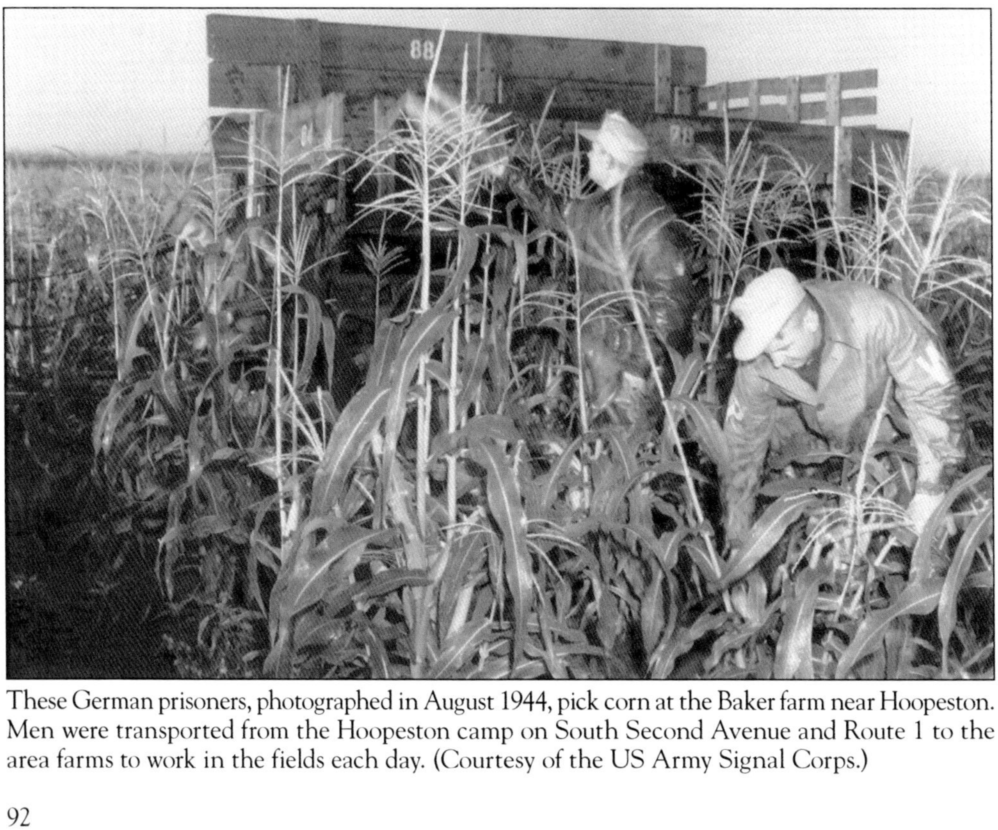

These German prisoners, photographed in August 1944, pick corn at the Baker farm near Hoopeston. Men were transported from the Hoopeston camp on South Second Avenue and Route 1 to the area farms to work in the fields each day. (Courtesy of the US Army Signal Corps.)

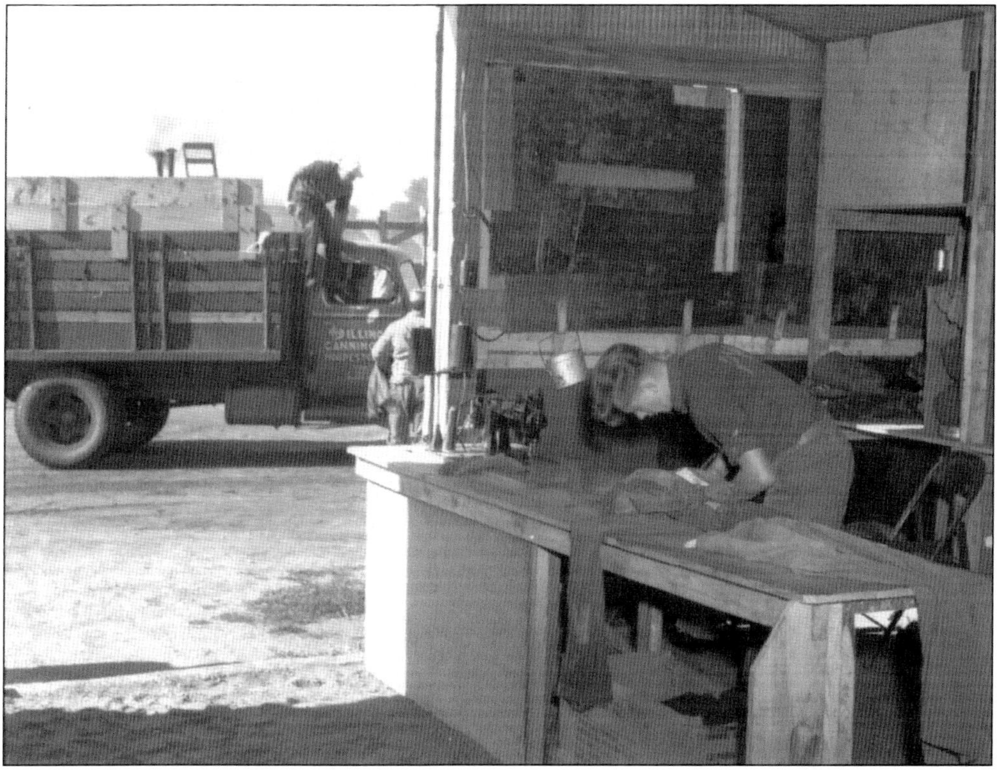

This young man, photographed in August 1944, was a tailor by trade, working on repairing clothing for his fellow prisoners of war. The small tailor shop was located inside the Illinois Canning Company farm building in Hoopeston. (Courtesy of the US Army Signal Corps.)

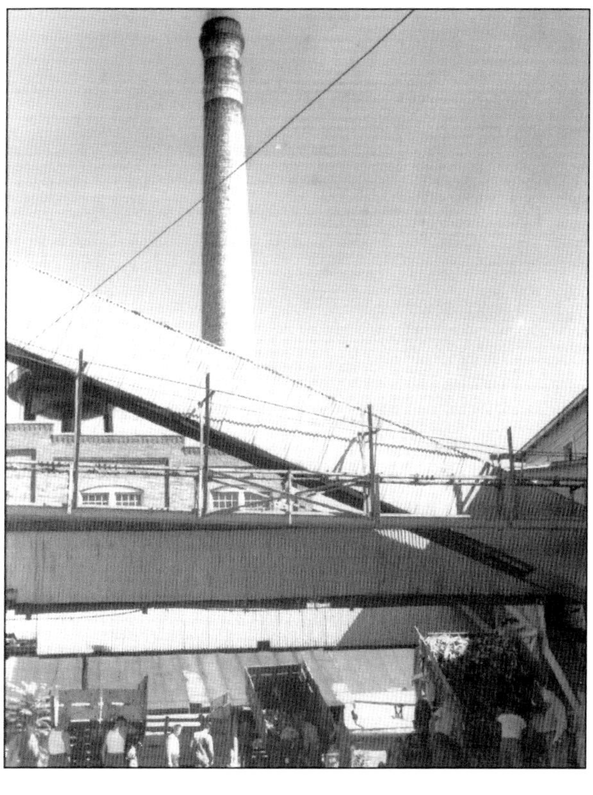

The German prisoners shown here in August 1944 are unloading corn trucks at the Illinois Canning Company site. Corn was brought in from area farms to be unloaded, shucked, cooked, and canned at the plant. (Courtesy of the US Army Signal Corps.)

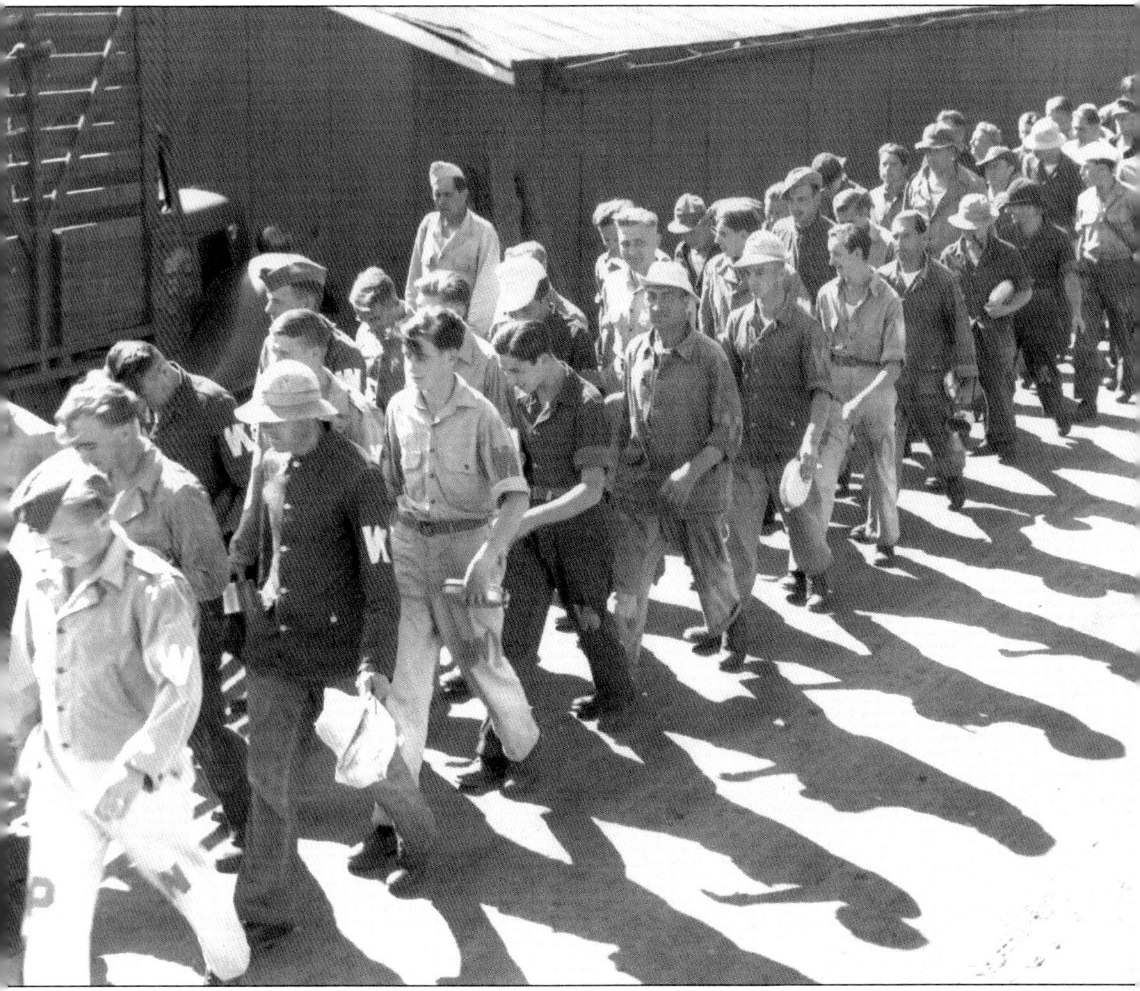

Young German soldiers leave the Hoopeston camp on Second Avenue in the early morning hours of August 1944 and march to area factories to work. Soldiers who requested to work in the fields were transported by vehicles. (Courtesy of the US Army Signal Corps.)

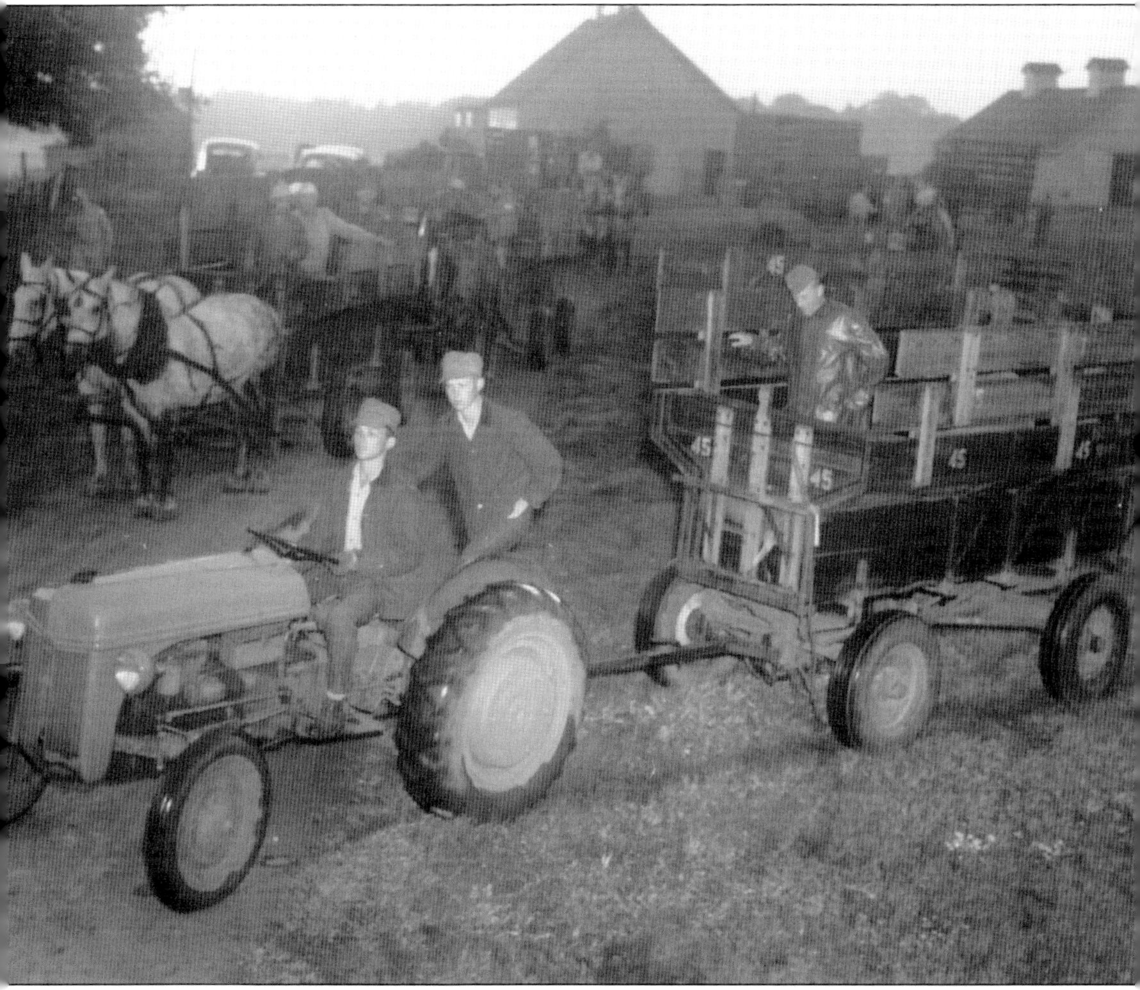

After a full day's work in the cornfields around Hoopeston in August 1944, these German prisoners file into vehicles at the Baker farm for the trip back to the Hoopeston camp on South Second Avenue. The Baker farm was one of several that used the prisoners to help harvest corn. (Courtesy of the US Army Signal Corps.)

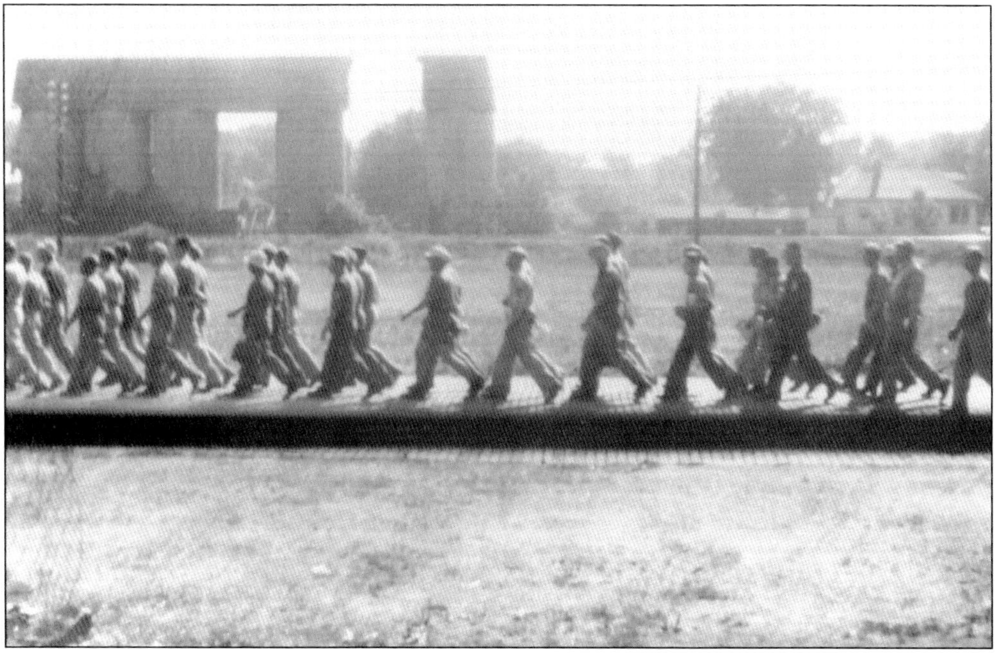

Glenna Powers took this photograph of German prisoners marching down First Avenue to the canning factories from inside her front door. According to the rules of the Manpower Commission, photographs of the prisoners were not allowed; however, many Hoopeston residents did take pictures. (Courtesy of Glenna Powers.)

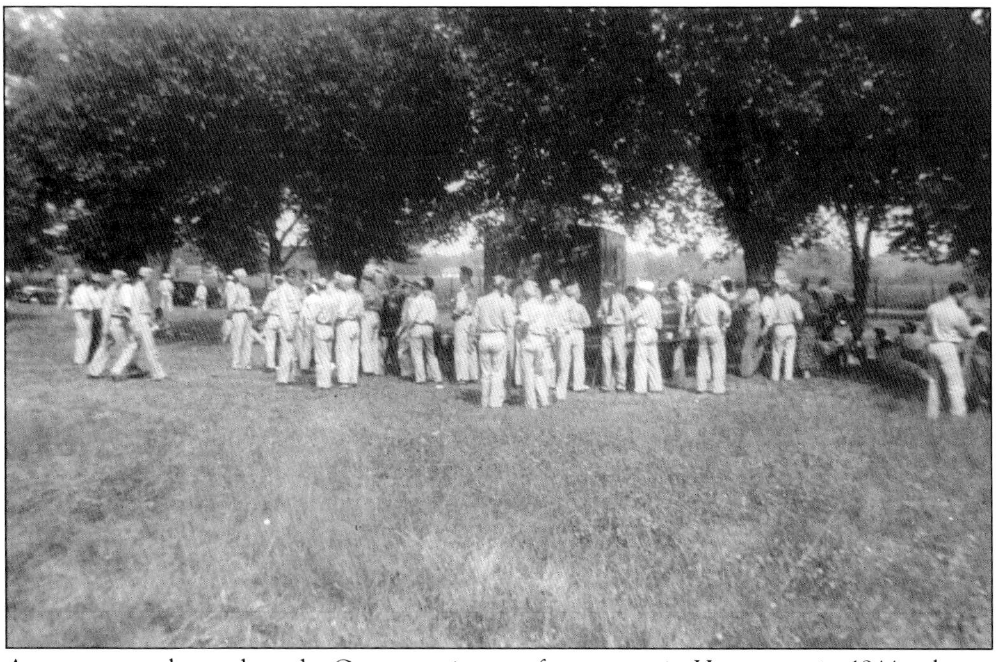

Army personnel, guards at the German prisoner of war camp in Hoopeston in 1944, relax at McFerren Park for a brief hiatus from the daily tasks of guard duty. The soldiers enjoyed the time at the park visiting amongst themselves and with the residents of Hoopeston. (Courtesy of Glenn Bloyd.)

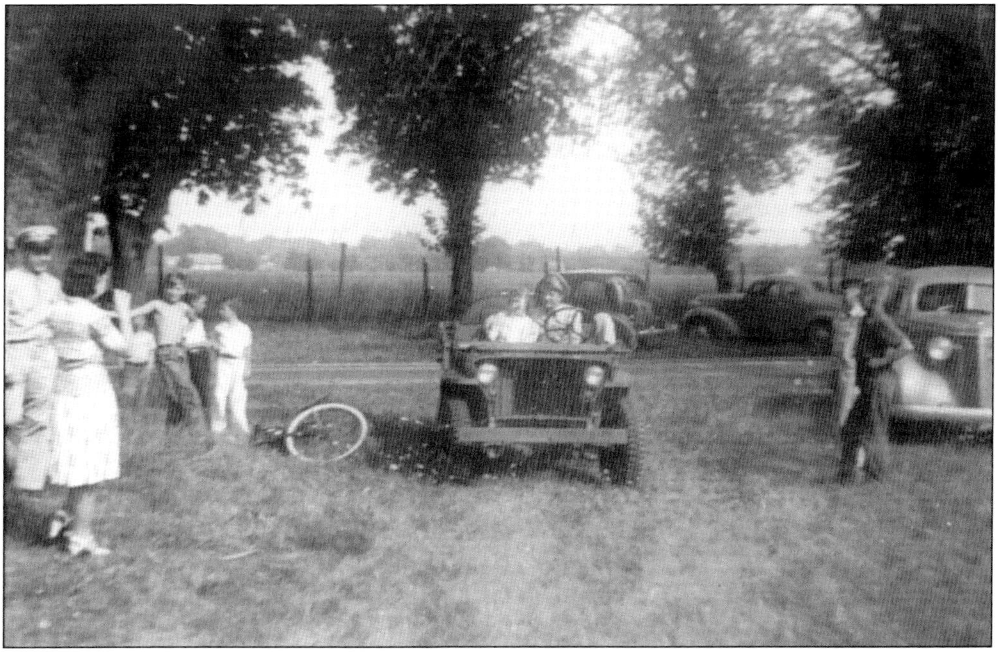

Area residents posed and visited with the young Army soldiers in McFerren Park during the soldiers' off-duty time. Many soldiers were far from loved ones and enjoyed the family atmosphere offered to them by the locals in the park. (Courtesy of Glenn Bloyd.)

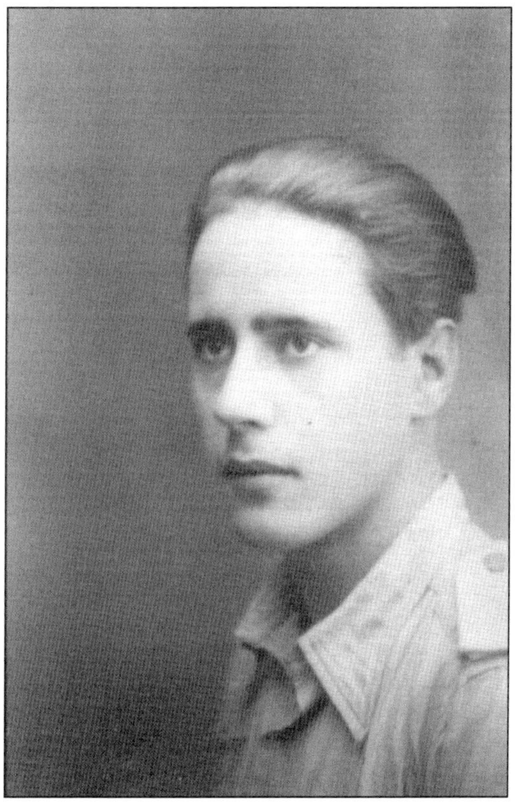

This photograph of Rudy Scholz, a German Montross (Marine), is the only portrait found of the men in Hoopeston. Scholz was among the first 75 German prisoners of war to arrive at the Hoopeston camp on April 26, 1944. He was also one of three who escaped in June of that same year. Two of the three men, Scholz and Julius Janisch, stole a vehicle owned by Ivan Fink to make their escape and were court-martialed. They were captured near Sullivan, Indiana, on June 11. Herman Kuzel hopped a train south and was captured June 13 near Brazil, Indiana. He was not court-martialed. (Courtesy of Rudy Scholz.)

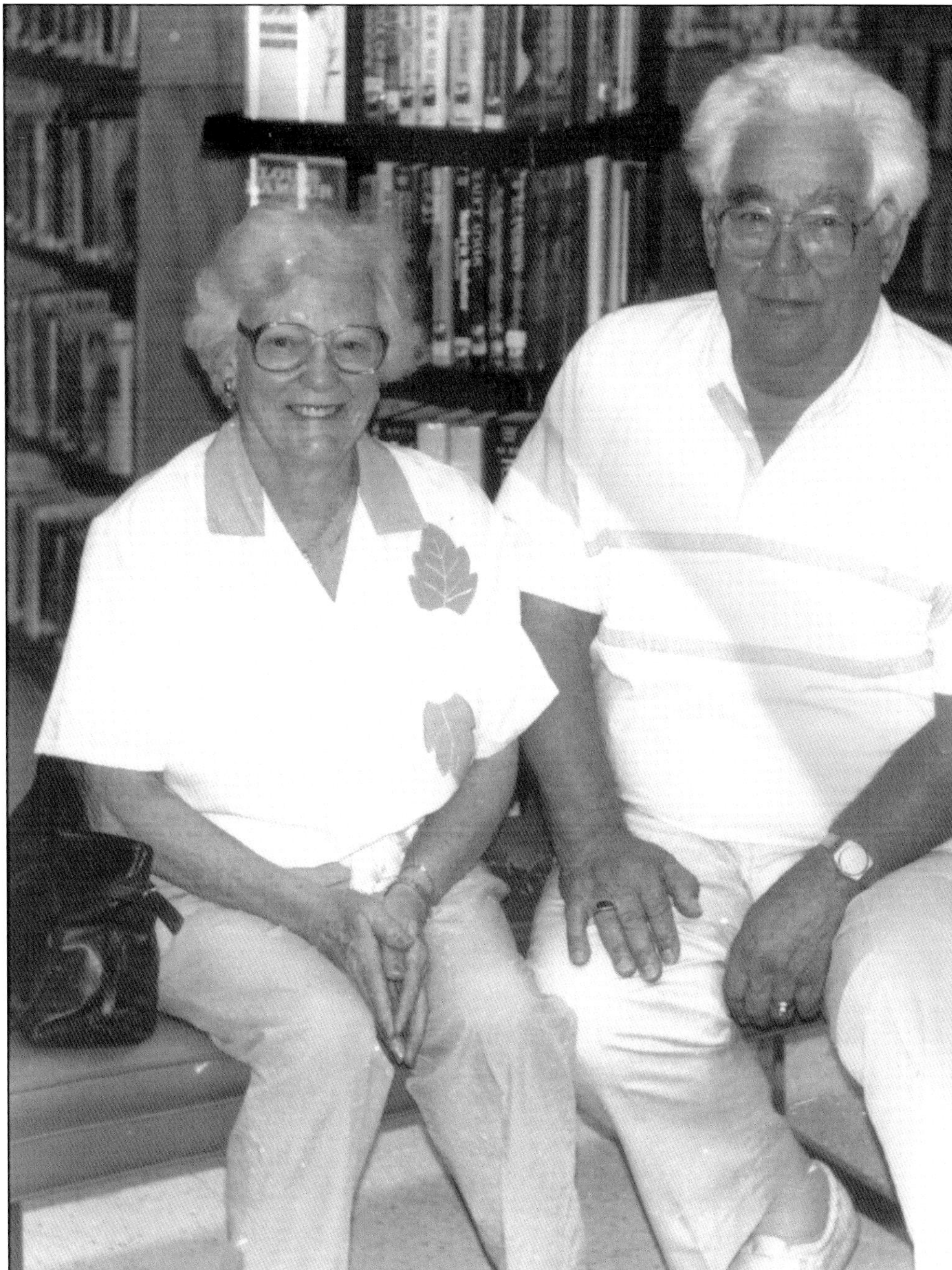

This photograph shows Kurt and Emilie Pechmann at the Hoopeston Public Library. Pechmann, captured in Italy, was a German prisoner of war in the Hoopeston camp during the summer of 1944. He returned to America in 1952 to start a new life with his wife, Emilie. Pechmann, owner of Pechmann Memorials Inc. in Madison, Wisconsin, returned to Hoopeston in August 1993 to visit. (Courtesy of the *Hoopeston Chronicle*.)

Nine

Hoopeston Fires

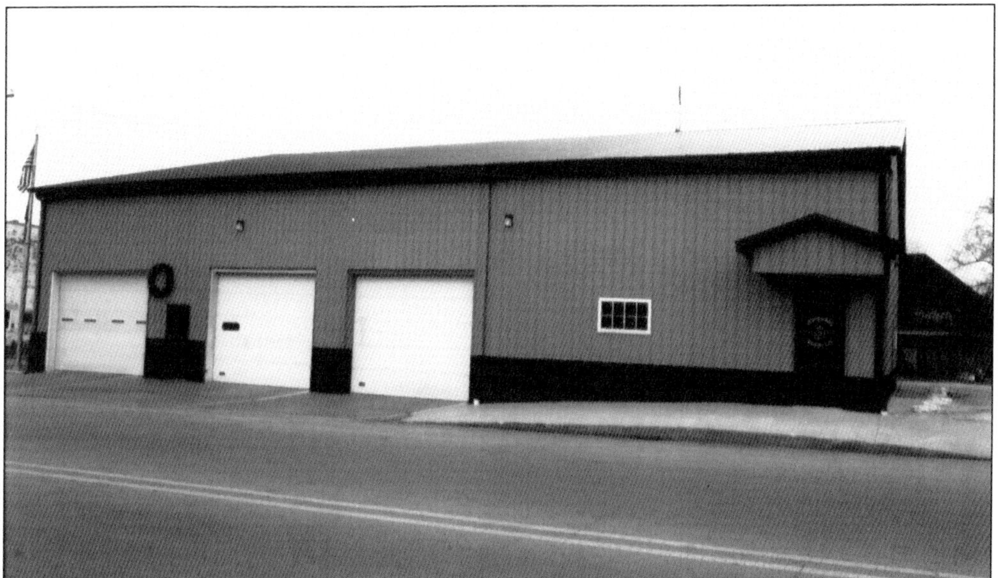

The Hoopeston Fire Department and City Hall, located on the corner of Seminary Avenue and Market Street, burned down in the early hours of February 25, 1924. Built by William Silver in 1897, the building housed the city hall, fire department, police department, and jail. The loss was said to be $45,000, though the city only had a $6,000 policy on the building and contents. The fire department remains in this location today.

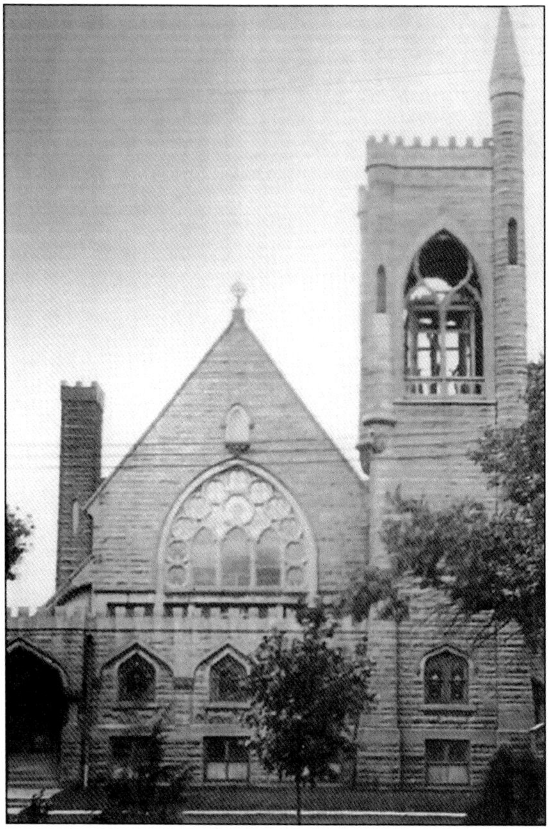

The Universalist church, built in 1886, was destroyed by fire in 1956. The only things saved from the church were the chimes, which were installed in the First Christian Church. (Courtesy of Tom Weber.)

The *Chronicle-Herald*, owned by Mills Publication, stood on First Avenue and Main Street and burned once in 1939 and again in the 1950s (when it was totally destroyed). The Hoopeston Fire Department's quick action in the 1950s prevented the same fate from befalling the Illinois Lumber and Coal Co. next door.

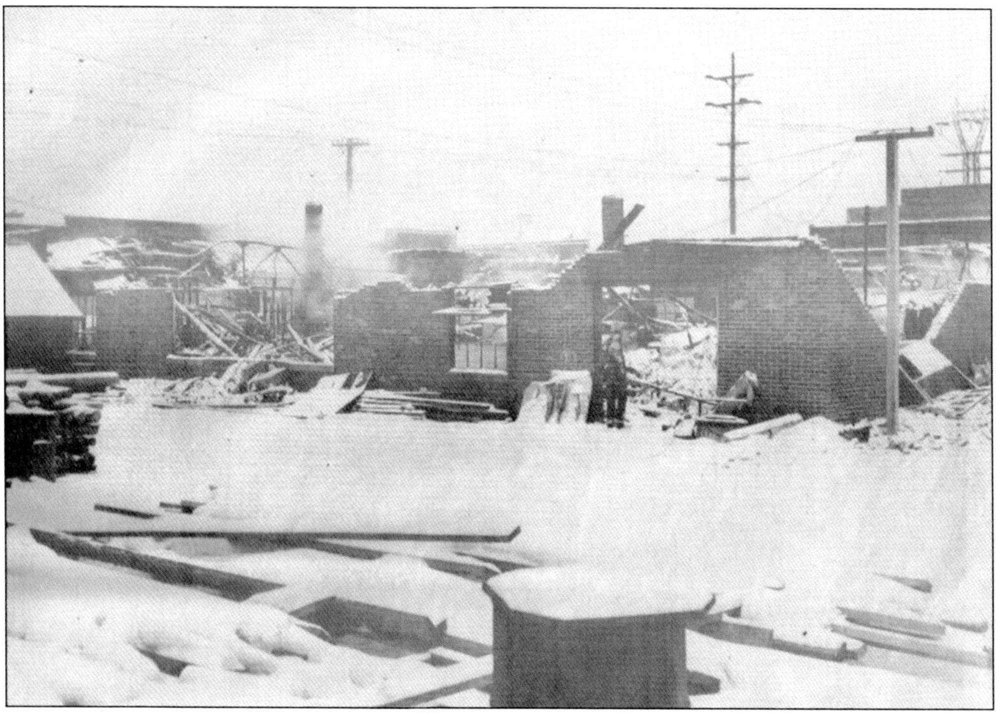

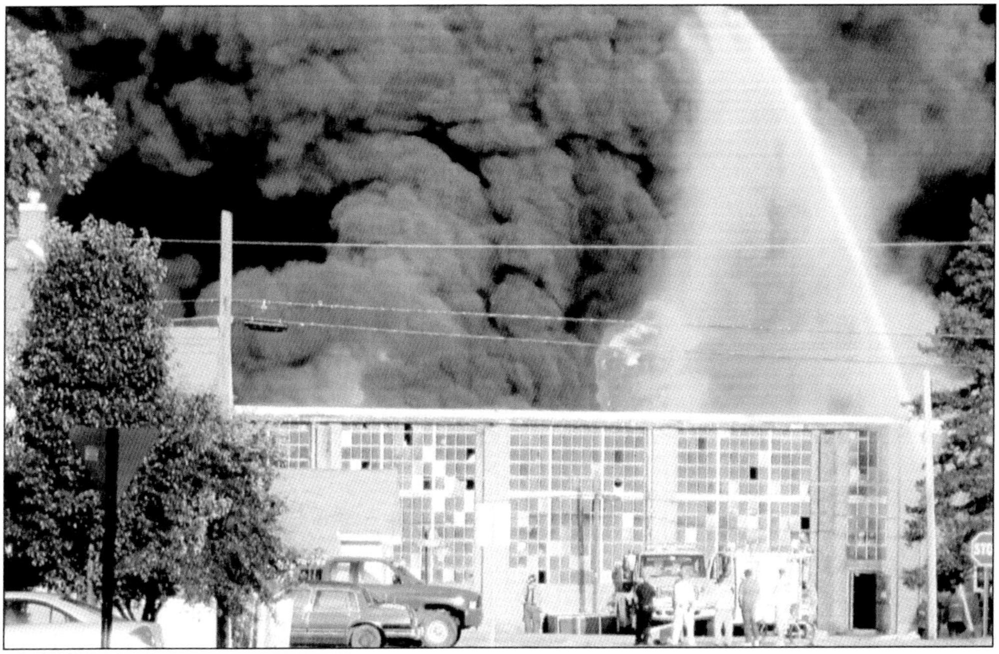

On June 19, 2013, firemen at the South Market Street entrance to the J&R Tire Recycling building try to contain the raging fire. This section is the middle of a three-block-long building that at one time housed Food Machinery Corporation, a 100-year old business.

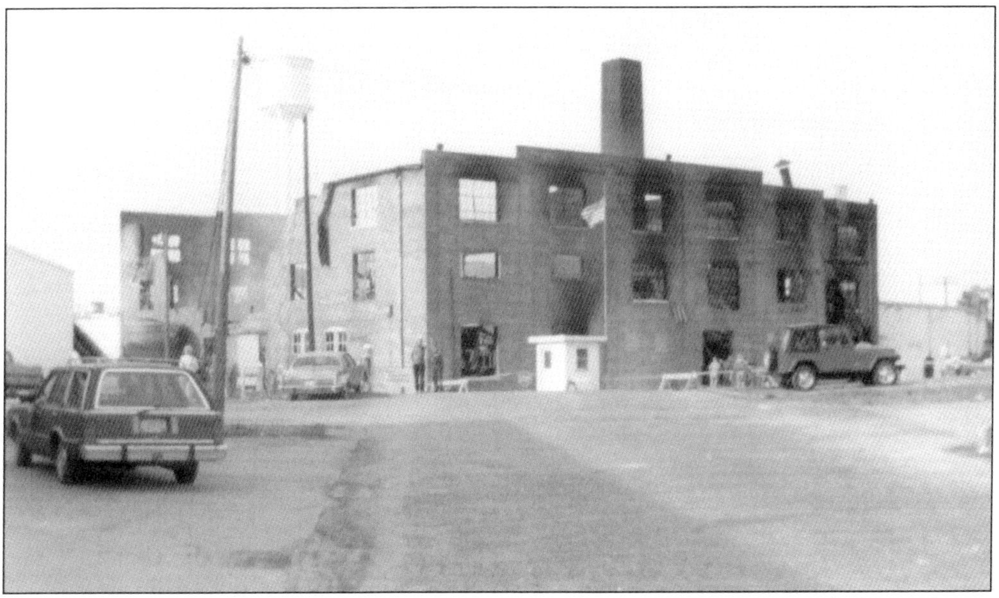

Stokely officials reported injuries to four employees in the September 11, 1992, boiler explosion and fire at the Hoopeston plant. The three-story building that housed the main office as well as a filling and sealing line were completely destroyed. A sales representative from a Decatur, Illinois, electrical firm received major burns and was the most seriously injured. The canning factory, originally known as the Hoopeston Canning Company, had burned once before in 1905 and been rebuilt in 1906. It remained in business until 1998 when the doors were closed by Chiquita Brands three days after they purchased it.

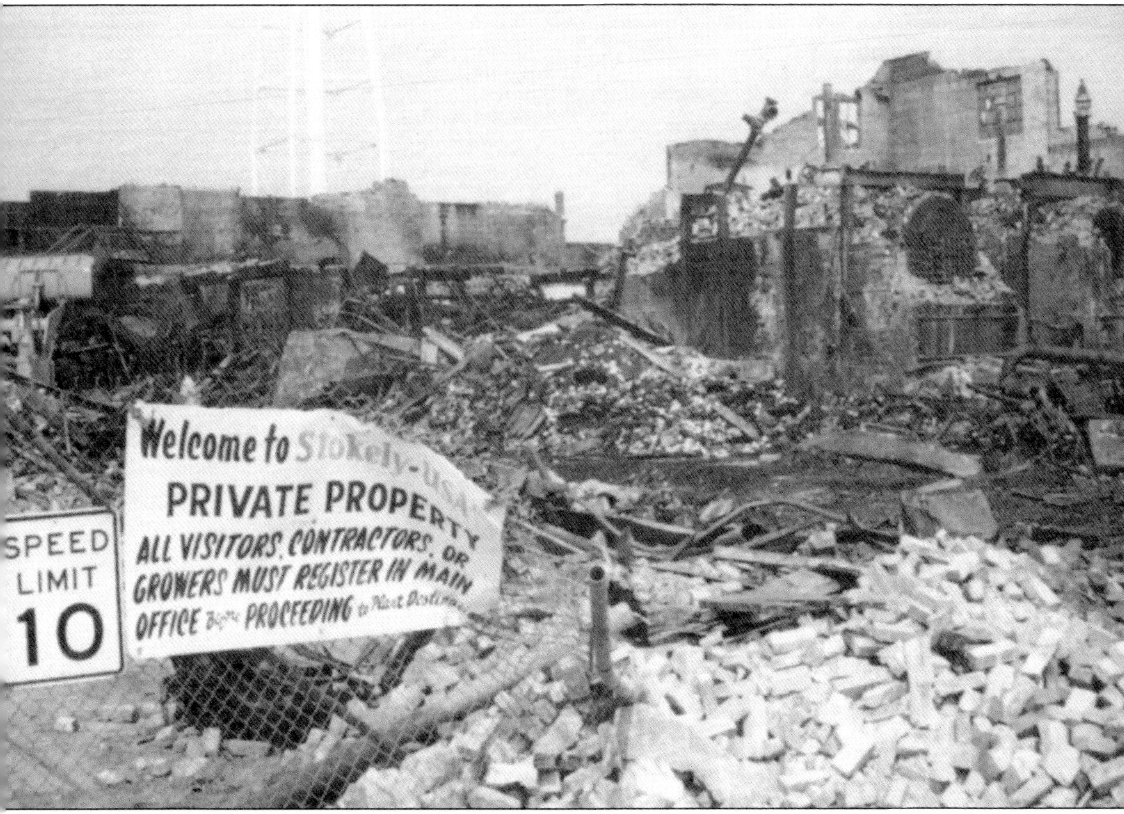

This photograph of the Stokely USA fire in 1992 shows the aftermath and the cleanup process that began shortly after the fire marshals inspected the building to determine the cause of the blaze. The structure was rebuilt in 1993 and closed in 1998.

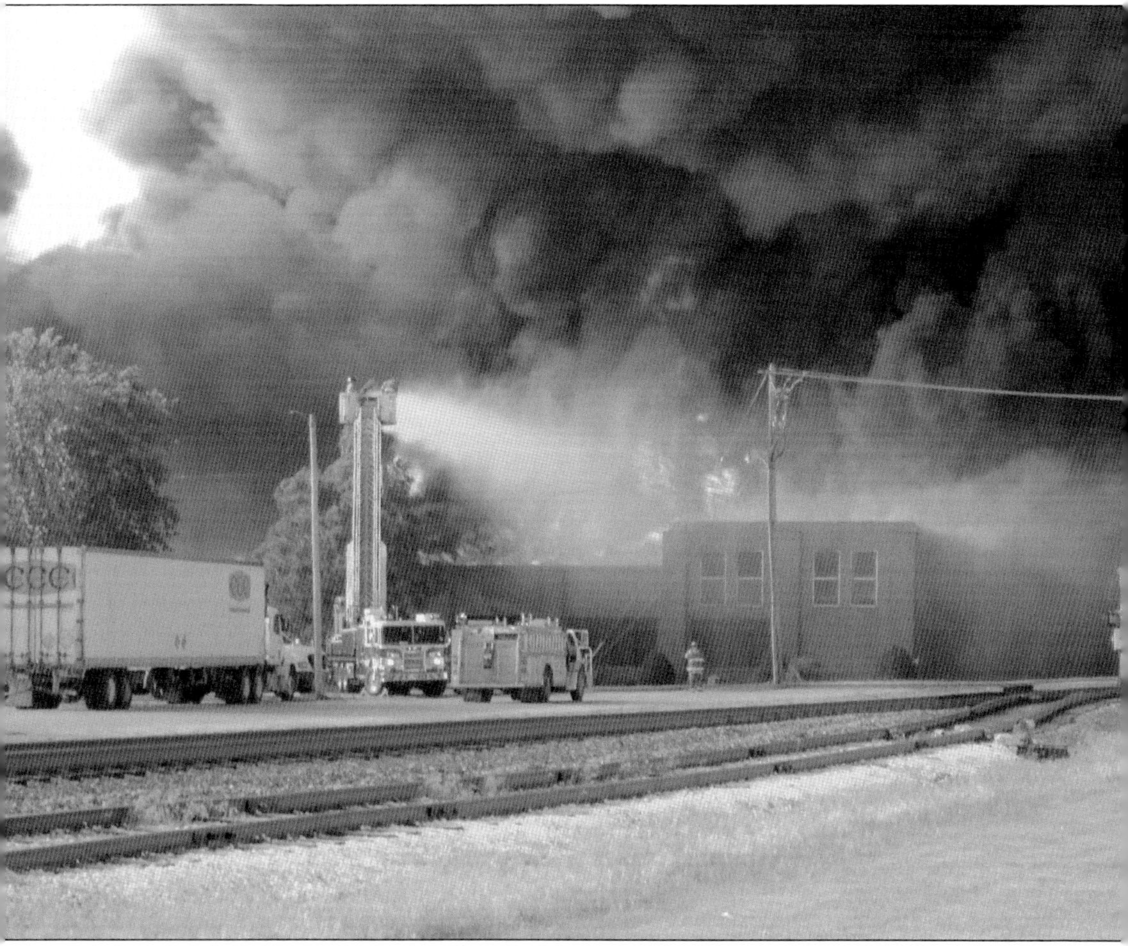

A&R Tire Recycling Service burned to the ground on June 19, 2013, when a spark ignited the dust as an employee worked on a motor. The fire spread throughout the three-block-long building. Toxic smoke and debris from the tires caused a five-block area to be evacuated. The blaze was fought by 24 fire departments, with aerial trucks from Watseka and Danville helping to prevent the fire from spreading to the three blocks of residential homes and businesses. A&R Tire Recycling Service was owned by Rodney Rogers.

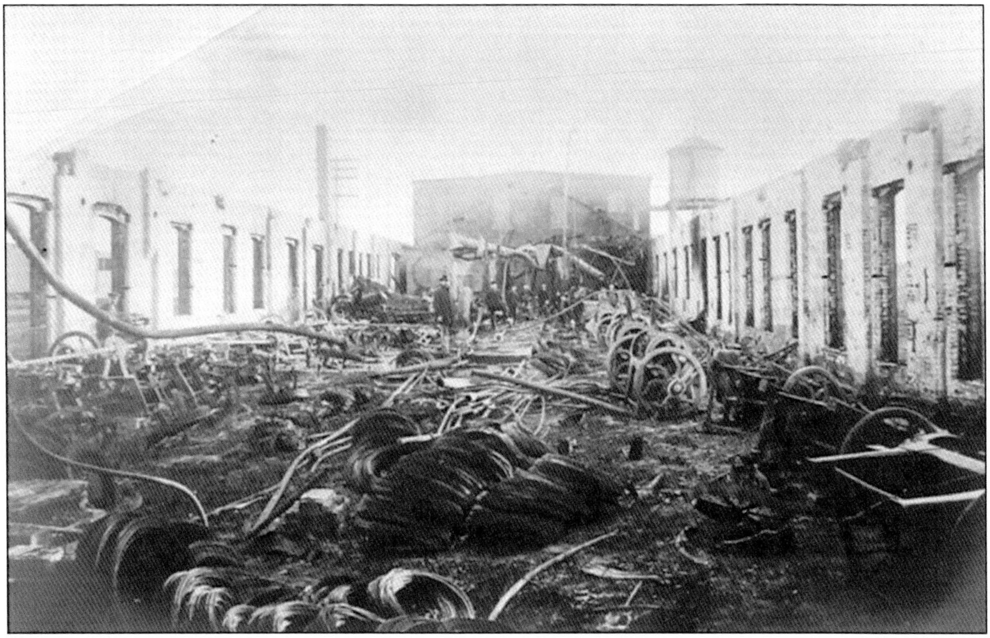

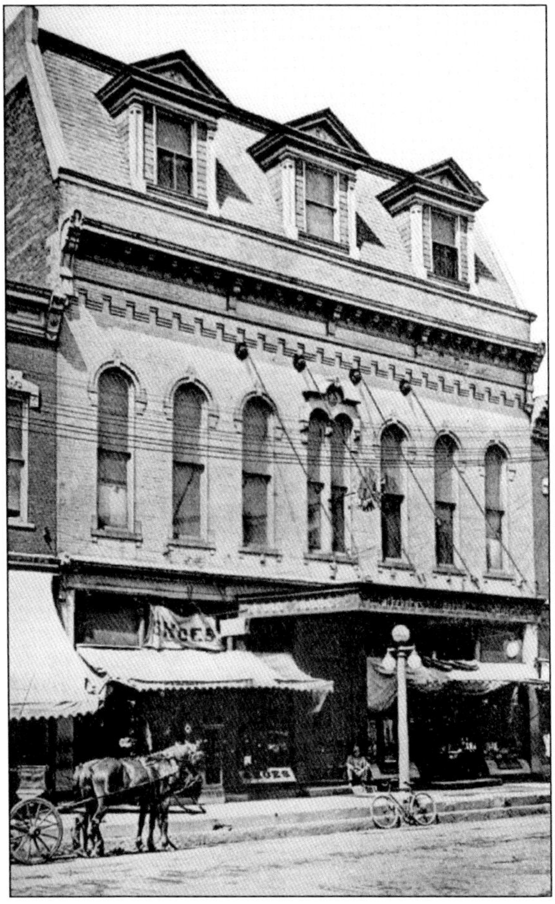

The Horse Nail Factory in Hoopeston burned to the ground on December 18, 1908. It was financed and managed by A.H. Trego, James A. Cunningham, John L. Hamilton, William Moore, Charles S. Cary, and W.W. Todd.

The McFerren Opera House is shown in this 1890s photograph. It was later destroyed completely in a fire that engulfed the entire block on January 20, 1937, along with the Hoopeston National Bank on the corner of Main and Market Streets, Spurgeons, Lester's, Blayney's, Nelson Hardware, Parrish Cafe, Ralph Kitchen Barber Shop, and Dollie Anne Beauty Shop. (Courtesy of the Hoopeston Historical Society.)

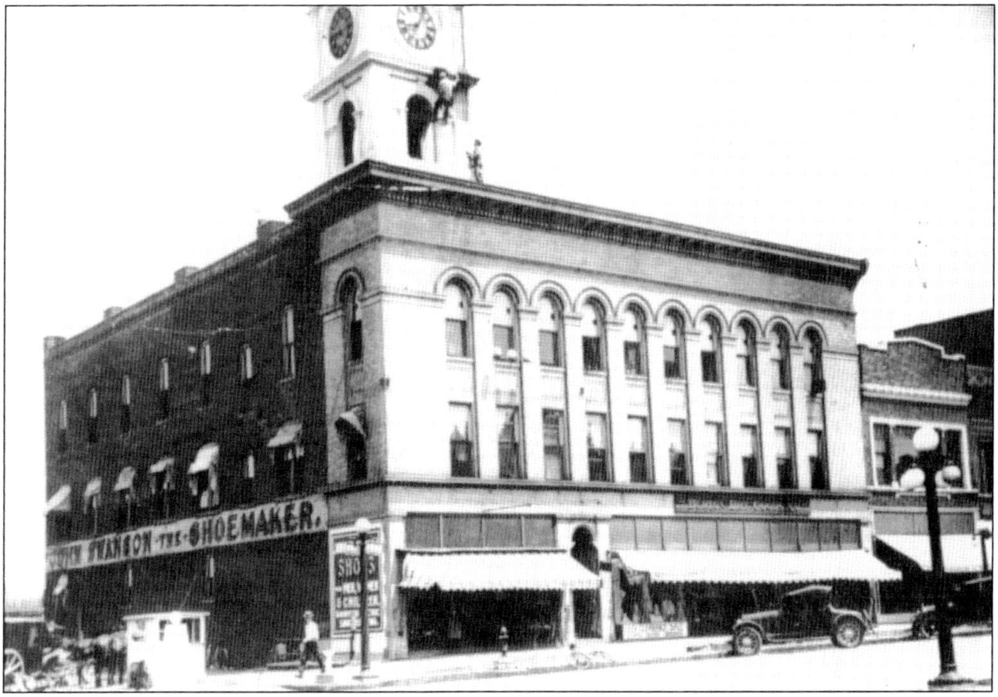

The town clock building, built in 1895, burned three times (it was rebuilt after the first two fires). It burned the first time in January 1905, the second time in June 1925, and the last time on April 7, 1947.

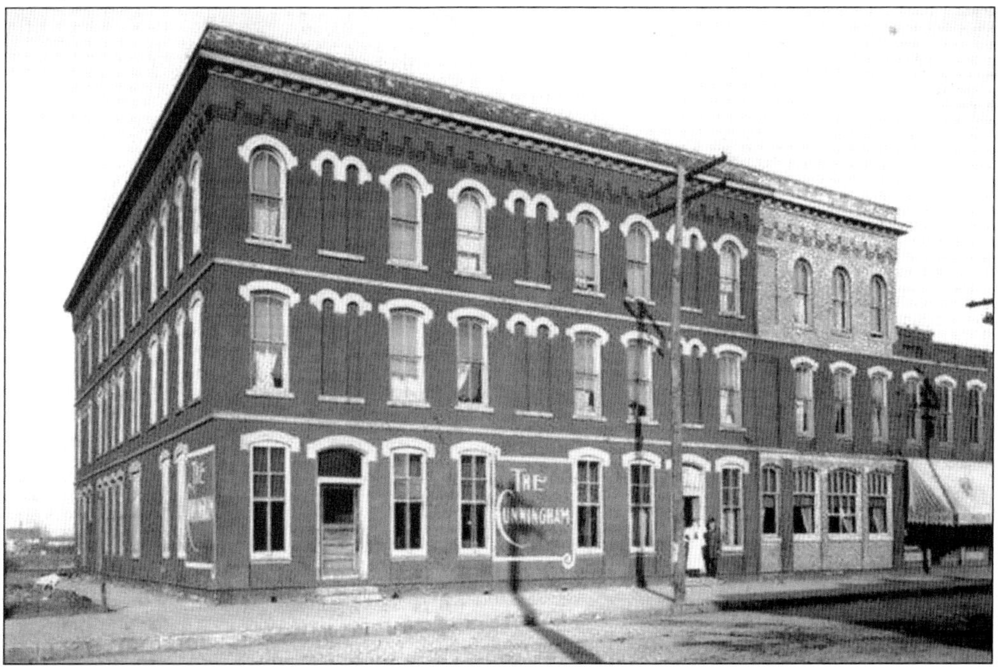

The Cragg Hotel, also known as the Arlington, the Cunningham, and the Cunningham-Cragg Hotel, burned in March 1965. It is now an empty lot in the 100 block of East Main Street next to the railroad tracks.

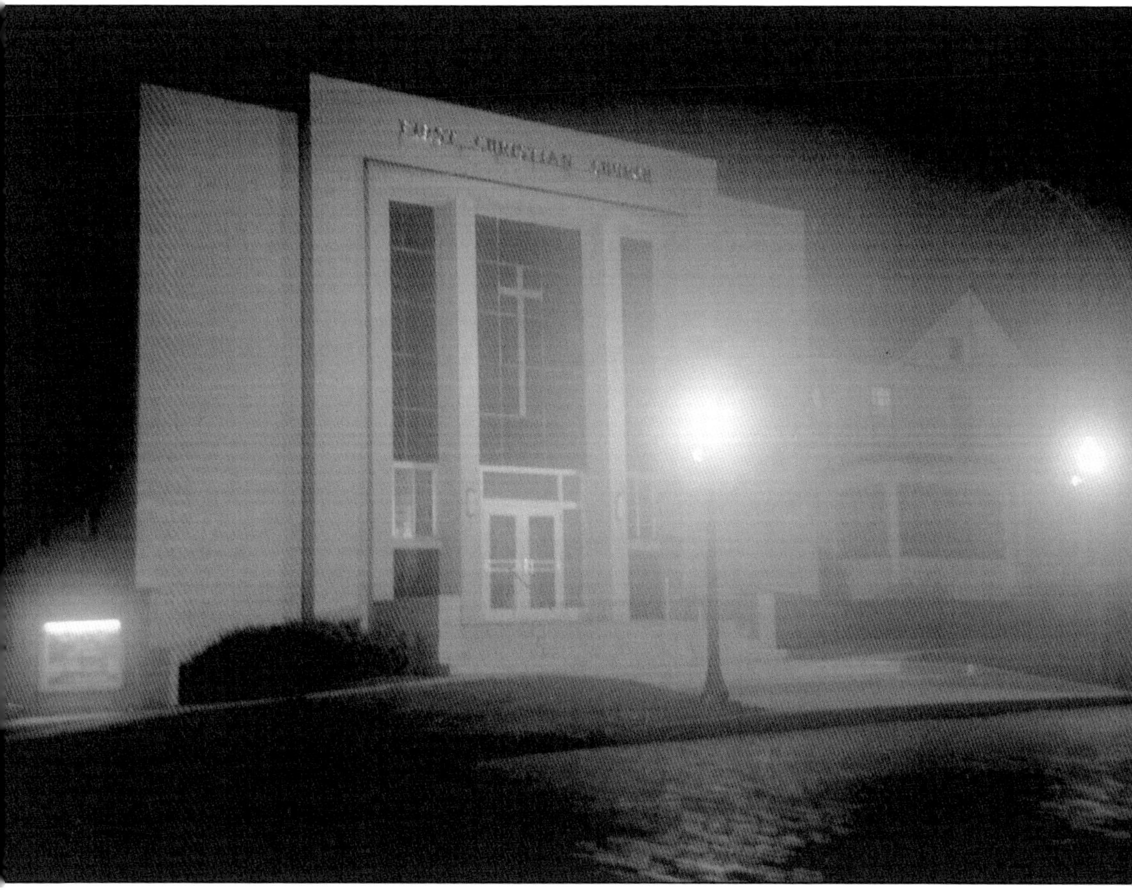

First Christian Church of Christ, organized in 1873 and shown here in 1971, was first located at 646 East Honeywell Avenue. A new church was built on the northeast corner of Main and Fourth Streets in 1899. The church burned entirely on December 17, 1953.

Ten

MISCELLANEOUS

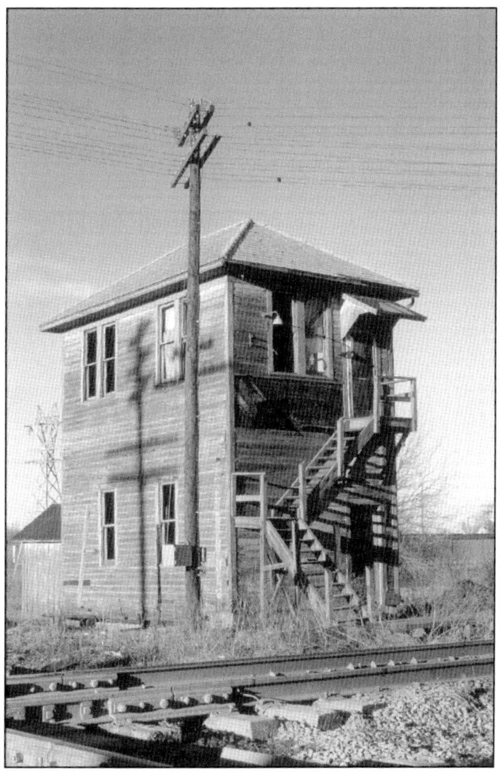

The switch tower for the railroads was located in the northeast corner of the railroad junction. This photograph shows the tower in the 1970s. (Courtesy of Scott Baer.)

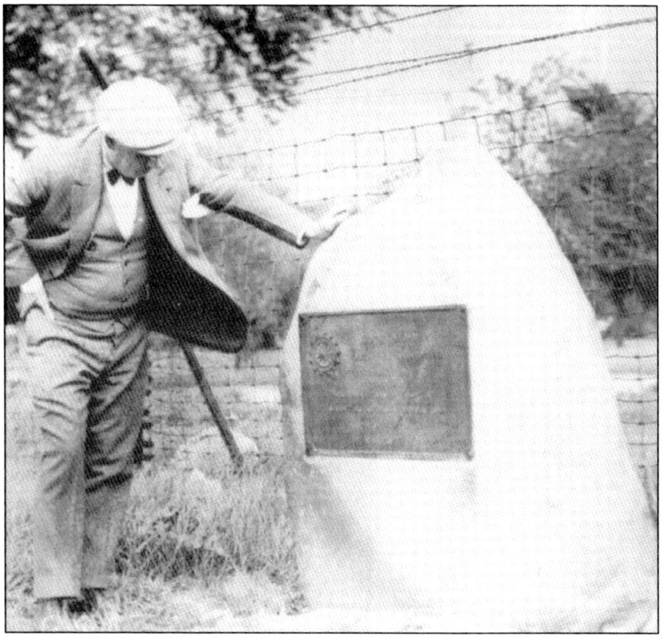

The Barbara Standish Chapter of the Daughters of the American Revolution erected a boulder in 1920 just west of the McFerren Park fence to memorialize the Old Hubbard Trail, as it was known 100 years ago. This road was used by Gurdeon S. Hubbard, an Indian trader, as he traveled from the Danville area in central Illinois to Fort Dearborn. It was later the Dixie Highway and is today known as Route 1. (Courtesy of the Illinois Department of Transportation.)

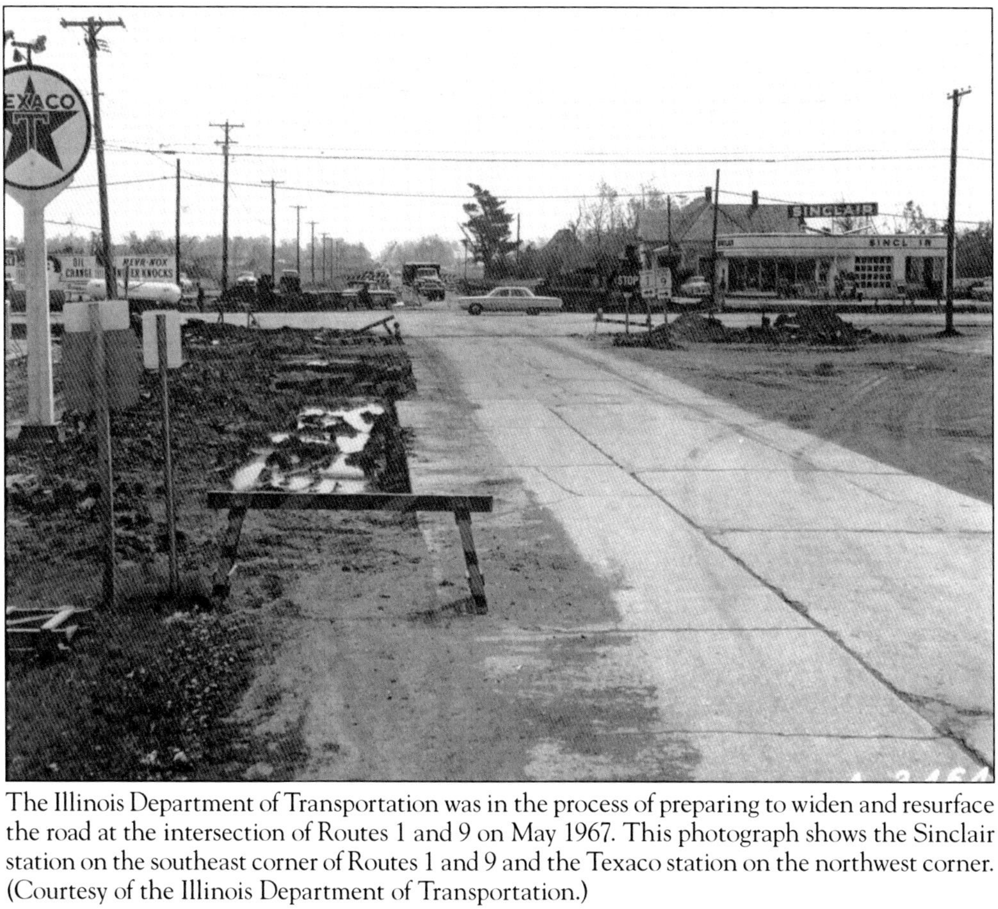

The Illinois Department of Transportation was in the process of preparing to widen and resurface the road at the intersection of Routes 1 and 9 on May 1967. This photograph shows the Sinclair station on the southeast corner of Routes 1 and 9 and the Texaco station on the northwest corner. (Courtesy of the Illinois Department of Transportation.)

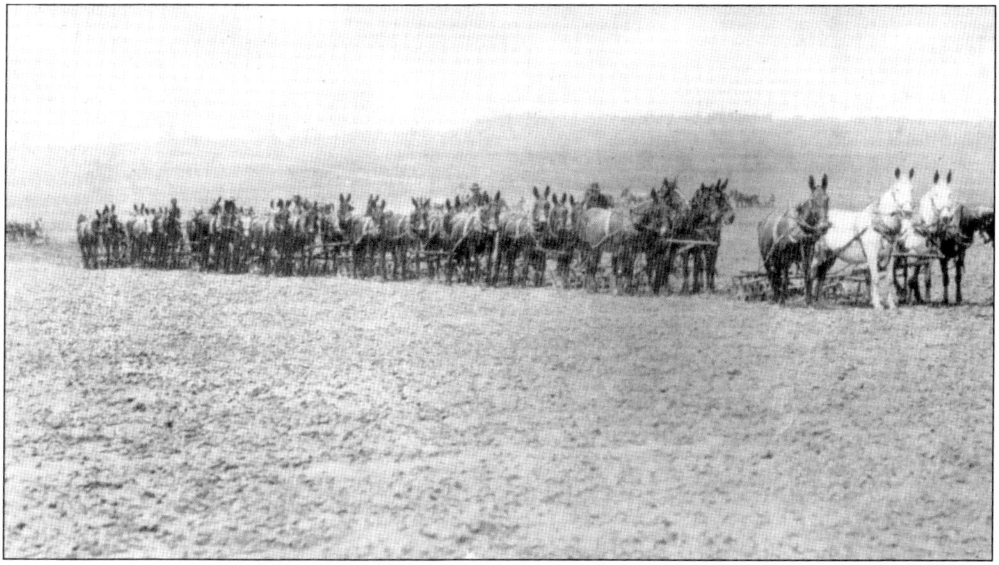

Disking fields in the 1920s was done with mostly mules and horses. Farmers would gather to help each other bring the crops in from the fields, fill wagons pulled by horses or mules, and take them to the canning companies in Hoopeston. (Courtesy of the Hoopeston Public Library.)

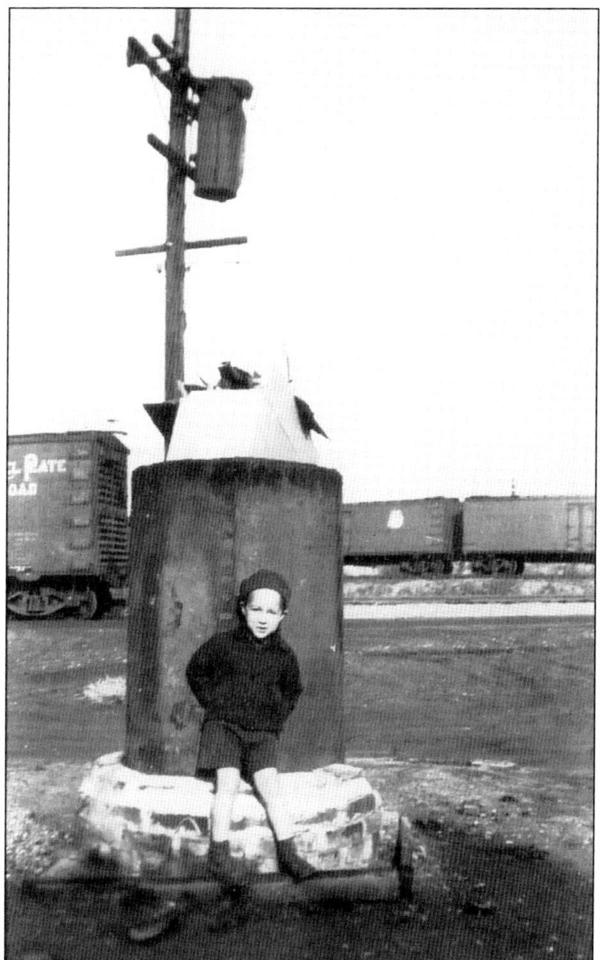

Mike Zook sits in back of Lester's Drug Store, with the Nickle Plate train parked behind him and a few cars sitting on the switch tracks in about 1950. Lucy Carlson, who worked for the Zook family when she first arrived in Hoopeston, was his nanny.

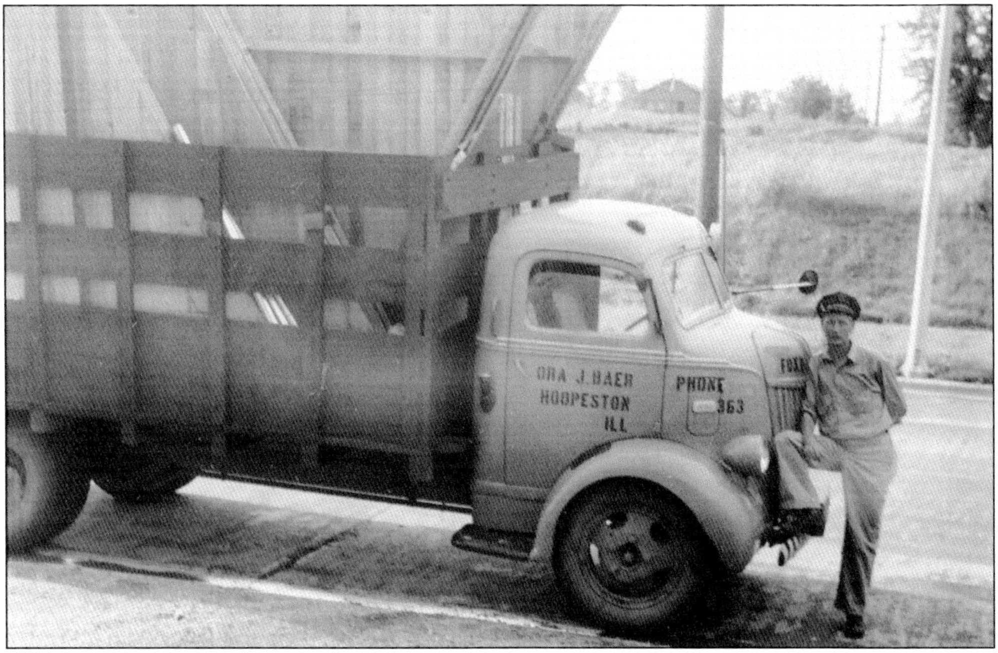

Floyd Foxworthy (1905–1986) was hired to drive the truck used to pick up the economy portable homes from the Economy Portable Housing Company in Chicago. Floyd was Ora J. Baer's construction foreman for over 20 years and was described by him as unfailingly punctual and trustworthy. (Courtesy of Scott Baer.)

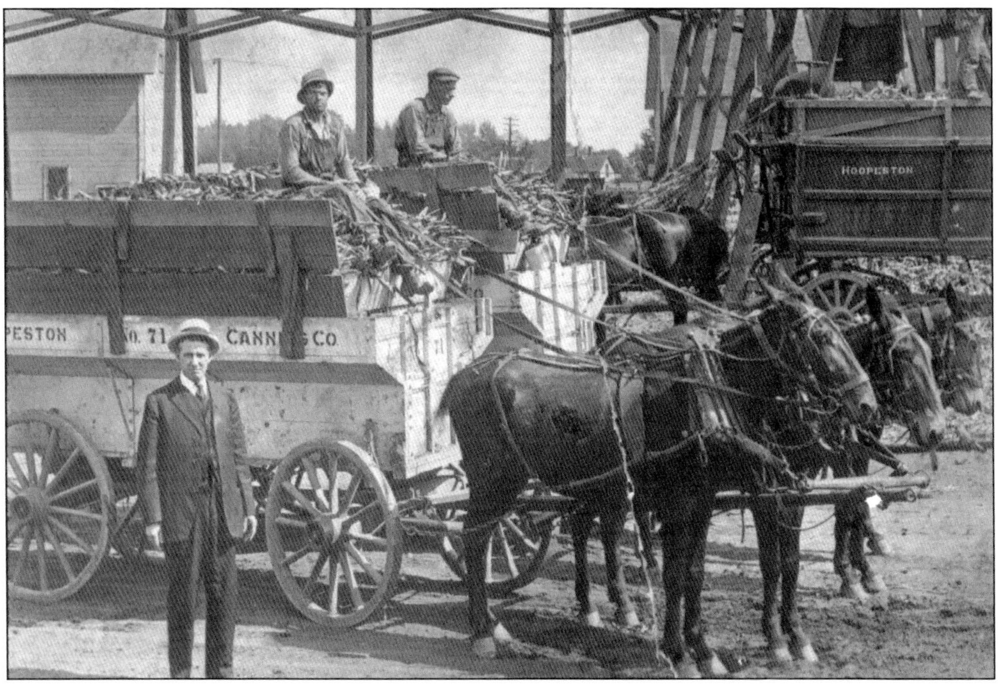

This 1900s photograph was taken during corn-packing season. Haulers with their wagons and horses pulled the harvested corn to the Hoopeston Canning Company to be unloaded, shucked by hand, run through the cutters, canned, and cooked.

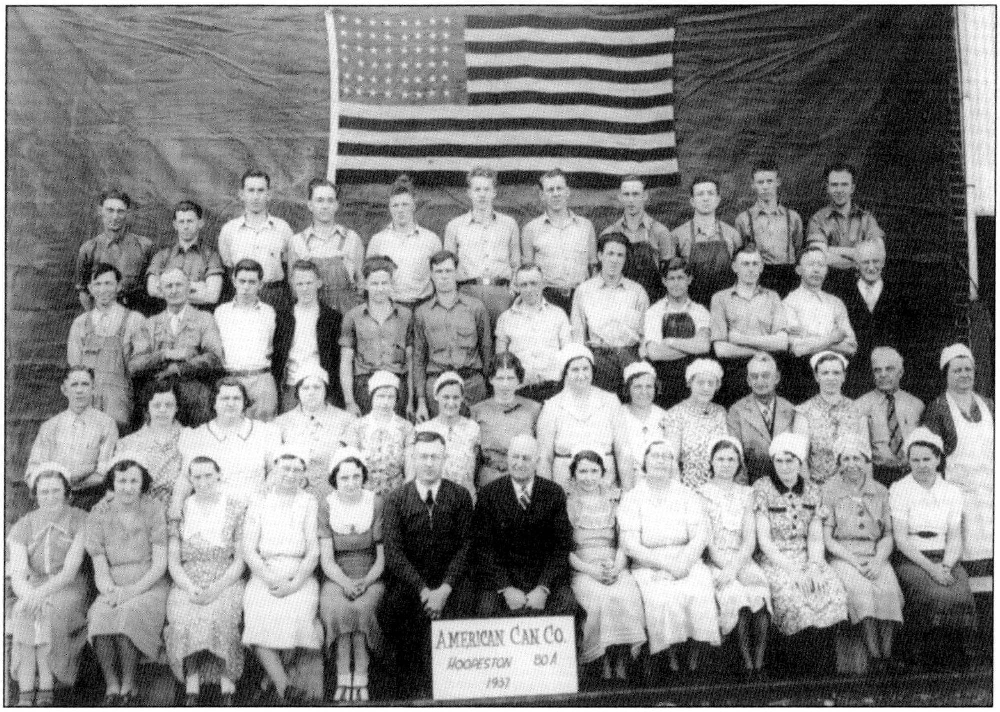

American Can Company staff and employees pose with bosses in front of an American flag in this 1937 photograph.

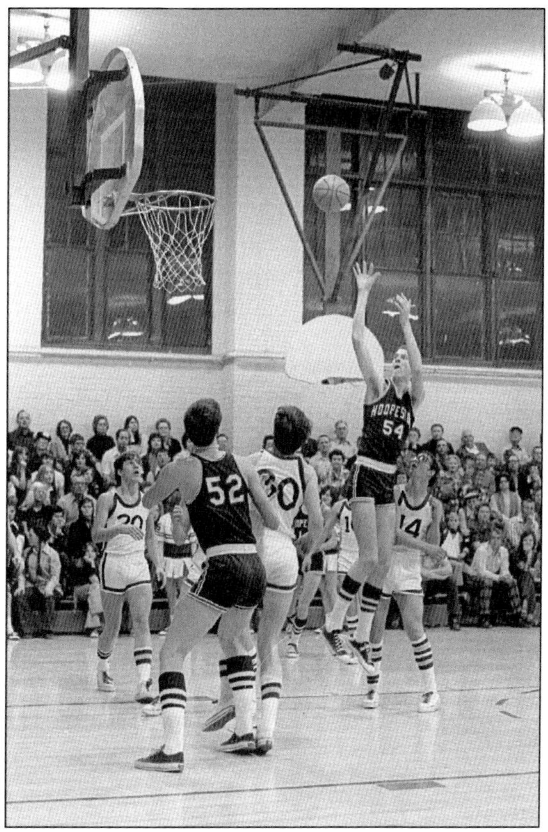

Scott Eells was one of the Cornjerkers' outstanding basketball players in his high school years. Shown in this 1975 photograph, Eells (54) is sending a ball to the hoop. Eells went on to play basketball for Purdue during his college years. (Courtesy of the Hoopeston School District.)

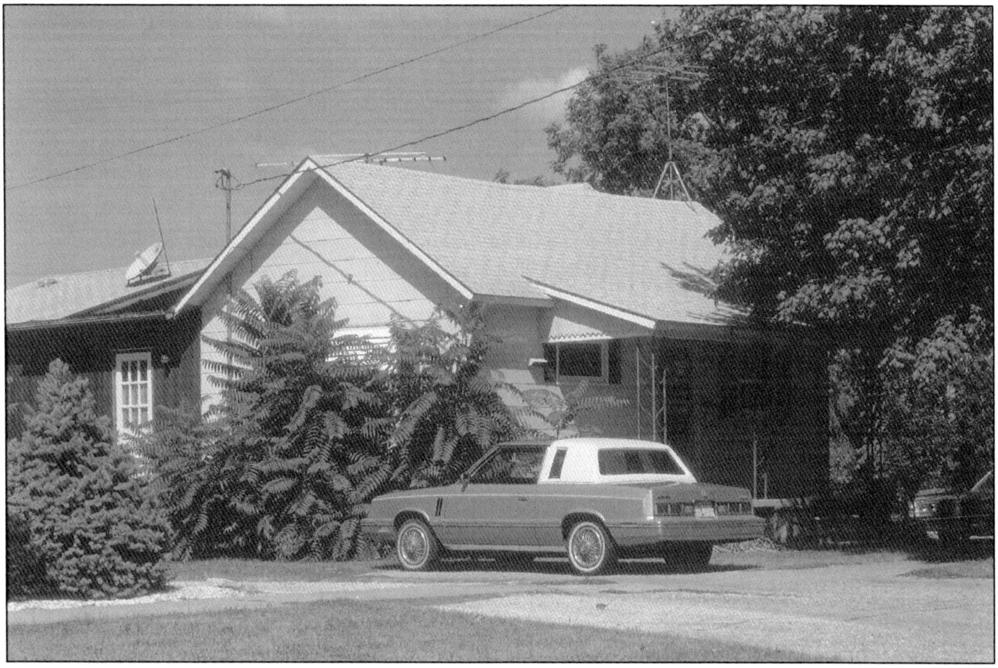

WHPO is Hoopeston's only radio station. This 1984 photograph is another view of the south side of the building on the corner of North Market Street and Wyman Avenue. (Courtesy of Scott Baer.)

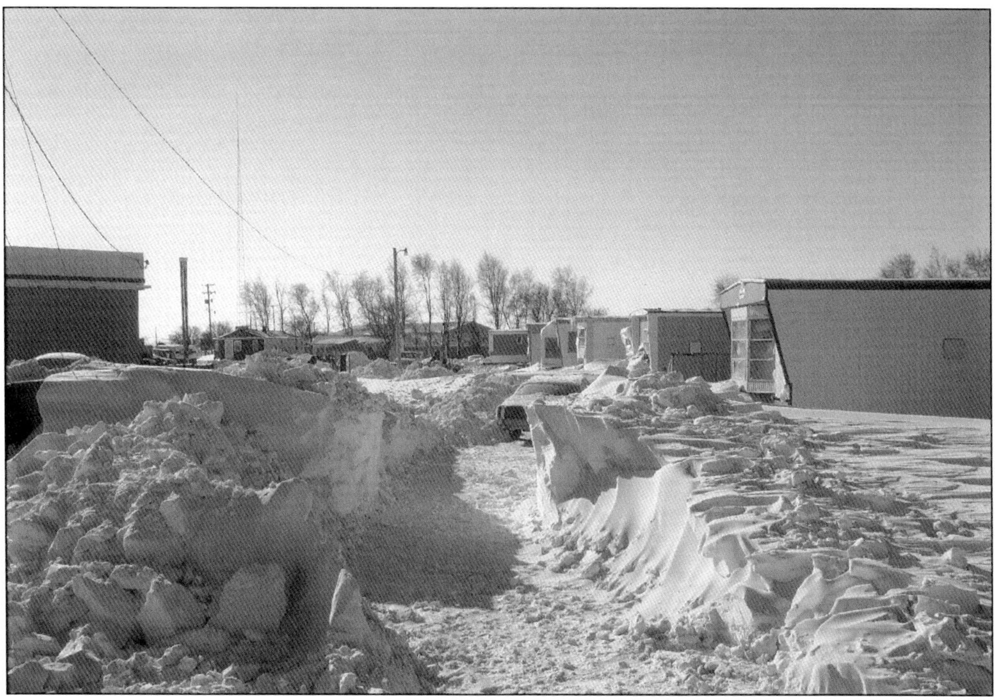

Baer's Trailer Park was a virtual nightmare with snowdrifts after the January 15–27, 1978, snowfall. This photograph shows a very small path for a vehicle after the snow. The record snowfall measured 28 inches. (Courtesy of Scott Baer.)

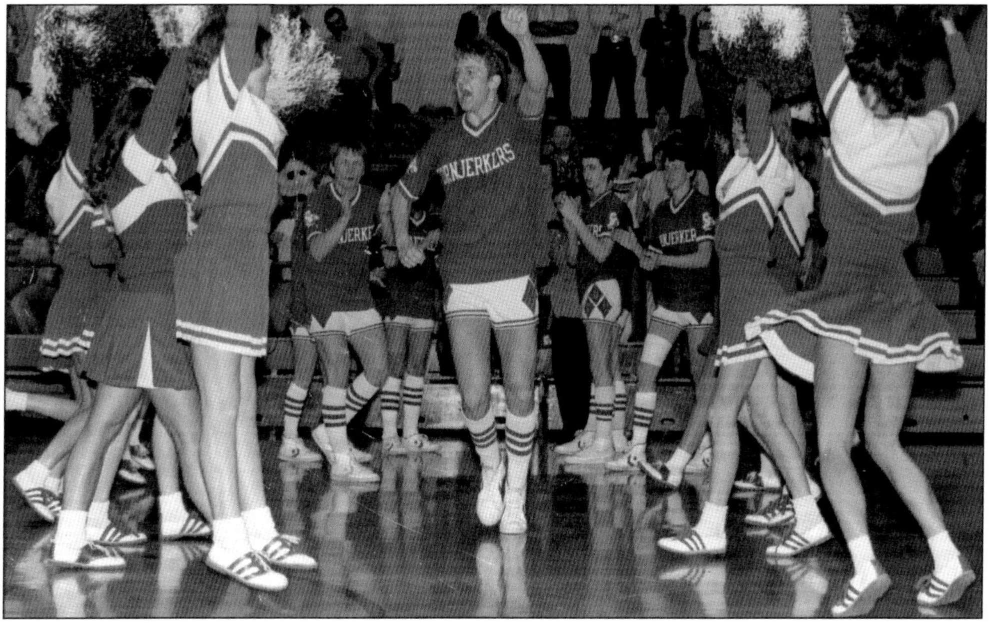

Thad Matta, shown in this 1970s photograph, graduated from Hoopeston. He was hired as a coach in July 2004 at Ohio State University and led Ohio State to five Big Ten conference tournaments and four Big Ten titles. (Courtesy of Hoopeston Area School District.)

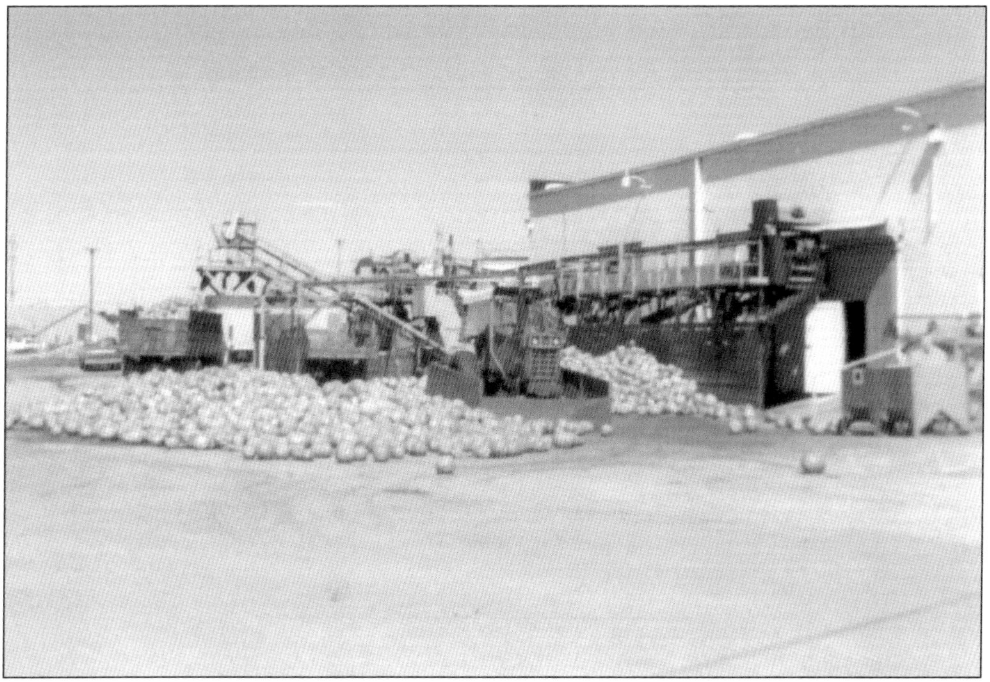

Pumpkins were canned in Hoopeston by Stokely USA. Area farmers contracted with Stokely to raise pumpkins for the company. This photograph, taken between 1980 and 1990, shows the dump area. (Courtesy of Nancy Thorn.)

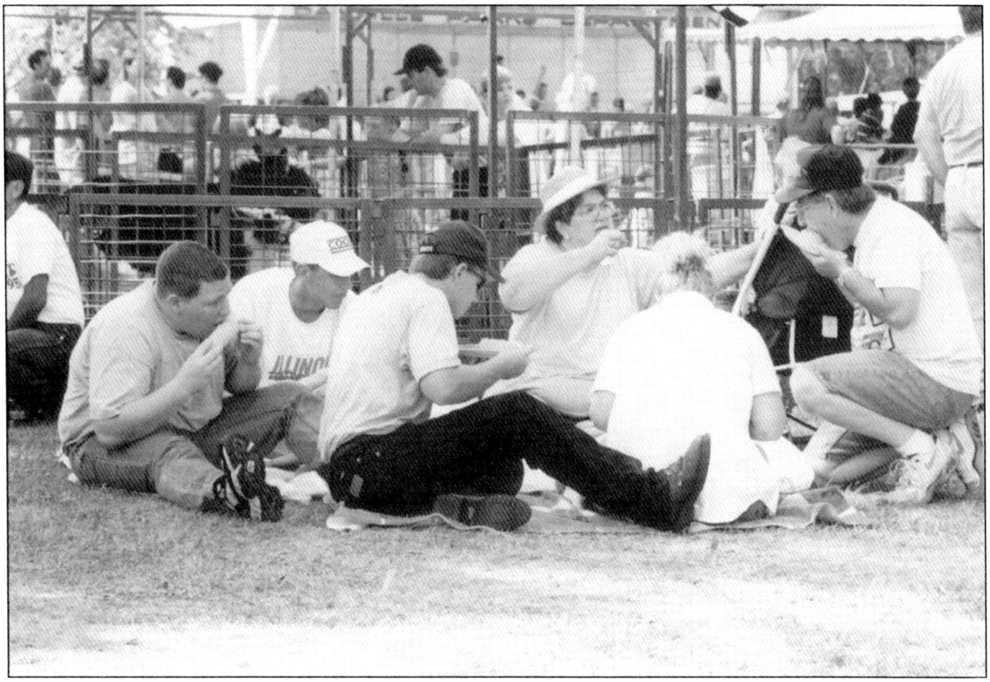

During the National Sweetcorn Festival, visitors stand in line for six ears of free sweet corn, which is cooked by a steam engine. This photograph shows visitors during the 1990s eating their corn. (Courtesy of Stephen and Holly Eyrich.)

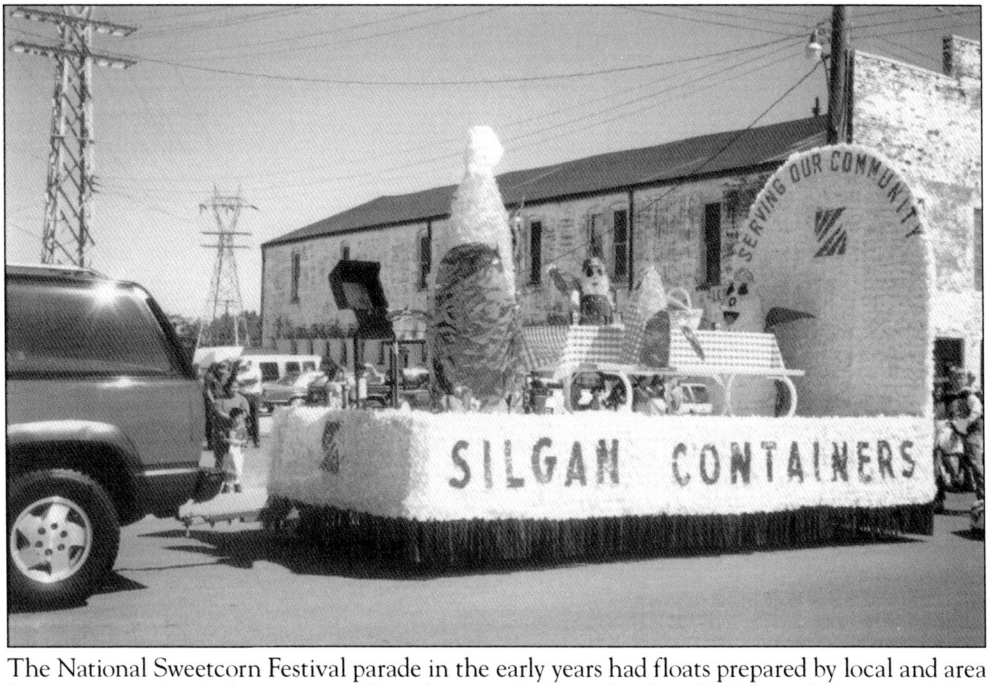

The National Sweetcorn Festival parade in the early years had floats prepared by local and area businesses as a kind of promotion. This photograph shows the float for Silgan Containers. Many businesses hired professional companies to build the floats for them. In later years, as the businesses closed or moved, the number of floats decreased. (Courtesy of Nancy Thorn.)

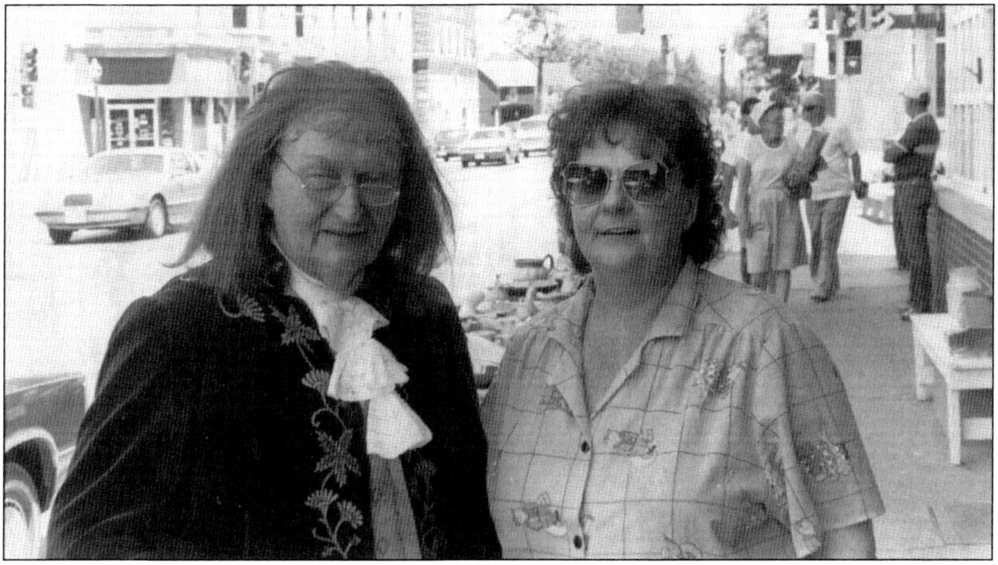

Ben Franklin visited Hoopeston during area events approximately 800 times. In this photograph, Franklin (portrayed by James A. Miller, 1925–1997) is speaking to a lady on Main Street. Miller recreated Ben Franklin while he was a member of the Scottish Rites Bodies Valley of Danville, Illinos. He was particularly popular with schoolchildren. (Courtesy of the Hoopeston Historical Society.)

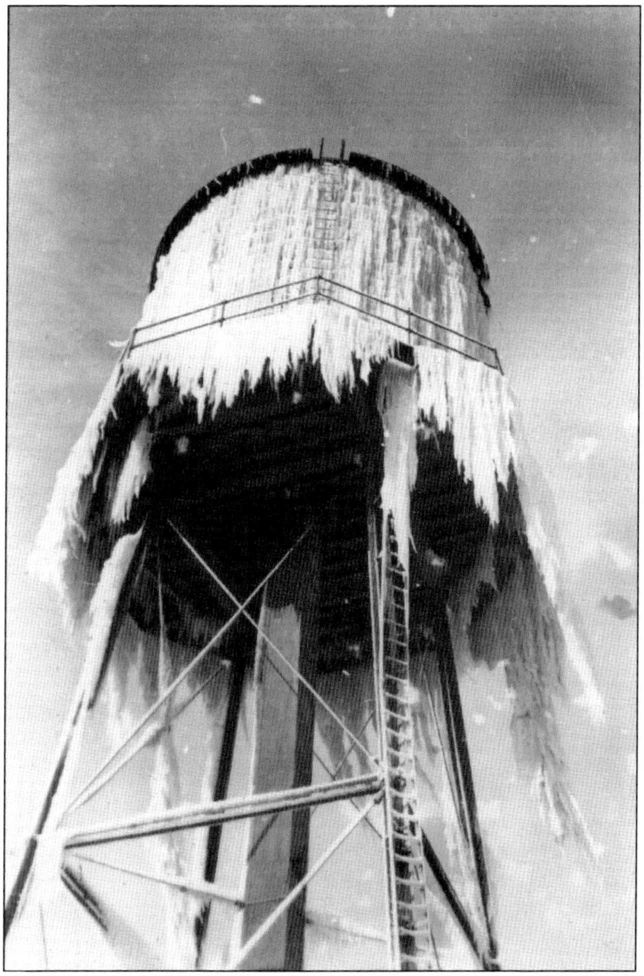

This American Can Company water tank photograph was taken on January 25, 1940. The temperature had dipped to 22 degrees, causing water to freeze into sheets of ice that hung several feet below the tank.

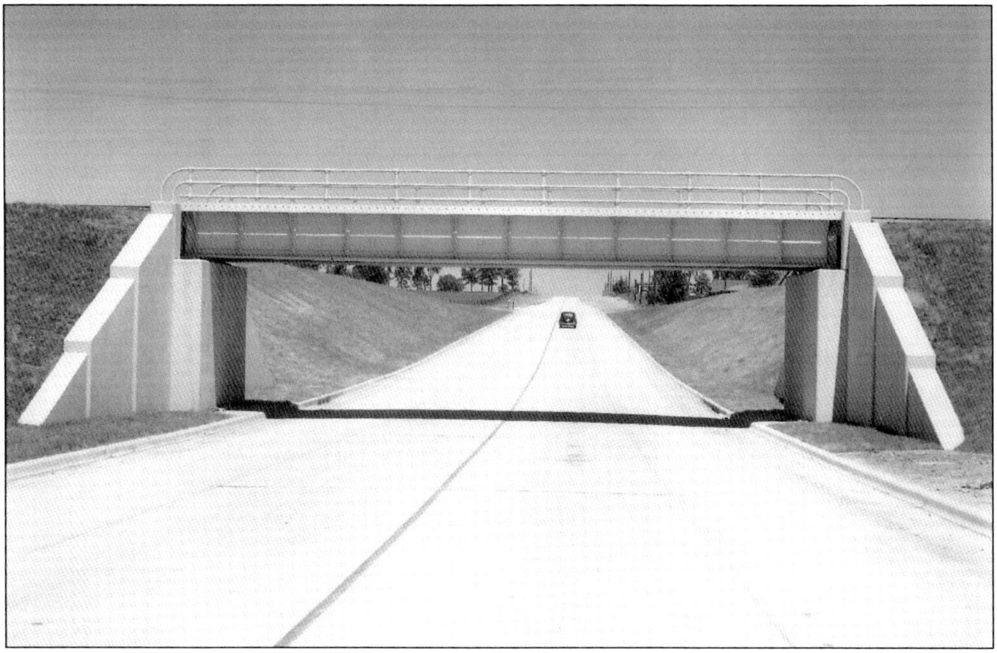

As rail crossings were a major hazard for motorists, the State of Illinois completed an underpass in Hoopeston at the New York, Chicago & St. Louis Railroad crossing, 25 feet north of the Route 1 and Main Street intersection in 1941. The trestle was removed in July 1990 after the tracks were abandoned. The Dixie Highway was also widened to 18 feet from Chicago to Danville, Illinois, in 1924. (Courtesy of the Illinois Department of Transportation.)

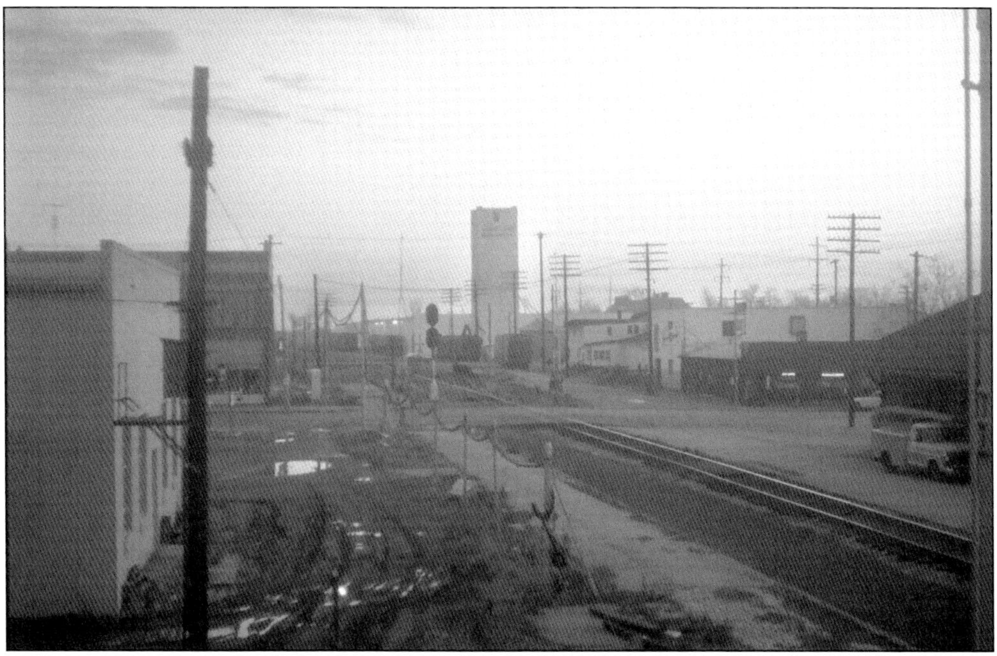

This southward view from the switch tower shows the back of Galloway's Machine Shop, the south corner of the train station, Ted's Drive-Thru, the back side of the *Chronicle*, and the Illinois Lumber Company. (Courtesy of Scott Baer.)

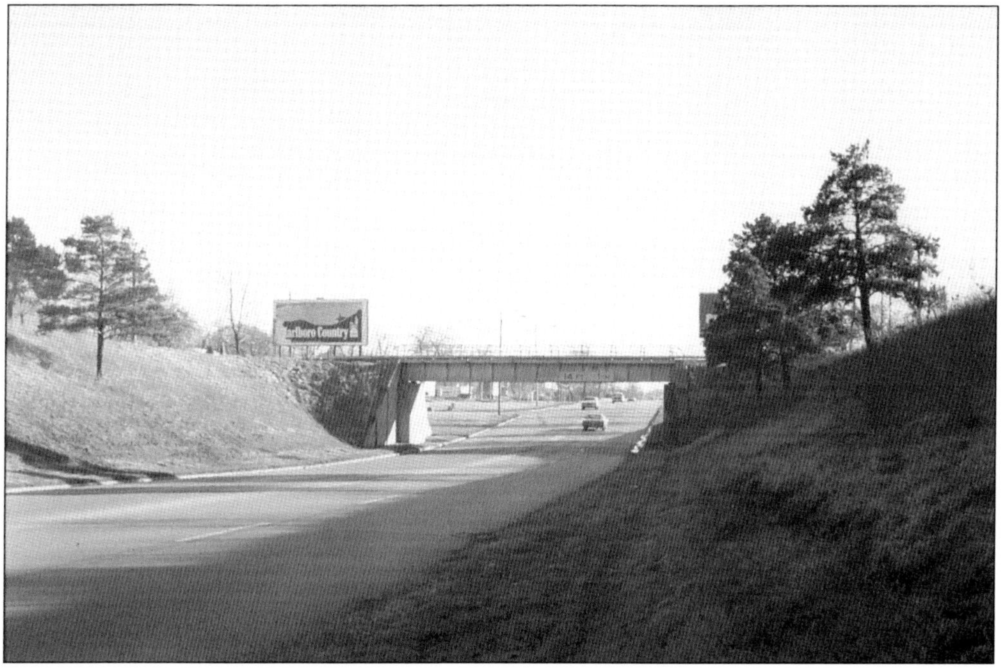

Seen here in the 1970s, the viaduct north of Main Street on Route 1 was well traveled with local traffic as well as Chicago traffic. The viaduct prevented traffic from having to cross the railroad tracks. (Courtesy of Scott Baer.)

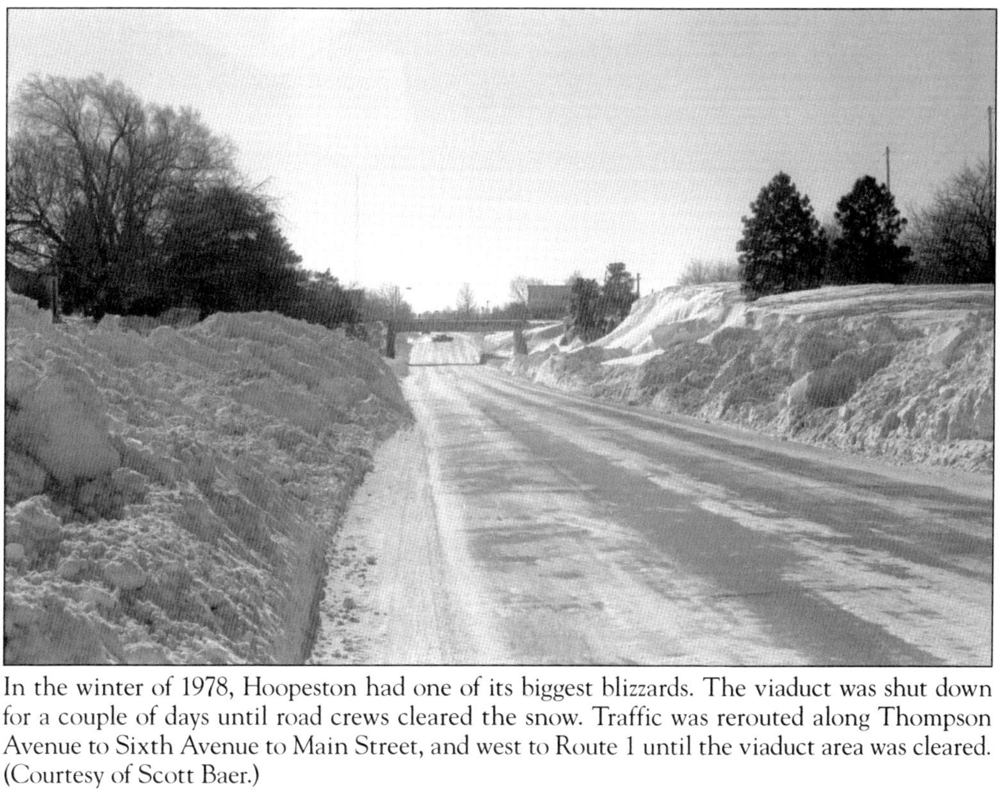

In the winter of 1978, Hoopeston had one of its biggest blizzards. The viaduct was shut down for a couple of days until road crews cleared the snow. Traffic was rerouted along Thompson Avenue to Sixth Avenue to Main Street, and west to Route 1 until the viaduct area was cleared. (Courtesy of Scott Baer.)

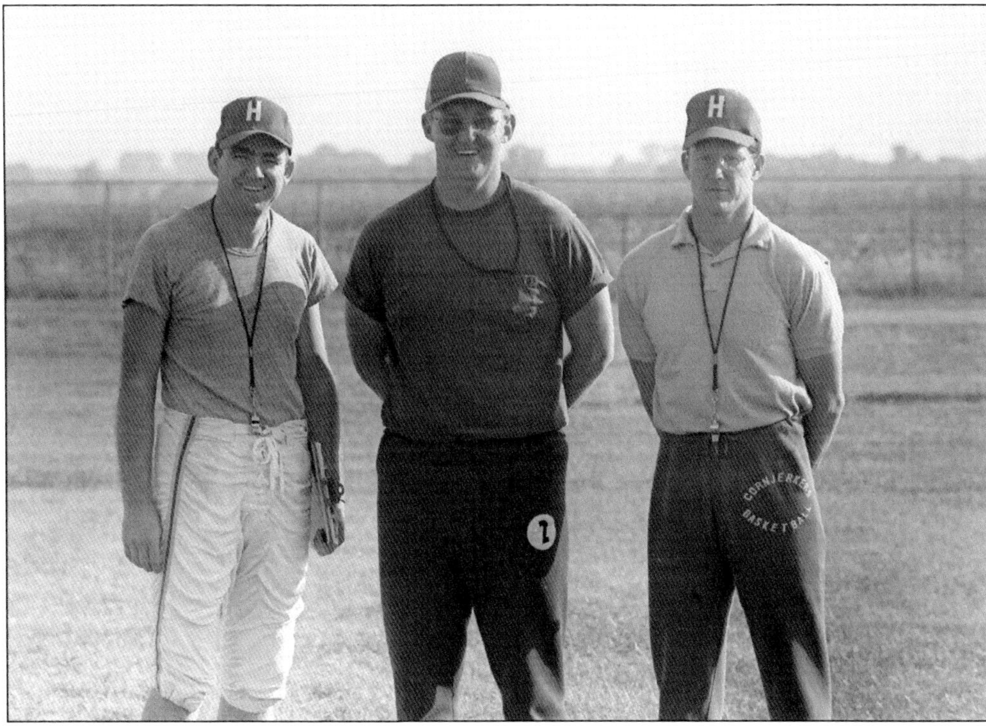

This 1975 photograph shows the Hoopeston High School coaches who led the sports program for Hoopeston (from left to right): Buddy Velasco, Jim Matta (father of Ohio State coach Thad Matta) and Ed Bird. (Courtesy of the Hoopeston School District.)

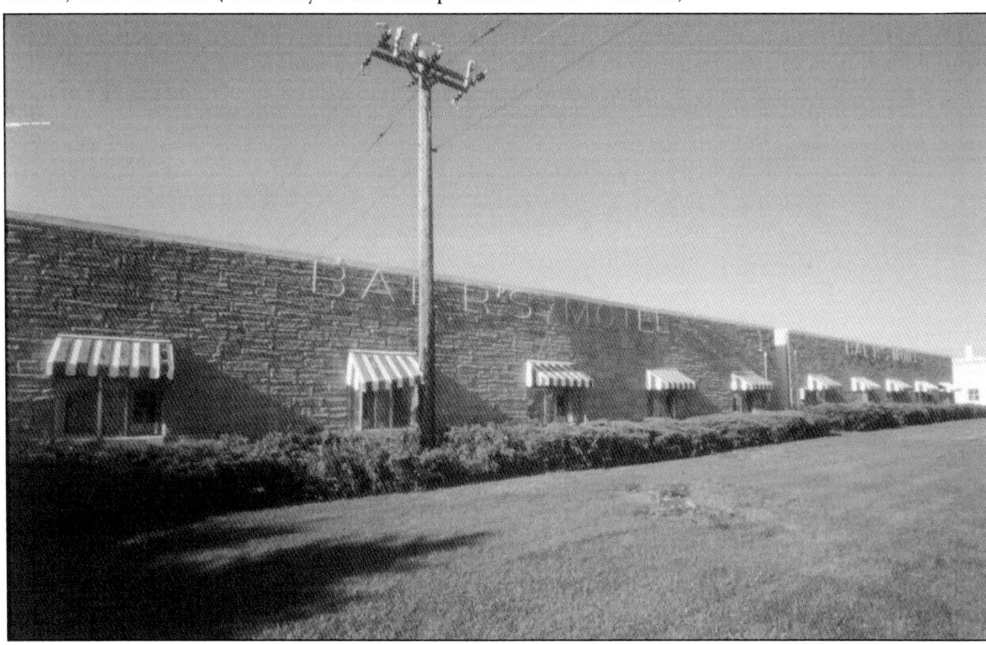

This view of Baer's Motel was photographed from the Route 9 side of the road in 1974. During the evening hours, the sign was lit up and could be seen as travelers came into Hoopeston. (Courtesy of Scott Baer.)

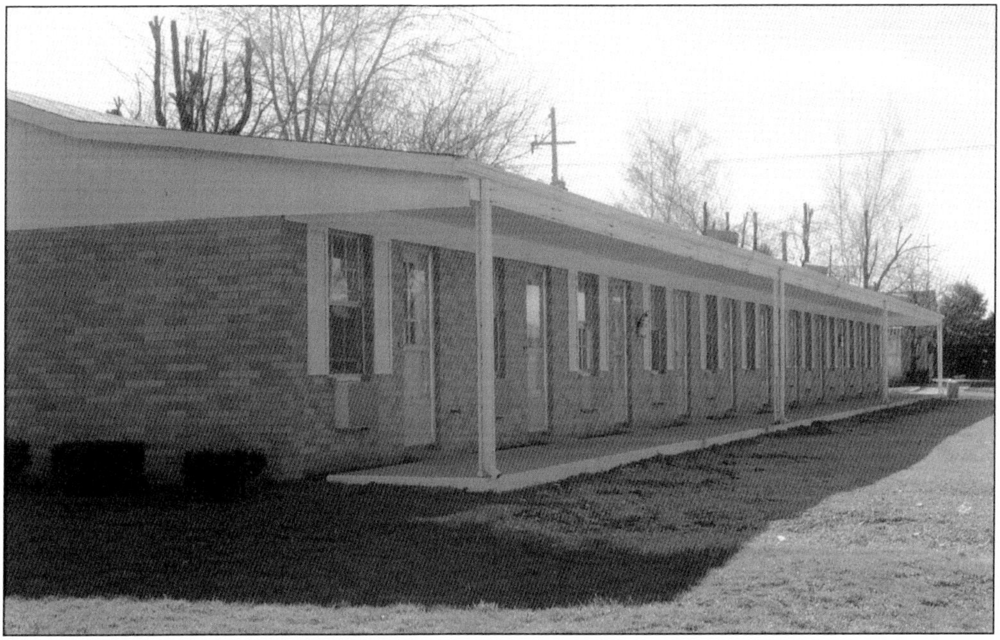

The north section of Baer's Motel in 1975 had several rooms that were rented either overnight or for a week or longer. (Courtesy of Scott Baer.)

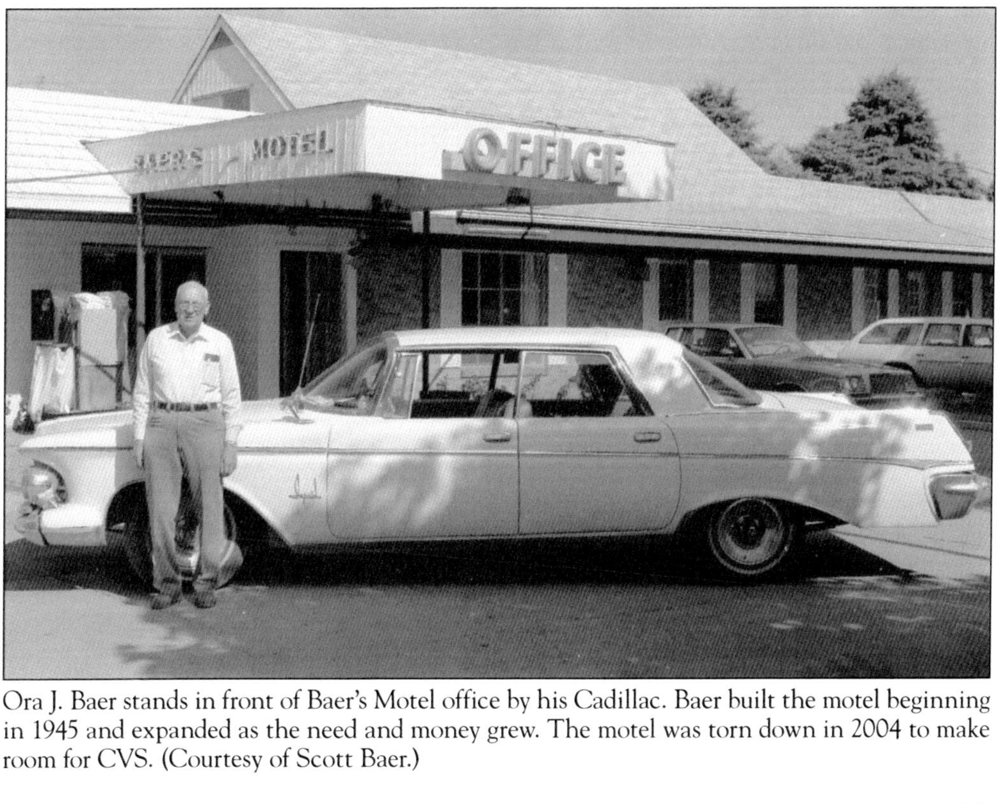

Ora J. Baer stands in front of Baer's Motel office by his Cadillac. Baer built the motel beginning in 1945 and expanded as the need and money grew. The motel was torn down in 2004 to make room for CVS. (Courtesy of Scott Baer.)

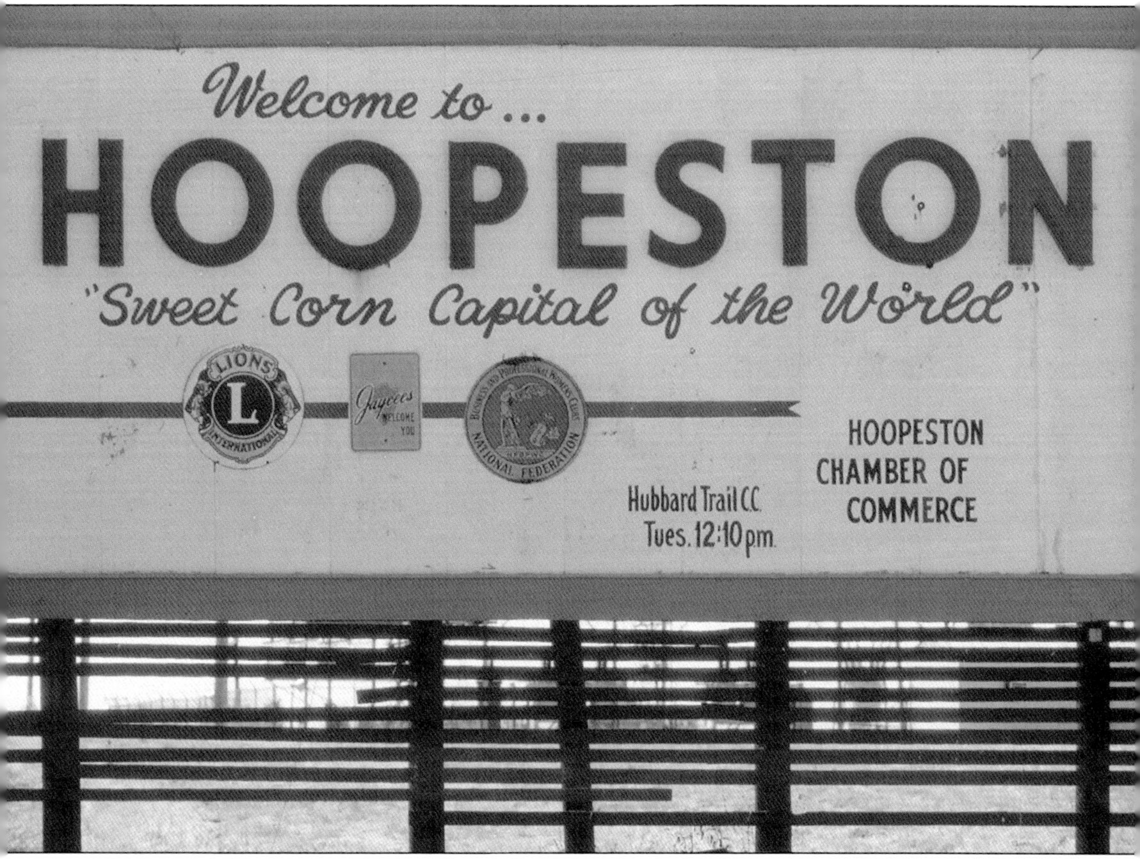

This 1984 Hoopeston sign was located north of town and was the first thing that welcomed travelers. The sign has since been replaced. (Courtesy of Scott Baer.)

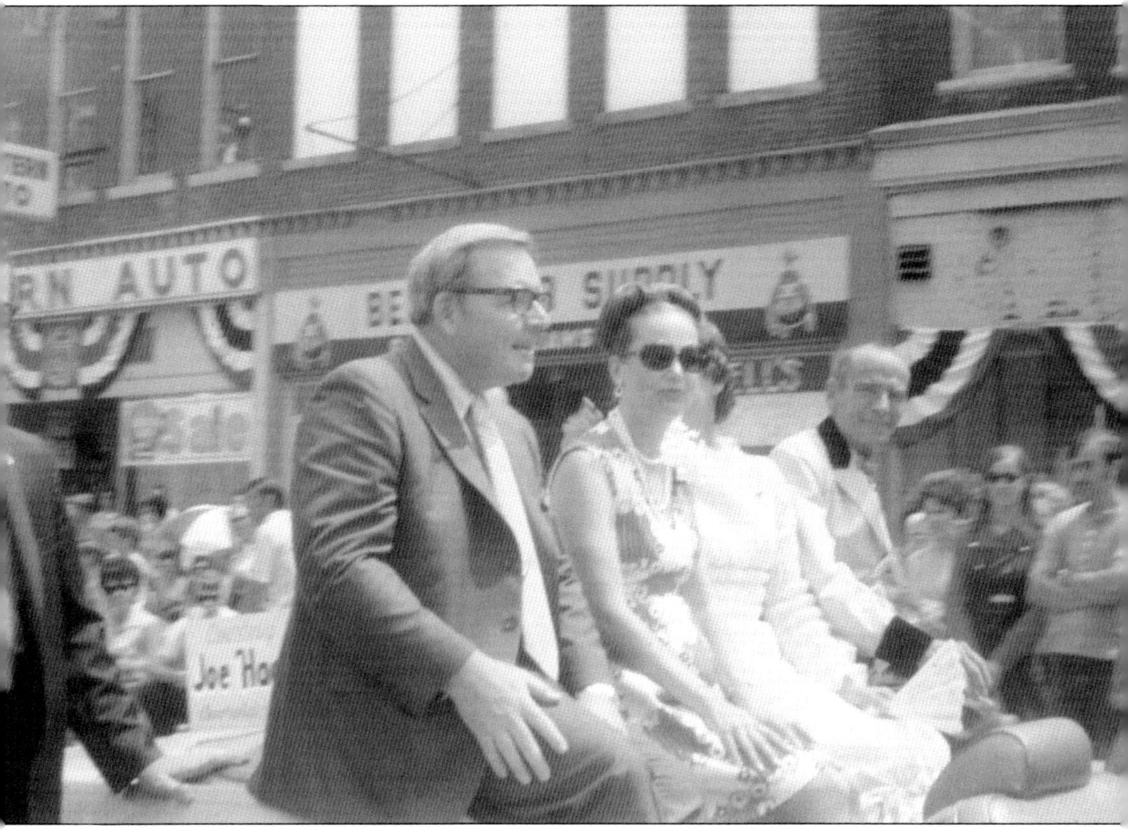

Riding in a parade car, Illinois governor Richard B. Oligivie (left), and Illinois senator Tom Merritt (far right), and their wives are shown during a parade celebrating the 1971 Hoopeston centennial. Senator Merritt lived in Hoopeston. (Courtesy of Scott Baer.)

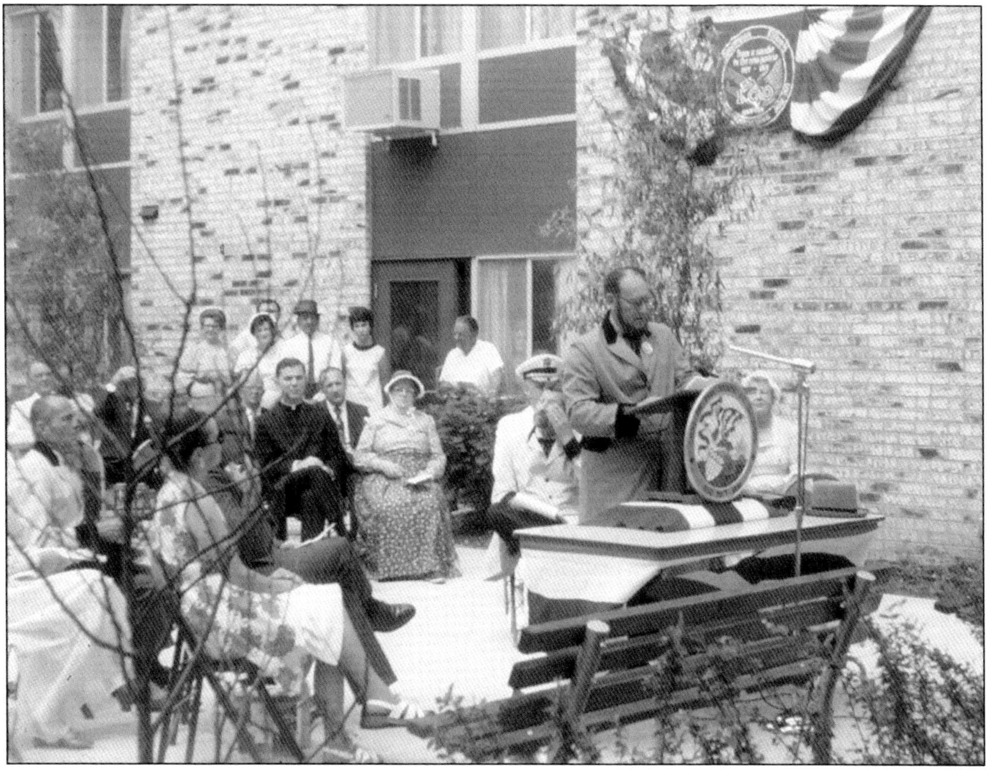

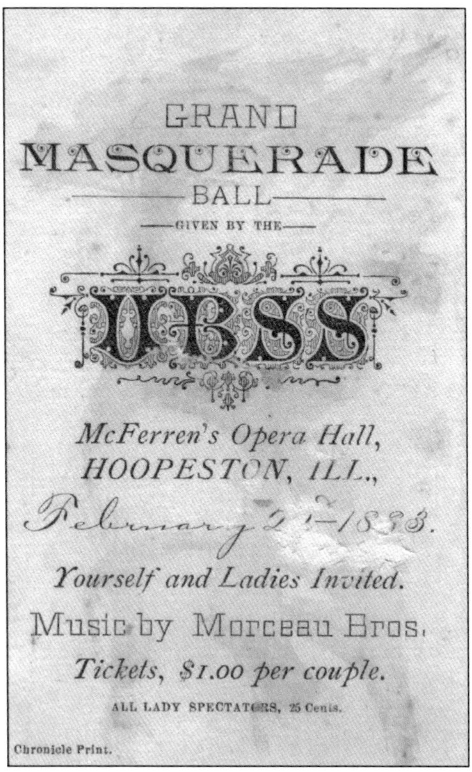
GRAND
MASQUERADE
BALL
GIVEN BY THE
UBSS
McFerren's Opera Hall,
HOOPESTON, ILL.,
February 25—1893.
Yourself and Ladies Invited.
Music by Morceau Bros.
Tickets, $1.00 per couple.
ALL LADY SPECTATORS, 25 Cents.
Chronicle Print.

Mayor Earl Smock is giving a speech at the Centennial Manor on East Honeywell Avenue during the 1971 Hoopeston centennial. Several ladies are shown dressed in 1871 period clothes. The mayor grew a beard, as did many men, for a centennial contest. (Courtesy of Scott Baer.)

This is Ella Roberts's invitation to a masquerade ball on February 25, 1893, at the McFerren Opera House.

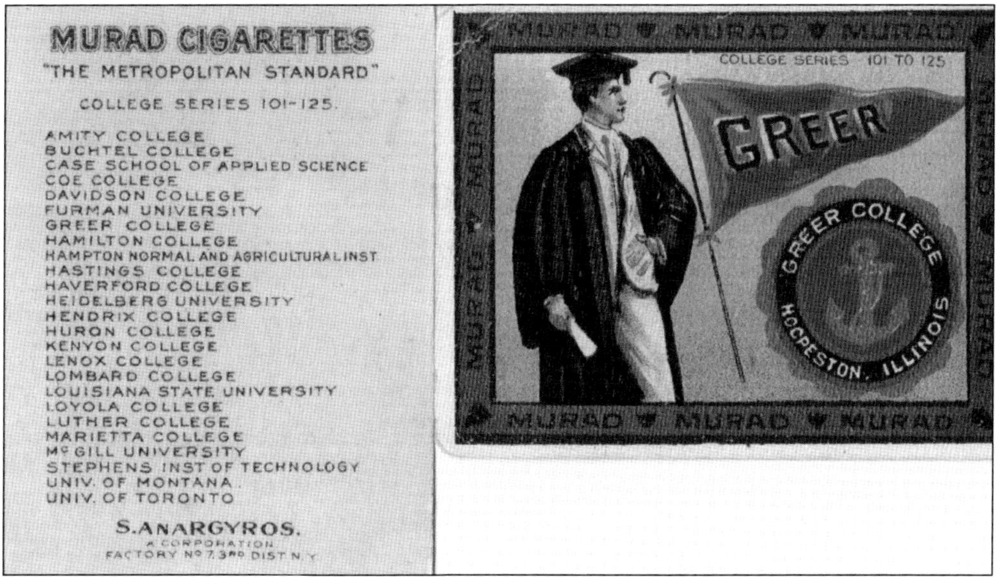

Murad Cigarette Company placed colleges on their cigarette packs in their college series during 1910. This advertisement shows John Greer College in Hoopeston, Illinois.

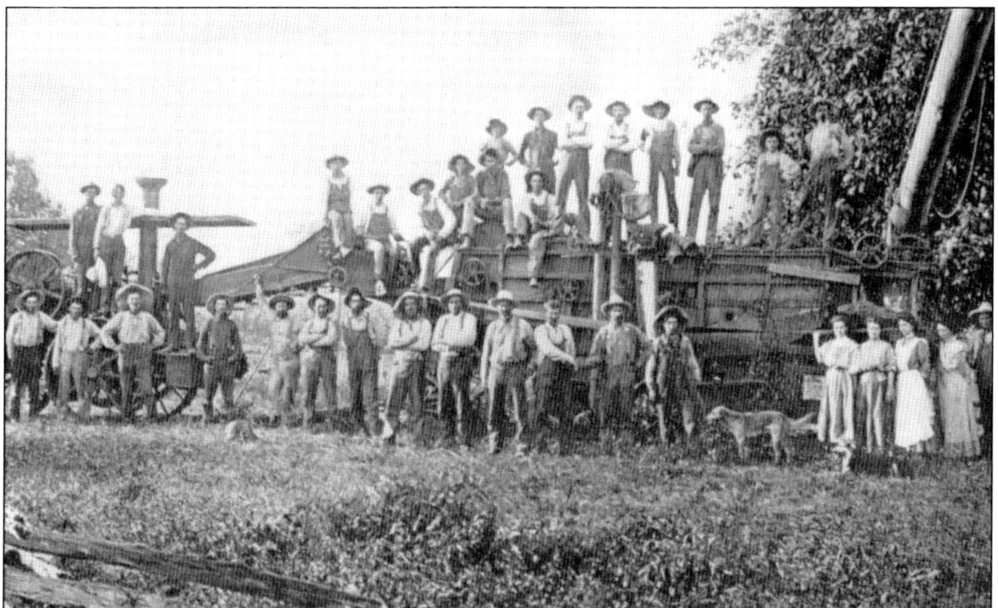

This photograph of a country scene in the 1900s field depicts the early threshing machines used during harvest. The men did the harvesting while the ladies made sure they had food during the long days of work.

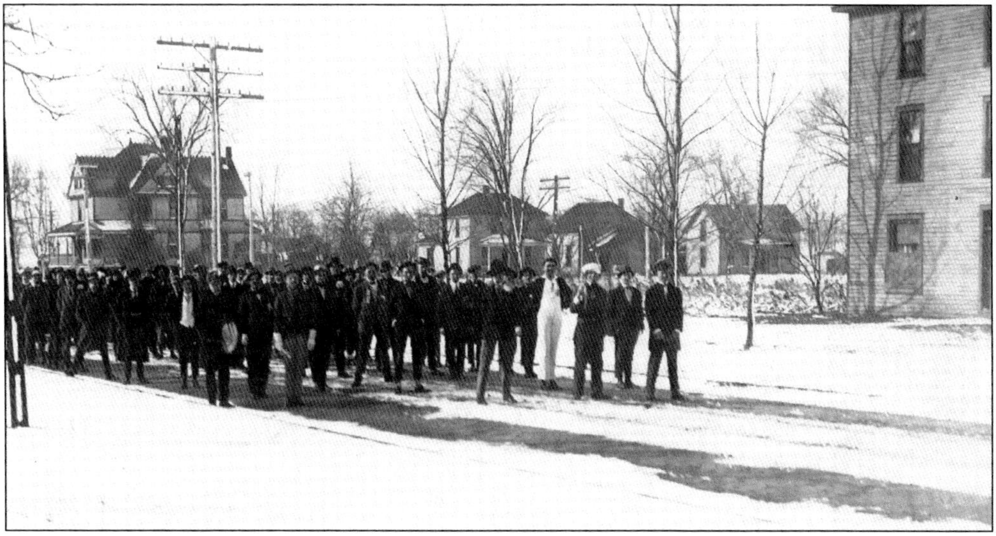

Hoopeston High School is having a "rough neck day" on March 16, 1916. Behind the students and to the left is the John Greer College president's house on Sixth Avenue and Penn Street.

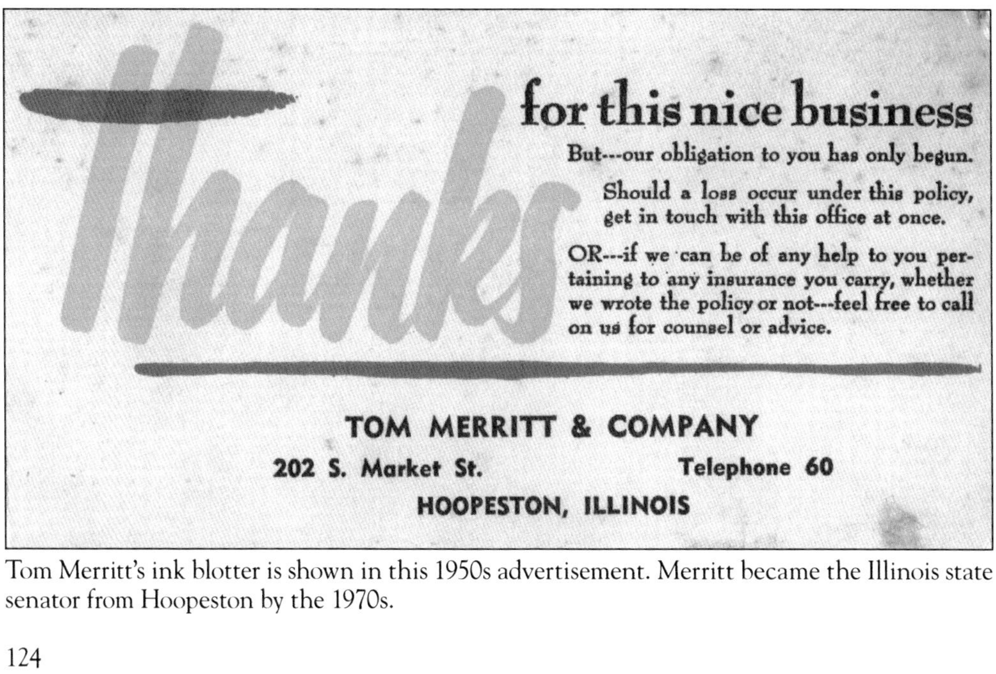

Tom Merritt's ink blotter is shown in this 1950s advertisement. Merritt became the Illinois state senator from Hoopeston by the 1970s.

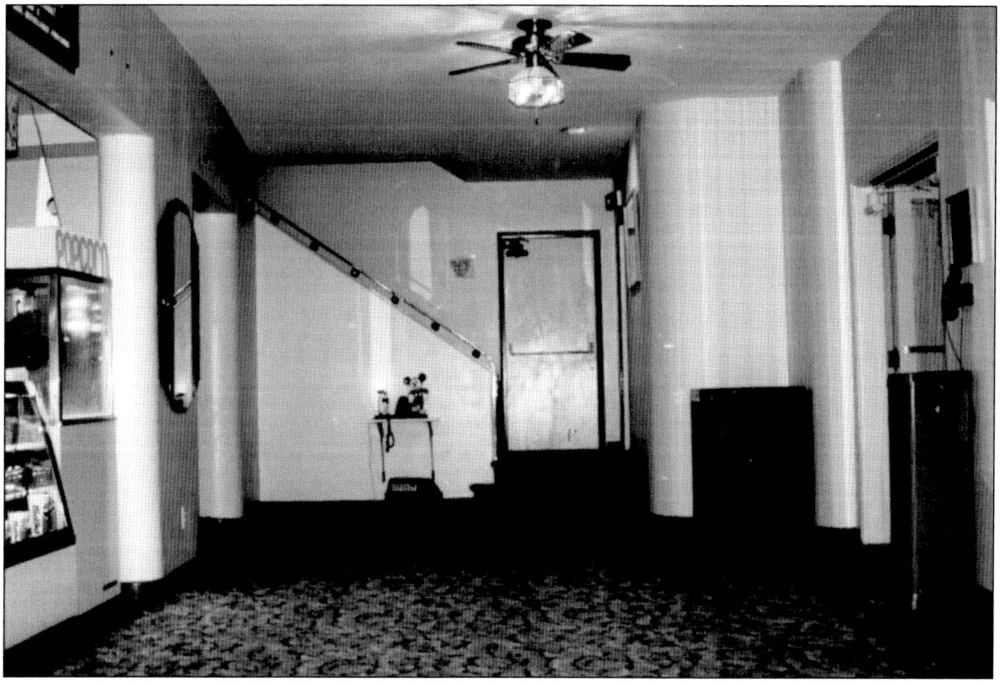

This photograph of the Lorraine Theatre lobby was taken in the 1940s or 1950s. The theater was remodeled in the Art Deco style by Alex Claussen, a Chicago theater designer and graduate of the Chicago Art Institute.

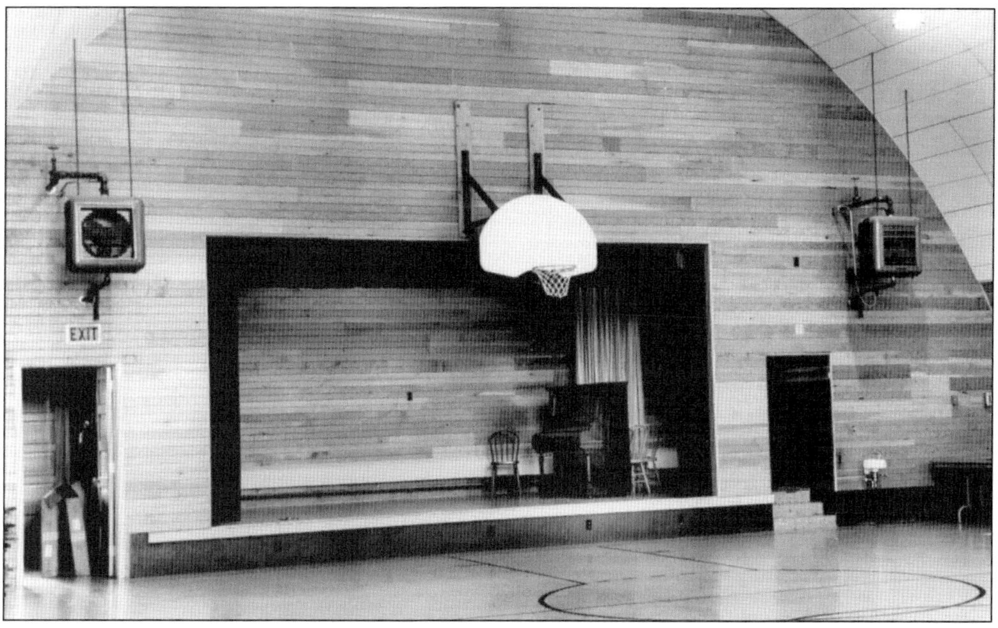

Lincoln Grade School's gymnasium, shown here, was built in the late 1950s or early 1960. Lincoln Grade School was located on First Avenue and West Lincoln Street. It housed first to eighth grades until 1956, when seventh and eighth grades were sent to the junior high. Lincoln was closed in 1969, and students went to the new John Greer Grade School. (Courtesy of Scott and Traci Brown.)

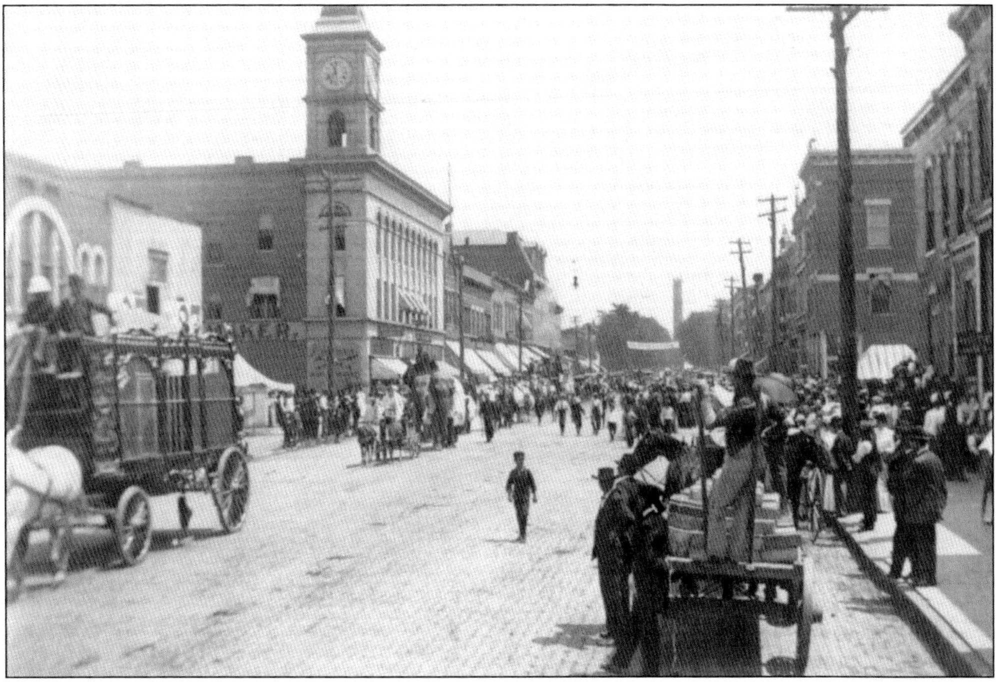

Solly Circus parades down the brick-paved East Main Street on November 11–12, 1925. Ira Owen Kreager American Legion Post 384 sponsored the circus as a special day for Hoopeston residents. In October of that year, the group also sponsored a Halloween party and dance for the town.

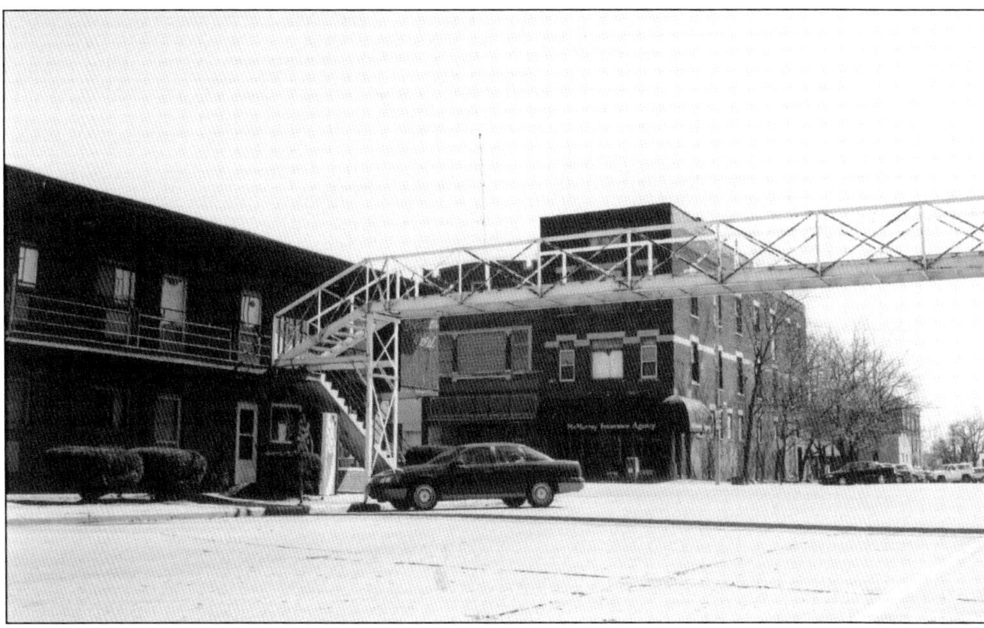

This photograph shows the walkway bridge over North Bank Street from the Downtown Motel leading to the second floor motel rooms across the street. Although used extensively until about 2000, it is considered unsafe to walk across now. In the background is McMurray's Insurance Agency.

ABOUT THE ORGANIZATIONS

BARBARA STANDISH CHAPTER NATIONAL SOCIETY DAUGHTERS OF THE AMERICAN REVOLUTION: The Barbara Standish Chapter was the first to organize in Vermilion County as part of the National Daughters of the American Revolution. It was organized September 8, 1905, and officially chartered October 4, 1905, with 18 member applications approved. It was the 32nd chapter in the state of Illinois. Current officers are Ruth Neathery, regent; Carol Livingston, vice regent; Nancy Thorn, treasurer; Carol Hicks, secretary; and Eileen Layden, registrar.

HOOPESTON HISTORICAL SOCIETY: The Hoopeston Historical Society, organized May 18, 1987, was chartered May 28, 1987. The first officers were Charlotte Russell, president; Carol Smith, first vice president; Dorothy Shuler, second vice president; Sally Keith, treasurer; and Barbara Lanie, secretary. Directors were Carl Weber, Gertrude Evans, and Elizabeth Chorney. Meetings are held on the third Monday of each month. The present officers are Tami Goin, president; Mary Jo Polson, vice president; Jean Minick, treasurer; and Carol Hicks, secretary. Board members are Jimmy Polson, Peggy Justice, and Linda Williams.

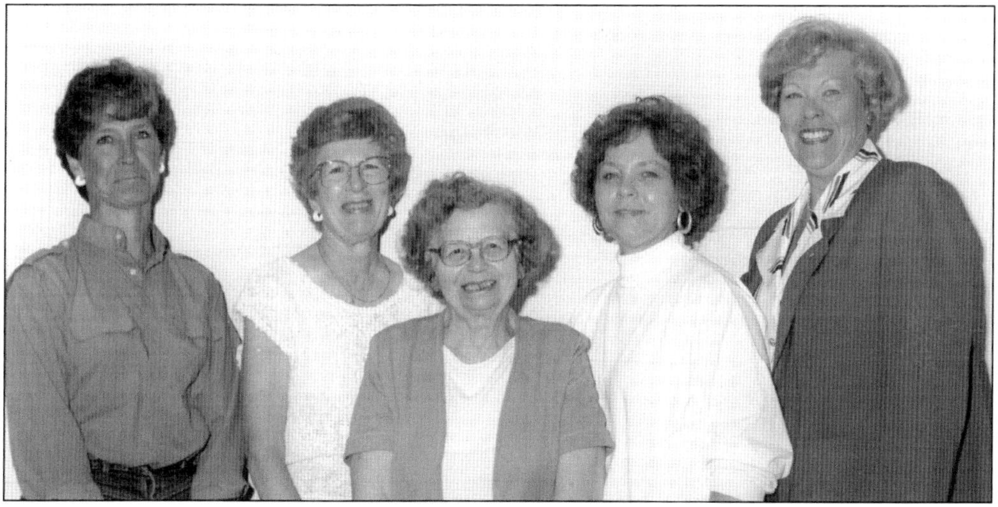

The new Hoopeston Historical Society was formed in 1987. The first officers, shown here from left to right, were Barbara Lanie, secretary; Carol Smith, first vice president; Dorothy Schuler, second vice president; Sally Keith, treasurer; and Charlotte Russell, president. (Courtesy of Hoopeston Historical Society.)

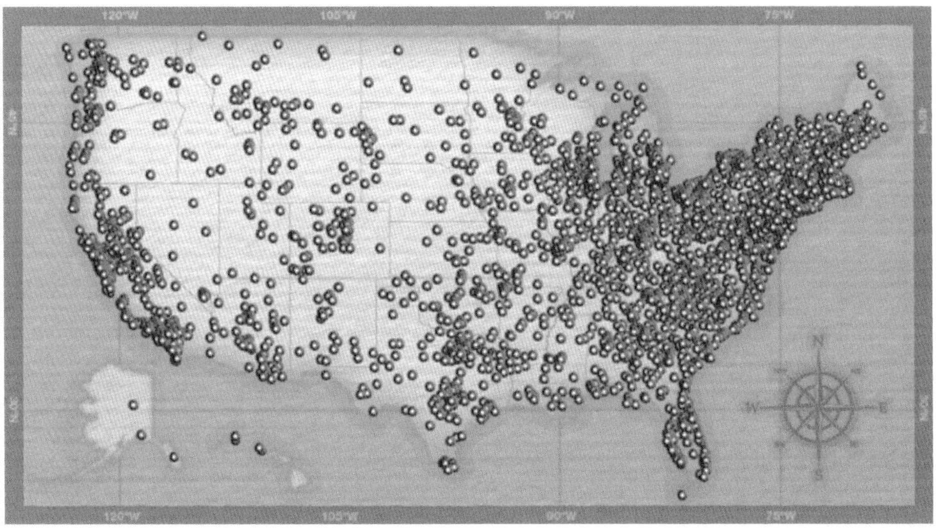